CONTINENTAL IDEALISM

Standard accounts of nineteenth-century German philosophy often begin with Kant and assess philosophers after him in light of their responses to Kantian idealism. In *Continental Idealism*, Paul Redding argues that the story of German idealism begins with Leibniz.

Redding begins by examining Leibniz's dispute with Newton over the nature of space, time and God, and stresses the way in which Leibniz incorporated Platonic and Aristotelian elements in his distinctive brand of idealism. Redding shows how Kant's interpretation of Leibniz's views of space and time consequently shaped his own "transcendental" version of idealism. Far from ending here, however, Redding argues that post-Kantian idealists such as Fichte, Schelling and Hegel, on the one hand, and meta-physical sceptics such as Schopenhauer and Nietzsche, on the other, continued to wrestle with a form of idealism ultimately derived from Leibniz.

Continental Idealism offers not only a new picture of one of the most important philosophical movements in the history of philosophy, but also a valuable and clear introduction to the origins of Continental and European philosophy.

Paul Redding is Professor of Philosophy at the University of Sydney and a fellow of the Australian Academy of the Humanities. He is the author of *Hegel's Hermeneutics* (1996), *The Logic of Affect* (1999) and *Analytic Philosophy and the Return of Hegelian Thought* (2007).

CONTINENTAL IDEALISM

IDEALISM

Leibniz to Nietzsche

Paul Redding

Routledge
Taylor & Francis Group

LONDON AND NEW YORK

This edition published 2009
by Routledge
2 Park Square, Milton Park, Abingdon, Oxon OX14 4RN

Simultaneously published in the USA and Canada
by Routledge
270 Madison Ave, New York, NY 10016

Routledge is an imprint of the Taylor & Francis Group, an informa business

© 2009 Paul Redding

Typeset in Goudy by
Taylor & Francis Books
Printed and bound in Great Britain by
TJ International, Padstow, Cornwall

British Library Cataloguing in Publication Data
A catalogue record for this book is available from the British Library

Library of Congress Cataloging in Publication Data
Redding, Paul, 1948-
  Continental idealism : Leibniz to Nietzsche / Paul Redding.
    p. cm.
  Includes bibliographical references and index.
  1. Idealism–History. I. Title.
  B823. R34 2009
  141–dc22

2008050314

ISBN10: 0-415-44306-7 (hbk)
ISBN10: 0-415-44307-5 (pbk)
ISBN10: 0-203-87695-4 (ebk)

ISBN13: 978-0-415-44306-7 (hbk)
ISBN13: 978-0-415-44307-4 (pbk)
ISBN13: 978-0-203-87695-4 (ebk)

CONTENTS

CONTENTS

vii

ACKNOWLEDGMENTS

The most valuable assistance I have received in thinking about the material in this book has come from the students at the University of Sydney who have found their ways into various courses I have taught there on these topics over the last decade and a half. If you somehow happen to be reading this, and recognize yourself in this description, please accept my warmest thanks. As always, I have greatly benefited from conversations (immediate and mediated by the written word) with a far greater number of people than I could thank individually. Were I to try and make a list it would definitely include Rick Benitez, David Braddon-Mitchell, Robert Brandom, Paolo Diego Bubbio, Bruin Christensen, Byron Clugston, Jean-Philippe Deranty, Moira Gatens, Stephen Gaukroger, Duncan Ivison, Jane Johnson, Jim Kreines, Simon Lumsden, David Macarthur, George Markus, Justine McGill, Douglas Moggach, Terry Pinkard, Robert Pippin, Huw Price, Philip Quadrio, Robert Stern, Andres Von Toledo and Robert Williams. Byron Clugston provided further invaluable help with the text, for which I am additionally grateful.

Further afield, I wish to thank Tony Bruce at Routledge for his enthusiasm and for his overseeing of this project from a stage in which it was little more than a vague, merely subjective "Vorstellung". In the course of this he elicited very helpful feedback and criticism from a variety of anonymous reviewers, and my thanks extend to them as well. I thank also James Thomas for his deft and sensitive editing of the manuscript. Large parts of the project were undertaken with the assistance of a Discovery Grant from the Australian Research Council, for which I am most grateful, as I am to the School of Philosophical and Historical Inquiry at the University of Sydney for providing the physical and scholarly support for work on this book. Support of a very different kind has come from my life partner, Vicki Varvaressos. For her presence I am eternally thankful.

INTRODUCTION

Idealism is a philosophy that has been out of fashion for more than a century—so far out of fashion and seeming so far off the table of defensible philosophical positions that many philosophers would probably be hard pressed to say anything much about it, even in criticism. Oddly enough, *idealism* has even tended to remain out of fashion despite a revival of interest in particular *idealists*, like the considerable revival of interest in both Kant, a "transcendental idealist", and the "German idealists", Fichte, Schelling and Hegel, who worked in his wake. Here, among those sympathetic to those philosophers, it is not uncommon to encounter *denials* that they were "idealists", even in the case of Hegel, who referred to his philosophy as "absolute idealism". The general idea seems to be that one must separate a philosopher that one wants to defend from the "*i*-word", given the simply irredeemable nature of idealism as a philosophical stance.[1]

One factor contributing to this strange state of affairs seems to be the peculiarity that a philosopher who did not use the term of his own philosophy has come to stand for many as the prototype idealist: George Berkeley, Bishop of Cloyne. That is, "idealism" seems to have come to be synonymous with "immaterialism", the term that Berkeley used to describe his own philosophy. The idea of Berkeley as the prototype idealist may be a conception most prominent in English-speaking philosophy, but clearly we cannot hold anglophones entirely responsible. Kant's transcendental idealism was, on its first appearance, linked by its German critics to the philosophy of Berkeley, and Kant himself, in the "Refutation of Idealism" added to second edition of the *Critique of Pure Reason*, held Berkeley to be a central representative of the idealism Kant was refuting.

In a letter to J. S. Beck, from 4 December 1792, we find Kant helpfully clarifying the relation of his idealism to Berkeley's immaterialism. Countering the claim of those who had identified his "critical idealism" with the philosophy of Berkeley, Kant explains: "For I speak of ideality in reference to the form of representation while they construe it as ideality with respect to the matter, i.e., ideality of the object and its existence itself" (Corr: 11.395). By appealing to the Aristotelian distinction between form and

1

matter, then, Kant, we might say, describes his philosophy as involving a *reversal* of Berkeley's "idealism". As a "material idealist", as an idealist *about* matter, Berkeley had reduced matter to ideas subjectively conceived, and so reduced matter to *mind*. But in contrast, Kant was an idealist about *form*, regarding both the spatiotemporal form and the conceptual form of objects as contributed by the knowing mind (as "mind-dependent") rather than as having independent *per se* existence.[2]

A number of central contentions of this book might be seen to grow from this point. The first is that the "transcendental idealism" of Kant and, after him, Fichte, as well as the variously "objective" and "absolute" idealisms that followed, can only be adequately understood against the background of Aristotle's "hylomorphic" form–matter distinction, a distinction which came from Aristotle's transformation of Plato's doctrine of "forms" or "ideas". But to invoke the relevance of such Platonic–Aristotelian notions in this context suggests that we align the thought of Kant in relation to that of Leibniz, who had constructed his "monadology" on a Platonic and Aristotelian basis, and who had also insisted on the ideality of spatiotemporal form. It is thus that Leibniz will be taken as the starting point of the tradition of Continental idealism as it is treated in this book. Another claim running through this work is that Kant's way of thinking about the ideality of form introduced an ambiguity into his approach to the ancient project of metaphysics that Leibniz had attempted to reconcile with the more nominalistic natural philosophy of his time. On the one hand, the thesis of the ideality of form led Kant to the idea that we can only know "appearances", and so to a type of scepticism with respect to the project of metaphysics conceived as knowledge of "things-in-themselves". But beneath this well-known picture of Kant as a type of metaphysical sceptic (that I characterise as the "weak" interpretation of transcendental idealism—"weak TI") was a *stronger* thesis ("strong TI"), which asserted that everything into which traditional metaphysics inquired and which it took to be ultimately real was, in some sense, mind-dependent, and did not have *per se* existence. On the interpretation presented here, the development of idealism in the post-Kantian period was to develop the programme of strong TI, the investigation of a world that was not "there anyway", but which had been constructed by the human mind throughout its own developmental history. The full-blown development of this programme was to be found in Hegel's idealist metaphysics of "spirit".

In the recent renaissance of scholarship on the post-Kantian idealist tradition, the essentially *anti-Berkeleian* thrust of its development has been well brought out. In Frederick Beiser's apt phrase, the post-Kantians were effectively consumed with continuing Kant's "struggle against subjectivism" (Beiser 2002), and the reanimation of the thought of Plato and Aristotle was central to this struggle. However, this appeal to a type of Platonist form of thought has tended to be made in opposition to the idea, stressed by *other* recent interpreters of Hegel, that the post-Kantians should be understood as having developed the "spirit" of Kant's transcendental idealist *critique* of traditional metaphysics, while being critical of its "letter". Here, I want to maintain, however, that the perceived opposition between a type of "non-metaphysical" or post-Kantian interpretation of Hegel, and an interpretation that stresses the Platonist and Aristotelian heritage of his metaphysics, is a false one. Putting both Kant and the post-Kantians in the context of Leibniz's attempt to rejuvenate the Platonist tradition in the context of emerging modern culture, and understanding what it might be to be an idealist rather than a realist about *form*, allows us to better understand the general orientation of the type of thought I call "Continental idealism".

Continental idealism: Some structural features

Continental idealism, as largely ignored and poorly understood, has acquired a stereotype that has come to occupy the gap within philosophy's historical consciousness. On the whole, such philosophy is "dark" and "obscure", its proponents given to mysticism and irrationalism, rather than common sense or science, interested in speculation and system-building over careful, piecemeal accumulation of knowledge, attracted to indirect, allusive and metaphorical forms of expression, and so on.

Like all stereotypes and caricatures, this one bases itself on and exaggerates certain recognisable features of its subject matter, and extrapolates these features out of any context or relation to opposing features. As a rhetorical device, it is typically used for the purposes of ridicule rather than criticism, *presupposing* rather than *arguing* that its target is ridiculous. Perhaps worst of all, reducing an opposing philosophical position to a dismissible stereotype can be a way of protecting one's own position from any awareness of how it may seem from an opposing point of view. Nevertheless, stereotypes only work to the extent that they employ *some* recognisable features or traits of their targets. So what are the traits of Continental idealism that underlie the stereotype? As a preliminary sketch I offer the following.

1. The stance of *rational reconciliationism*—the irenic intention to reconcile conflicting stances or orientations towards the world, rather than simply take sides. For example, to reconcile the claims of modern science and religion, traditional philosophy and science, religion and philosophy, and so on. Thus Leibniz can be interpreted as attempting to reconcile the modern mechanistic worldview of Galileo and Newton, with ancient Greek metaphysical notions based on the Aristotelian concept of "substance"; Kant, as trying to reconcile the existence of *moral action* with the *causally determined world* of Newtonian science; Hegel, as attempting generally to reconcile opposed *philosophical points of view* by appealing to a "dialectical" theory of the unity of opposites, and so on.

2. A conception of the *perspectival* nature of perceptual knowledge. The idea that perceptually based knowledge was in some way shaped by the conditions affecting the knower was conveyed by Leibniz with the metaphor of "perspective", and the Kantian successor to this notion involves his account of conditions of experience and knowledge. But any *awareness* that our empirical knowledge is "perspectival" presupposes the existence of a type of knowledge that, by being freed from the limitations of perception, is freed from such perspectivity. In both Leibniz and Kant, it is the role of concepts to free knowledge from these limitations.

   Such a concern with the conditions of knowledge, I suggest, runs through the idealist tradition and prompts a series of attempted resolutions in which the trope of the "perspectival" is organised around two axes. The first contrasts the *perspectivity* of *human* knowledge with the purported *non-perspectivity* of the purely conceptual knowledge attributed to God. This distinction could be articulated in different ways. For example, Leibniz had conceived of the difference as one of *degree*, while Kant conceived of it as a difference in *kind*. The second axis along which this problem gets considered is that of the relationships *among* the finite perspectives as instantiated by socially related and interacting individuals. Here the perspectivity affecting any *individual* knower is sought to be mitigated, not by appeal to aperspectival knowledge but by their consideration of claims issuing from *different* perspectives. Thus the nature of the social relations within which individuals are embedded and the question of their capacity to acknowledge the claims of others come to have bearing on their capacity to transcend their own perspectival limitations.

3. An appeal to elements from the *Platonist and Neoplatonist tradition* to be opposed to the strongly nominalist and voluntarist characteristics of emerging modern philosophy. This is particularly found in Leibniz and Hegel, and draws on various features not only of the thought of Plato himself, but especially later Neoplatonists, both pagan (such as Plotinus and Proclus) and Christian (such as Meister Eckhart, Nicholas of Cusa and Jacob Böhme). Among the features characterising the thought of this tradition are (a) a prioritising of the role of concepts and inferences in the generation of knowledge over the role of sense experience; (b) a rejection of the *nominalist* ontology underlying empiricism, and an attraction to a *holistic* and *organicist* view of knowledge and the cosmos; (c) a prioritising of *aesthetic* dimensions of experience, seen as relevant to the intellectual grasp of holistic unities; and (d) a rejection of the strongly *transcendent* and *personalised* conception of God of orthodox Christianity, and a tendency to a more "Platonic theology", equating the deity with the processes of reason itself.

4. The assertion of *"idealism"* over *"realism"*. This has to be understood in relation to traits 2 and 3, as these elements give rise to a form of

"idealism" that is very different from the nominalist philosophy of Bishop Berkeley, with which it is often confused. First, the continental "idealist" position, with its Aristotelian "hylomorphic" dimension, is not a form of Berkeleian "immaterialism", and can be compatible with the view that modern science gives us a genuine (albeit partial and one-sided) view of the world and ourselves. Furthermore, one consequence of Kant's *reversal* of Berkeley's immaterialism was that Kant was explicitly an idealist about the issue on which Berkeley was a *realist*—"spirit", in its divine and finite forms—putting idealism at odds with orthodox Christian theology. In this way, idealism can be seen as an alternative to the "spiritual realism" with which it is commonly confused.

All these might be contrasted with what are characteristically taken as the features of mainstream English-speaking philosophy (especially what has become dominant in the "analytic philosophy" of the last hundred years)—thus, with the tendency of philosophy (1) to align itself with the outlook of modern science *against* religion and ancient philosophy; (2) to favour a predominantly *empiricist* conception of knowledge based on a model of perceptual knowledge; (3) to reject as wrong-headed the sorts of pre-modern conceptions of existence as found in Platonism and Aristotelianism; and (4) to align itself with a materialist realism (or "naturalism"), conceived of as opposed to "idealism" as found in Berkeley, that is, as opposed to *spiritual* realism.

1

THE SEVENTEENTH-CENTURY BACKGROUND TO THE EMERGENCE OF CONTINENTAL IDEALISM

1.1 Early-modern theology and natural philosophy

The development of modern natural science, we are told in influential accounts like those of Alexander Koyré (Koyré 1957) and Thomas Kuhn (Kuhn 1957, 1962), was a revolutionary rather than a cumulative affair. Very crudely, the geocentric cosmology that the medievals had inherited from ancient Greece was not *simply* a set of beliefs about which cosmic bodies moved and which were at rest. Rather, it was a complexly organised structure—a "paradigm" in Kuhn's account—incorporating physical, epistemological and metaphysical aspects. Furthermore, this structure had become invested with rich *theological* significance, as dramatically exemplified by Galileo's trial in 1633. Among the features of Aristotelian thought that had to be overthrown in order for the new cosmology to emerge was Aristotle's account of the nature of *space*, and it would be in the context of arguments over the new conception of space that Continental idealism would be born.

For Aristotle, the most basic notion was not that of "space" but "place"—*topos* (Morison 2002). Place was a fundamental concept in the explanation of movement because the elements that made up the terrestrial realm—earth, water, air and fire—were all accorded natural "places" to which they would move if unimpeded. Pick up a sod of earth, release it, and, of course, it will move *downwards*. Light a fire, and it will be observed that its flames move *upwards*. The explanations for phenomena such as these appeal to the natural places of elements. Earth has its natural place at the centre of the cosmos, fire has its natural place away from the earth in a layer or shell surrounding it, the layer containing the orbit of the sun, while water and air naturally layer themselves between these two places. Furthermore, in the Aristotelian cosmos there was a differentiation between the sublunar and superlunar realms, with different forms of explanation applying to each. The sublunar, effectively *terrestrial*, realm was the realm of generation and decay, while the superlunar or *celestial* realm was one of constancy and perfection. In the former, motion was between fixed places and, effectively, linear; in the latter, the movement of more perfect bodies, such as that of the stars, was circular, as that is the only form of motion that can go on eternally in finite space. As the derivative term, space was just the totality of differentiated *places*.

Within the scientific cosmology that unfolded between Copernicus and Newton and that came to replace the ancient geocentric view, there were no differentiated "places" in Aristotle's sense: space, as finally established by Newton, was "isotropic". That is, "space", rather than place, was conceived of as singular, infinite and uniform, and so with no inherent *directions*. Without fixed given places, there could be no "up" or "down", as there was in the geocentric cosmos; there could only be the non-subjectively oriented property of tri-dimensionality. Aristotle had been well aware that the notions "up" and "down" had a perspectival character in as much as the direction that was "up" for an observer located on one part of the earth would be "down" for another located on the *opposite* side of the earth. Nevertheless, this did not imply that they were simply relative *to* the observer (Phys: 205b34). "Up" was the direction of the natural movement of fire: effectively the direction of lines radiating from the centre of the cosmos to its periphery. "Down" was the opposite direction. And the centre and the periphery of the cosmos were real, objective places.

Aristotle's was not the *only* view of the nature of space that had been developed in the ancient world, and he had worked out his conception of space as a finite totality of places, against rival views such as Plato's, as found in the *Timaeus*, or those of the atomists. Moreover, after Aristotle, quite different conceptions of space could be found among the Stoics. Importantly, the earlier Platonist view also underwent recurrent revivals and modifications which were meant to allow it to answer various of Aristotle's criticisms. Such Neoplatonist views in particular would contribute substantively to the conception of space central to the establishment of modern science in the sixteenth and seventeenth centuries. In the sixth century, Philiponus had argued in a very un-Aristotelian and seemingly "modern" way that space was "a certain interval, measurable in three dimensions, incorporeal in its very nature and different from the body contained in it".[1] Later, in the fifteenth century, the fundamentally egocentric nature of the Aristotelian conception was exposed and criticised by Nicholas of Cusa, who conceived of space as an "infinite sphere" whose centre is everywhere and circumference nowhere,[2] suggesting that the very idea of a "centre" of the universe was a relativistic or perspectival one. The "centre" was just where the observer was located, and so Cusa claimed that regardless of *where* an observer were located throughout the universe, it would appear to that observer that they were *at* the "centre". With this conception, Cusa is commonly regarded as looking forward to and, in a way, anticipating, the heliocentric cosmology later to be established by Copernicus (Koyré 1957: 6–24), but Cusa's thought seems to work on the deeper level of the conceptualisation of the space of the universe itself, and to anticipate later questions concerning the relation of "relative" to "absolute" space. Copernicus reversed the earth-centred view of the cosmos by making the earth revolve around the sun, but this meant that the universe remained finite and still had a centre—the sun. But Giordano Bruno, inspired in part by Cusa, radicalised Copernicus' move by infinitising the universe and depriving it of both a boundary and a centre, making available the modern infinite and homogeneous conception of space.[3]

Against such "modern", "reflective" views, it is common to think of Aristotle's account as, in a sense, *naïvely* in accordance with first appearances. It is easier and more natural to think of the earth at rest and the sun, moon and stars as moving about it, rather than thinking of the earth as just another planet orbiting the sun in the way that the moon orbits the earth, and the sun as just another star. But in other ways Aristotle's account of space as the finite totality of differentiated places was counterintuitive. First, Aristotle argued against the atomists' concept of the *void*. One reason for this followed from his concept of substance (*ousia*): How could there *be* a void, if a void is *nothing* rather than *something*? Space had to be *something*, so it had to be a plenum rather than a void.[4] But the impossibility of a void for Aristotle also followed from the tight conceptual linkage between place and movement. There could be no directionality in space conceived without substances of any kind *in it*. The other counterintuitive consequence of Aristotle's notion of space concerned the incoherence of the idea of any space *beyond* the outer sphere of the heavens. "It is clear", Aristotle puts it in *On the Heavens*, "that there is neither place nor void nor time beyond the heavens" (OH: 279a12). Against this, the Stoic view could seem more natural: the earth-centred cosmos with its surrounding shells was itself *surrounded* by empty space.

It is commonly argued that the dominance of the Aristotelian conception of space had prevented the application of geometry to cosmology, despite the sophistication of the Greek developments within that branch of mathematics. Plato had advocated the application of mathematics to understanding the cosmos for reasons that would become familiar from the modern point of view. For Plato it was *measurement* that was to provide the means of correcting knowledge that was tightly tied to the phenomenal qualities of appearance.[5] However, *Aristotelian* cosmological space, according to Max Jammer, could not be geometrised: "How could Euclidean space, with its homogeneous and infinite lines and planes, possibly fit into the finite and anisotropic Aristotelian universe?" (Jammer 1954: 26). Thus, such a project of mathematising the world came to be rejected by Aristotle as well as by the atomists and the Stoics (Funkenstein 1986: 34), and it had to wait for Newton to carry it out systematically and coherently. However, Newton had to have available to him an adequately de-Aristotelianised conception of space to do this.

In the complex story of the development of the notion of infinite space in the early-modern period, it is usual to point to the role of ancient texts that had been unavailable to the West during the Middle Ages but that had become available during the sixteenth and seventeenth centuries, often through the influx of intellectuals into Western Europe after the fall of Constantinople in 1453. According to Edward Grant, appeals started to be made to "ancient Greek authors (Plato, Proclus, Epicurus, the Stoics, Hero, Simplicius, Plutarch, Philoponus, Hermes Trismegistus, etc.), the Church Fathers, Cabbalists" and other non-scholastic authors who "quickly took their places alongside, and often replaced, long-standing and revered authorities" (Grant 1981: 182–83). Among these, however, "Plato was the central figure in the powerful eclectic philosophies that were developed in opposition to the dominant Aristotelian natural philosophy and cosmology of medieval and early modern scholasticism" (ibid.). Among the most immediate Platonic influences on Newton for his conception of space would seem to be the Cambridge Platonist, Henry More,[6] and the relevance of this concept of space involved extended well beyond the science of physics.

1.2 Henry More and Newtonian "spiritualism"

More had been primarily interested in theological rather than natural scientific issues, and had dedicated much of his life to combating what he saw as the atheistic view of the world implied within the writings of contemporaries like Descartes, Hobbes and Spinoza. The Renaissance had witnessed increasing interest in occult phenomena, and in a way not unusual for the time More appealed to a variety of supernatural and occult phenomena involving witchcraft and the actions of demons and spirits of various kinds, in his attempts to refute atheistic materialism (AAA: bk 3). Such phenomena he accounted for in terms of a theory of *spirit* developed in opposition to Descartes. In Descartes' classical dualist ontology, body is conceived of as extended substance and mind as non-extended *thinking* substance. For Descartes, not only are all bodies extended, all extension is *bodily*—that is, there is no extended empty space. Like Aristotle, then, Descartes had argued *against* the notion of void space: all space must be occupied by *something*, just in the way that our ambient space, for example, is occupied by air.

For More, Descartes' "nullibilist" views had disastrous consequences for the idea of God, as they implied either that God *was* a material body (an inference drawn by Spinoza) or that God was nowhere and, hence, was *nothing*. Against Descartes, then, More argued that spirits were incorporeal *extended* substances. It was the fact of their extension that allowed the understanding of how it was that they could interact with each other *and* with material objects. It was this attribution of extension to spirits that had allowed him to think of void space in a new way, and, apparently taking the idea from cabbalistic writings,[7] he conceived *space itself* as a spiritual substance, or as an attribute of a spiritual substance. More now had an answer to one of Aristotle's original arguments against the very concept of empty, matterless space. Space had to be *something* rather than *nothing* because it had properties such as tri-dimensionality, and only something could have properties. In short, space could be conceived as *infinite* and as *singular* because it was an *attribute of God*. This idea was important for Newton.[8]

In his mathematised physical theory, Newton was reliant on the distinction between relative and absolute motion. The argument had been made for centuries that the movement of, say, a boat on a river could be understood differently if one considered it relative to the flowing water or relative to the riverbank. Newton needed to resist the inference that all movement was thereby relative to that of some other body. At a physical level, he employed a thought experiment involving the rotation of water in a rotating bucket to try to argue the case for motion that could be considered absolute rather than relative to some arbitrarily chosen framework (MPNP: vol. 1, 6–12). At a metaphysical level, however, he needed a conception of space that would make sense of the idea of absolute space within which the question of any object's motion or rest could be answered definitively. More's Neoplatonic understanding of space, as an attribute of God, answered that need. Edward Grant sums up the relation between Newton and More:

> Newton's public utterances on the relationship of God and space would appear to link him clearly with Henry More. Does this signify, then, that for Newton, as for More, God is an extended and dimensional being? It would appear so. If Newton conceived infinite, extended, void space as God's attribute, it surely follows that God is an extended being.
>
> (Grant 1981: 244)[9]

After Newton, the success of his physics seemed to provide a retrospective justification for the conception of *absolute* space as a type of infinite, empty container, at least until the late nineteenth century, when the issue of absolute space again came under attack in a development that eventually led to modern relativity theory. However, while this "empty container" view of space is commonly understood as "Newtonian", it should be remembered that for Newton himself, space was not empty. Rather, for him just as for More, space was *full*—it was full of God. And while Newtonian physics is now commonly taken as an exemplification of a naturalistic attitude to the world, if we look to Newton's own conception of the science he was developing, it presupposed a metaphysics that could not be further opposed to naturalism—in the conception of absolute space at the core of the theory, it presupposed a form of metaphysical *spiritualism*.

We might think of the "spiritualist" features of Newton's natural philosophy that linked him to More as including the following related features. The most fundamental reality is a spiritual being, God, which, among other things, is an extended nonmaterial substance whose extension simply *is* the absolute space and time, which are the ultimate presuppositions of physical science. This God is the most fundamental reality in the sense that the material world that exists *in* space depends on him as both its creator and as its ruler. First, as dependent on its creator, matter has no necessary existence, we can conceive of absolute space as empty, and it is within God's power to have *not* created the material world, that is, to have *not* put matter into space. (In contrast, we cannot conceive of the absence of space itself.) Next, neither does matter have the autonomous power to *act*: it is an inert, "dead" stuff moved around by a force external to it. This force is the will of God. The laws according to which matter moves—the laws we know as Newton's laws—are laws decreed by God, analogous to the laws decreed by a king. God can act *on* matter because he is present everywhere throughout the absolute space in which matter moves. And just as this ubiquity secures his omnipotent capacity to act, it secures his omniscient capacity to know what happens in at every point of the extended world.[10]

Newton's theocentric metaphysics, with its picture of a divine ruler issuing laws for the material world, was not without political significance for a society that had emerged from a protracted civil war. Radical Republicans had been attracted to heterodox forms of Christianity in which the relation borne by God to the world was differently pictured (Jacob 2006). Among the heterodox Puritans during this period can be counted the "Behmenists", so-called because inspired by the writings of the German mystic Jakob Böhme, who pictured the world as in some sense alive and self-organising. On this picture, rather than being externally imposed, natural laws were emergent from material nature, a view that was, of course, more favourable to their Republican sympathies.[11]

The difference between these theological views in fact went back to the first centuries of Christianity. Newton's God as omnipotent creator and external lawgiver was effectively the God of St Augustine. The God of the Radicals was, like that of Böhme, closer to the "Platonic theology" of the pagan Neoplatonists Plotinus and Proclus, for whom the material world was an "emanation" from the divine "One", rather than a creation of a God like that of Augustine.[12] It is even controversial as to whether the One of the Neoplatonists can be considered to be a "mind" in any currently accepted sense,[13] but even if considered a mind it was one without a *will*, a divine faculty added by Augustine. The incorporation of Greek philosophy into the idea of God that the early Christians had inherited from their Jewish tradition can hardly be expected to have been a smooth one, and the theoretical wars of medieval theology had displayed a wide variety of possible Gods reflecting a wide array of possible human outlooks as to their relation to the world as a whole.

Newton, a man with very distinct theological and political views of his own,[14] was thus willingly enlisted on the side of those who had supported the reestablishment of the monarchy and then continued to wage a culture war against what was seen as the dangerous pantheist ideology of the Radical Republicans. Margaret Jacob has summed up the doctrines preached by theologians such as Richard Bentley, Samuel Clarke and Williams Whiston, who aligned themselves with Newton:

> They extolled the virtues of self-restraint and public-mindedness, while at the same time assuring their congregations that prosperity came to the virtuous and that divine providence permitted, even fostered, material rewards. The same providence that generates the mechanical laws at work in the universe oversees the workings of society and government, and men must see to it that they conform their political and economic actions to the stability and harmony decreed by supernatural authority. While tolerating doctrinal differences among Christians themselves, reasonable people must acknowledge a vast cosmic order, imposed by God, and attempt to imitate it in society and government.
>
> (Jacob 2006: 63)

1.3 Leibniz, Clarke and Berkeley on space and God

Newton's conception of space was one of the issues on which his bitter dispute with Leibniz was to turn, a dispute ultimately played out in the exchange of letters between Leibniz and Newton's follower, Samuel Clarke (L-C). Relations between Newton and Leibniz had become acrimonious over the issue as to which of them was the actual discoverer of the calculus, but larger issues than this separated the two men. In fact, we might take the dispute between Newton/Clarke and Leibniz as emblematic of an emerging distinction between what would come to be known as anglophone and "Continental" styles of thought. One convenience of this lies in the fact that another critic of Newton's absolutist account of space was the Irish philosopher George Berkeley (1685–1753), Bishop of Cloyne, whose "idealism" is often erroneously taken as a model for our understanding of the idealism of the Continental tradition.[15] An examination of the differences between the Berkeleian and Leibnizian criticisms of Newtonian realism about space and time will thereby provide a way of grasping the significance of the post-Leibnizian tradition.

As we have seen, Newton's conception of space as an infinite, potentially "empty" container had not been easily won, and far from free from its own peculiarities and paradoxes when probed. In particular, Newton had felt the need to underlay his concept of absolute space with an account of something, God, filling it, to respond to the "nullibilist" question. Leibniz was to reject Newton's conception of absolute space, arguing for a conception of space as *relational*. That is, for Leibniz the very ideas of space and time were simply abstractions from relations of coexistence or succession between objects (or more accurately, between the representations making up the contents of particular "monads"). This was a type of nullibilism: absent the objects, simply nothing would be left—nothing *rather than* "space", in Newton's sense. In the exchange with Clarke, Leibniz criticised both Newton's conception of space *and* the conception of God linked with it. Moreover, this opposition to Newton's *spatial* realism would, with Kant, come to be linked to an opposition of the "spiritual realism" associated with Newton's view of space. Following recent treatments of the development of Kant's critical philosophy, I will argue that his move to transcendental idealism was in part triggered by his realisation that his own *early* philosophical position (in which he tried to combine elements of Newton and Leibniz) entailed the type of crude popular form of spiritualism found in More, with its connections to belief in occult phenomena. In Kant's case, this position would be personified in the figure of Emmanuel Swedenborg (1688–1772) who, like More, was a believer in various types of "spiritual" occurrences.[16]

Both Leibniz (and after him, Kant) and Berkeley were critical of Newton's conception of space and time. But, as might be expected, while Leibniz's objections were "rationalist" ones, Berkeley's were of an "empiricist" nature, and this gave very different meanings to their respective anti-realist or "idealist" views about space. In the correspondence with Clarke, Leibniz based all his rationalist criticisms on one or other of his two fundamental principles, those of non-contradiction and sufficient reason, as he mentions in his second letter (L-C: L2.1). Consider the objection to the conception of absolute space that Leibniz makes in his third letter to Clarke, that runs along the following lines. If God created the material universe in an infinite space, then he would have had to place it *somehow* or *somewhere* in that infinite space, but "it is impossible that there should be a reason why God, preserving the same situations of bodies among themselves, should have placed them in space after one certain particular manner and not otherwise" (ibid.: L3.5). The argument is repeated *mutatis mutandis* for time. "Supposing anyone should ask why God did not create everything a year sooner, and the same person should infer from this that God has done something concerning which it is not possible that there should be a reason why he did it so and not otherwise" (ibid.: L3.6). In short, if God had created the world at *some particular time* within the infinite span of time, say on

4 July 6342 BCE, he would have needed a *reason* for doing it then, rather than at some other time. But nothing could *count* here as a reason, and to think of God as acting *arbitrarily* would be to impugn his rationality. The intended lesson is that this whole way of thinking of space and time leading to this conundrum is misguided. Leibniz puts forward his own relational theory of space as a way of avoiding these unacceptable results.

Clarke's reply to Leibniz on this point has various aspects, but it is pursued along two related themes. The first concerns the limits of *our* knowledge—"God may have very good reasons for creating this world at this particular time he did" (L-C: C4.15). The next concerns the *unlimitedness* of God's will. Leibniz's argument, Clarke states, "would prove that whatever God can do he cannot but do ... making him no governor at all but a mere necessary agent, that is, indeed, no agent at all but mere fact and nature and necessity" (C4.22–23). Indeed, the sufficient reason that Leibniz seeks "is often times no other than the mere will of God" (C2.1).

Clarke's objections to Leibniz are revealing in terms of Clarke's implied theology. Behind his objections lies the stance of theological "voluntarism", a stance that had become explicit in the thirteenth century, as a reaction to the influence of Aristotelianism as found in the views of Thomas Aquinas. As will be seen, the significance of voluntarism as a position the Continental idealists opposed is crucial for understanding this movement, and here they tapped into a long-standing anti-voluntarist tradition. In German-speaking regions of Europe especially, anti-voluntarist ideas were transmitted through late medieval figures like Albert the Great and Meister Eckhart,[17] and it was the tradition from which the "oppositional" thoughts of Jakob Böhme had sprung. It was to be especially influential among the post-Kantian idealists, and so a short detour into the theological disputes of late medieval Christianity is therefore warranted.

A forerunner to late medieval voluntarism is found in the conception of God in St Augustine, Bishop of Hippo (CE 354–430), who, while greatly influenced by the pagan Neoplatonists, had rejected the characteristic Greek optimism in the powers of human reason. In Janet Coleman's words, such a conception of human rational powers was regarded "as part of a perverse human fantasy of self-perfection, self-sufficient omnipotence and self-dependent autonomy. Ancient ethics exemplified man's original sin, that of pride which rejoices in private goods and a perverse self-love" (Coleman 2000: 393). It was this critical attitude to the limits of human reason that was to emerge once again in the thirteenth century, as manifested in the Condemnation of 1277, in which Etienne Tempier, Bishop of Paris, condemned the entertaining of a variety of philosophical ideas that had been reintroduced from pagan sources into contemporary theology. Included in the condemnation was Thomas Aquinas, who had died just three years earlier. The beneficiaries of the voluntaristic condemnation of Aquinas' Aristotelianism were nominalists such as Duns Scotus and William of

Ockham, and the consequences for the development of Western culture have been the focus of considerable attention.

In the early twentieth century, the French physicist and historian of science Pierre Duhem claimed that the orthodox and voluntaristic insistence on God's absolute power from the late thirteenth century had liberated European thought from the constraints of Aristotelianism and opened up the possibility of natural science (Duhem 1985). More recently, Hans Blumenberg has also appealed to the importance of Bishop Tempier's condemnation, but giving it a somewhat wider significance to that afforded by Duhem. For Blumenberg, "This document marks the exact point in time when the interest in the rationality and human intelligibility of creation cedes priority to the speculative fascination exerted by the theological predicates of absolute power and freedom" (Blumenberg 1983: 160).[18]

The church's insistence on God's absolute power was in effect a move against that type of *non-voluntarist* versions of Christian Platonist thought in which *ideas* were conceived of as equally real as the divine *mind* that thought them and were not, as in Augustine, reducible to the subjective thoughts of God. On this model God was in the position more of the *demiurge* of Plato's *Timaeus*, but such a conception was interpreted by the voluntarists as placing a limitation on God's power. For Ockham, for example, the only law to which God was himself subject was the law of non-contradiction, and some medieval voluntarists did not even admit of *that* constraint.[19] But this voluntaristic model of God was explicitly challenged by Leibniz: "people have pleaded the irresistible power of God ... and have assumed a despotic power when they should rather have conceived of a power ordered by the most perfect wisdom" (Th: 53). For Leibniz, God acts according to *two* basic principles, the law of non-contradiction and the law of sufficient reason: the former represents a type of *metaphysical*, and the latter, a type of *moral* necessity. The idea of God's being subject to moral necessity seemed to place constraints on the possible universes that he might have created, but such "constraints" are only a measure of his goodness.[20] God *could have* created other possible universes, if it were not for the fact of his divine justice, which implied that he create the *best* of all possible worlds. Indeed, this was the one he *had* created: *this* world *was*, as he famously argued in the *Theodicy* of 1710, the best of all possible worlds.[21]

Leibniz's Platonistic anti-voluntarism was, then, just the sort of view that Bishop Tempier had attempted to eliminate from Christendom in 1277 because it placed restrictions on God's power. And Leibniz's belief that humans could work out *from reason alone* certain facts about how the world must be was just the sort of view condemned by Tempier as exemplifying the sin of "pride". For the nominalists, the omnipotent will of God was beyond human comprehension, and so reason must give way to revelation. However, a radically *secular* version of such a voluntaristic anti-Platonic, anti-Aristotelian view was to appear in the seventeenth century in the thought of Hobbes, a thinker against whom Leibniz would oppose his own philosophy.[22] In short, in *Leibniz's* opposition to Newton's conception of space we find the implicit opposition of a Platonist to Newton's voluntaristic theology. What, however, was the nature of *Berkeley's* opposition to Newton's spatiotemporal realism?

Berkeley's opposition to Newton's conception of absolute space flowed from a very different source to that of Leibniz: it was a consequence of his radical *empiricism*. Starting from the assumption, found in Descartes and Locke, that what we are aware of in the first instance is our own subjective *ideas*, Berkeley, in his *Principles of Human Knowledge* (of 1710), argued against the legitimacy of the inference to something outside the mind that corresponded to and was causally responsible *for* those ideas, the inference central to Locke's account of our knowledge of the external world through experience. For Berkeley, Locke's inference to material bodies simply contravened his empiricist criterion of knowledge. If all we can experience are our own ideas, the inference to the material bodies that "caused" them cannot be made, as we can have no independent knowledge of their existence.

Berkeley's attack on Newton's conception of absolute space proceeded from the same radically empiricist standpoint. Void space is not perceptible, so we "cannot even frame an idea of *pure space*, excusive of all body". Here we think we do so, on the assumption that "every noun substantive stands for a distinct idea" (PHK: §116). Those in the grip of the notion of void space are essentially caught in a dangerous dilemma. They are led to think that "either real space is God, or else that there is something beside God which is eternal, uncreated, infinite, indivisible, immutable" (§117). And not only is there no *space*, there are no created material bodies *in* space. Bodies are just collections of ideas.

At around the same time as the exchange with Clarke, Leibniz commented on the radical philosophical position that the twenty-five-year-old Berkeley had put forward in *Principles* a few years before, correcting Berkeley in the terms of his own "monadology":

> There is much here that is correct and close to my own view. But it is expressed paradoxically. For it is not necessary to say that matter is nothing, but it is sufficient to say that it is a phenomenon, like the rainbow; and that it is not a substance, but the resultant of substances, and that space is no more real than time, that is, that space is nothing but the order of coexistents, just as time is the order of things that have existed before [subexistentia]. ... Badly, or at least in vain, he rejects abstract ideas, restricts ideas to imaginations, and condemns the subtleties of arithmetic and geometry.
>
> (PE: 307)

Here Leibniz alludes to the central metaphysical claim of *Principles*—the claim that "matter is nothing", Berkeley's "immaterialism". This is the doctrine often taken as definitive of idealism, despite the fact that Berkeley himself never describes his position as "idealist". But Berkeley's immaterialism is in fact a consequence of his underlying *spiritual realism*. For Berkeley, the underlying reality on which the existence of everything depends, the underlying substance, is the mind of God. Metaphysically, then, Berkeley's position was like that of Newton, except more radical. Newton had not *denied* matter, but had simply given it a dependent ontological status. It was the creation of God. But as Leibniz stresses, Berkeley had *denied* matter, and made it a *fiction*, and the grounds for this denial was, like his denial of space, his radical *empiricist* rejection of abstract ideas.

Exactly how to understand Berkeley's overall immaterialist claim is controversial. On the popular view, Berkeley has, in a very counterintuitive way, simply denied the reality of a *world* outside the individual mind. On other, more sophisticated readings, however, his philosophy is compatible with common sense, as what he rejected was not ordinary objects outside the mind, but simply something like Locke's unperceivable material substratum, in which perceivable properties are thought to inhere. On this reading, then, he did not reduce the world to the perceiver's subjective mental states, as is commonly claimed.[23] But even on this reading, Berkeley was still committed to a radically *spiritualist* ontology. He fully acknowledges the non-dependence of "external" objects on my individual will:

> whatever power I may have over my own thoughts, I find the ideas actually perceived by sense have not a like dependence on my will. When in broad day-light I open my eyes, it is not in my power to choose whether I shall see or no, or to determine what particular objects shall present themselves to my view; and so likewise as to the hearing and other senses, the ideas imprinted on them are not creatures of my will.
>
> (PHK: §29)

However, he interprets this in terms of their dependence on *another* will: "There is therefore some other will or spirit that produces them" (ibid.: §29). That is, he still requires the perceived properties to be supported by some substrate analogous to Locke's "I know not what", and this substrate is interpreted as a *spiritual* one, the mind of God.

Berkeley's radical rejection of "abstract ideas", such as the Lockean notion of substance or matter and Newton's conception of space—the stance that Leibniz describes as his "restricting ideas to imaginations"—reveals the radical *nominalism* of Berkeley's underlying position, the relevance of which was forcefully argued in the latter part of the nineteenth century by the American pragmatist philosopher C. S. Peirce. For Peirce,

Berkeley's metaphysical position was an extreme version of "that strange union of nominalism with Platonism" that was recurrent within British philosophy (Peirce 1992: 85).[24] Focusing on the *nominalism* of Berkeley's position will allow us to get a clearer sense of what the Continental idealists were committed to, given their strong *anti-nominalist* stand, a stand relating to their *anti-voluntarism*. In brief, my argument will be that in the wake of *Leibniz*, Continental idealism was characterised by an anti-nominalist opposition to empiricism, and that in the wake of *Kant*, a critique of the metaphysical conception of *spirit* or *mind* as a type of nonmaterial substance. It was in virtue of its attempt to extract itself from these two features of Berkeleian idealism that post-Kantian idealism could be construed as a "struggle against subjectivism" (Beiser 2002).

On Peirce's account, Berkeley stands at the end of a line of thinkers originating with the medieval nominalist William of Ockham and passing through Thomas Hobbes and John Locke. William of Ockham (1280–1349) was the most radical critic of the Aristotelian views of "realists" such as Aquinas. For "nominalists", like Ockham, "universals" (Platonic ideas) were only *names*. In the world itself, there were only particular objects—particular dogs, particular chairs, particular clouds, and so on—and above and beyond these, no separate *kinds* of objects, no "genus" dog, chair or cloud. Ockham's move was to consider a mental content as a *logical term*, akin to an element of language, which, "instead of existing on paper, or in the voice, is in the mind" but which "is of the same general nature, namely, a sign" (Peirce 1992: 93). While his realist opponents had taken universals to be *real*, in the sense of things *in the world*, Ockham's idea of the mental contents as akin to words or signs opened up the possibility that what had "universality" was the mental content itself, not what it stood for. With this, Ockham was, according to Peirce, "the *venerabilis inceptor* of a new way of philosophizing which has now broadened, perhaps deepened also, into English empiricism" (ibid.: 95).

In Peirce's reconstruction, Hobbes had generalised Ockham's move and "carried the nominalist spirit into everything,—religion, ethics, psychology, and physics" (Peirce 1992: 95), and Locke had, in turn, added a "sensationalist" aspect to Hobbes's by identifying Ockham's original mental "words" with the sensations or "sensory ideas" of which one was immediately aware in conscious experience. With this, mental contents, that had been conceived of as *word-like* in Ockham, were now conceived to be more *picture-like*. From such a Lockean starting point Berkeley now went beyond Locke by denying that we can even form any abstract general ideas at all (ibid.: 95–96).[25] Berkeley even criticised Ockham, Peirce points out, for having admitted general terms into the mind. All this is a consequence of the fact that, as Leibniz put it, Berkeley "restricts ideas to imaginations".

Leibniz, as we will see, was attracted to just those elements of Aristotelian "substantial forms" of which Berkeley was the radical critic.

Moreover, Leibniz was intensely critical of the other side of the nominalism of thinkers like Ockham and Hobbes, their *voluntarism*—the voluntarism we see too in Newton and Clarke. But Berkeley equally shared in this voluntarism, as it is central to his spiritual realism. Thus he posited two different ontological kinds: "Thing or being is the most general name of all, it comprehends under it two kinds entirely distinct and heterogeneous, and which have nothing in common but the name, to wit, *spirits* and *ideas*." And the fundamental distinction between these two types of thing is that "the former are *active, indivisible substances*: the latter are *inert, fleeting, dependent beings*, which subsist not by themselves, but are supported by, or exist in minds or spiritual substances" (PHK: §89). This identification of spirit with *activity* had been expressed forcefully in Berkeley's earlier notebooks in terms of an identification of the *spirit* with the *will*: "The Spirit the Acting thing—that which is Soul and God is the Will alone. The Ideas are effects, impotent things" (WGB: vol. 1, 87).[26] However, if God is omnipotent, then presumably he is not a *perceiving* being—in any case, he must not perceive in the way we finite spirits do, given the passivity that is at its core. And indeed, consistent with this idea, Berkeley says of God in the *Three Dialogues*, that he "perceives nothing by sense as we do; [his] will is absolute and independent, causing all things, and liable to be thwarted or resisted by nothing ... God Knows, or hath ideas; but His ideas are not conveyed to Him by sense, as ours are" (TD: 86–87).

Taking Berkeley as a model on which to understand the idealism of the philosophers in the Continental tradition from Leibniz onwards is thus a bit like taking an emu as representative of the class *Aves*. The idea that Berkeley is an "idealist"—a classification that was not Berkeley's and that has been denied by some of his most adept followers[27]—is possibly so deeply entrenched in the anglophone philosophical vocabulary to be immovable. But if we do use this word of Berkeley, we should consciously avoid drawing any inferences for the stance of the Continental idealists. (Consequently, in this work, I use "idealist" only in referring to the latter, and refer to Berkeley as a "spiritual realist".) To understand the philosophy of the Continentals, we should forget about Berkeley and turn to the first genuine representative of this tradition, Gottfried Wilhelm Leibniz.

2

THE MONADOLOGICAL WORLD OF GOTTFRIED WILHELM LEIBNIZ

Gottfried Wilhelm Leibniz (1646–1716) was born in Leipzig into a scholarly and noble family just before the end of the Thirty Years War (1618–48) that had torn apart the German states. His father was the Professor of Moral Philosophy at the University of Leipzig, and his mother was also from an academic family. Accordingly, Leibniz had a very broad education and throughout his life was active in a vast number of diverse intellectual areas. Much of his life was spent working in various official capacities in courts in Europe, including those in Paris, London and, for the greater part of his mature life, Hanover.

Central to Leibniz's philosophy was the project to reconcile religion, ancient metaphysics and modern science. He was a major innovator in mathematics (inventing calculus at the same time as and independently of Newton) and logic (anticipating the type of "algebraic" formalisation of logic later developed in the nineteenth century), but importantly, he also sought to rework ancient Aristotelian and Platonic ideas such that they could be made compatible with the developing physical sciences. Here, his influence was central to the development of a conception of science in Continental Europe that differed from the more mechanistic tradition found in Britain.

Many of his distinctive ideas about the nature of substances, and some of the very peculiar consequences of these ideas, seem to be entailed by the logical conceptions he ultimately took from Aristotle and Plato. Kant's later criticisms of Leibnizian metaphysics were, in turn, bound up with his criticisms of these logical conceptions.

2.1 Leibniz's monadological world

Leibniz is best known for his elaborate "monadological" metaphysics, a view in which the universe is ultimately made up of extensionless but active, simple substances which, in his later writings, he called "monads"— "the true atoms of nature ... the elements of things" (M: §3). This idea of a monad developed from his earlier notion of individual *substances*, the notion of *substance* being taken over from Aristotle (Mercer 2002). But equally, Leibniz seems to have taken over central elements from the philosophy of Plato and later Platonists.[1]

Donald Rutherford has helpfully described Leibniz's conception of individual substance in terms of the following features (Rutherford 1995: 133–37). Individual substances

(a) are independent, or have *per se* existence. An army, for example, is *not* a substance, because its existence depends on the existence of the soldiers making it up. In contrast, substances are radically independent of the existence of things *other than* themselves (with the exception of God);

(b) are the intrinsic sources of action to which appeal is made in all explanations. Substances are the ultimate explanatory principles of other things. Because substances *are* independent, one cannot appeal to any factor external to them to explain *their* behaviours;[2]

(c) endure through change. We think of substances enduring through changes in the properties they possess but which are not essential to them. A piece of wax remains *the same* wax through the changes of its properties resulting from heating it, for example;

(d) have *true* unity. Things such as armies or animal herds, the existences of which depend on component things (the soldiers making up the army, the animals making up the herd), have only *accidental* unity. Individual substances have true or *per se* unity;

(e) are the subjects for individuation—each individual substance is individuated from others by the *kind* of substance it is (is individuated by its "form" or "species"). No substance, then, can be regarded as a bare something—a *bare this*—but is always an instance of a kind. It is always a *this such* (this soldier, this cow, etc.). Individual substances are *infirmae species*, the lowest species on the Tree of Porphyry.

While these five features are largely as found in Aristotle, two other more distinctly Neoplatonist characteristics of substance are introduced by Leibniz. Each substance is

(f) "pregnant with its own future"—that is, all the temporal phases of a substance are internally connected, such that the entire future of an individual substance is somehow implicitly contained within it at any one instant. Linked to this characteristic is the notion that

(g) each substance is said to "express the entire universe". Every substance is ultimately connected with *every other substance* in the universe such that a change in the state of *any one* will be reflected in the state of *every other*. Leibniz expresses this in terms of a "harmony" between the states of all substances in the universe, as coordinated by laws originating in the mind of God.[3]

We might characterise these last two features as expressing distinctively *modern* ideas, in contrast to the more traditional "Aristotelian" conceptions of substance reflected in characteristics (a) to (e), since in Leibniz it is connected with the idea that the universe can be understood in terms of the operation of *simple* and *universally applicable laws*, an idea that is characteristic of scientific approaches to the universe found in early-modern thinkers such as Copernicus and Galileo. Standardly, early-modern advocates of the new cosmology of the infinite, "open" universe have been seen as having been strictly *opposed to* the Aristotelian view of the "closed" cosmos that had dominated in the medieval period. But while Galileo and other early-modern thinkers such as Thomas Hobbes thought of themselves, with their mechanical accounts of the universe, as *rejecting* Aristotle, Leibniz attempted to give an *alternative interpretation* of the mechanical approach to the universe by *integrating* or *reconciling* the new view with Aristotle's, by modifying Aristotle's in various ways, as reflected in (f) and (g). But as we will see, Leibniz seems to have brought about this *modernising* modification of the Aristotelian approach by synthesising it with other aspects of ancient philosophy, in particular, ones belonging to *Platonic* forms of thought, especially as developed by the Neoplatonists, Plotinus and Proclus.

2.2 Leibniz, the new physics, and the divine orderliness of the universe

As we have seen, Aristotle had thought of *space* as a combination of differentiated *places*, and one way this was expressed was in his idea of a radical ontological divide between the realms marked by the orbit of the moon. For Aristotle, the earth exists at the centre of the cosmos, and it is populated by *imperfect* substances (such as human beings and other living things) subject to generation and corruption. In contrast, all things existing beyond the orbit of the moon (i.e., belonging to the supralunar realm), such as the stars, are perfect and incorruptible substances. This difference is reflected in the behaviour of the elements of the terrestrial or sublunar and the celestial or supralunar realms, respectively: the natural motion of terrestrial bodies as linear; that of celestial bodies, circular.[4] In contrast to Galileo's later mechanics, with its principle of inertia, in Aristotle's physics all movement requires a mover, and so Aristotle had posited an ultimate source of such movement. This is God (*theos*), the "prime mover", who exists at the "outer sphere" of the cosmos and who is responsible for the diurnal rotation of the stars. God himself, however, was himself "unmoved".

In the physics developed by Galileo and Newton to go with the new cosmology of Copernicus and Bruno, the same laws were seen as applying throughout this now infinite universe and there were no fixed *places* in the universe (such as a centre and an edge), as presupposed by the sub- and supralunar distinction in Aristotle. But while the new cosmological system within which the evolving universal form of mechanical explanation could progressively synthesise terrestrial and celestial phenomena was indeed new, it was, as a general cosmological picture, not unprecedented. Platonists like Nicholas of Cusa could draw upon both ancient resources such as the cosmology found in Plato's *Timaeus*, which was far more "celestial" than its Aristotelian rival, and forms of Christian Neoplatonism that had incorporated the views of Plotinus and Proclus. The "infinite-circle" trope which Cusa had applied to the universe had been drawn from the early fourteenth-century Dominican mystical theologian, "Meister" Johann Eckhart (c. 1260–c. 1328), who had used it of God.

While some conservative contemporaries of Leibniz, such as his teacher Jakob Thomasius, had rejected the new scientific world view in order to hold onto the older Aristotelian ideas, Leibniz *embraced* the new style of thinking as found in Galileo, Descartes and Newton, according to which the elements of the world are perceived as interacting under universally applicable laws. Like Newton himself, he thought of the universal laws describing the movements of bodies in the world as decreed by God, and it was the same Neoplatonic elements that had gone into Newton's natural philosophy that allowed Leibniz to transform the Aristotelianism to which he adhered. Thus Loemker has noted that to the extent that the eclecticism of seventeenth-century thinkers like Leibniz had sought for unifying principles, "it assumed the form of Christian Platonism," a system of thought whose "intricate threads of influence" had linked "the Franciscans, the Brothers of the Common Life, Nicholas of Cusa, and the Florentine Academy to Bruno, Campanella, and Descartes" (Loemker 1961: 332). Thus, when the focus shifts to such attempts to unify Aristotelian natural philosophy with the resources of Christian Neoplatonism, the transition from "closed cosmos" to "infinite universe", as stressed by thinkers such as Thomas Kuhn, need not look quite as radical and anti-Aristotelian as it is commonly portrayed. As Eckhard Kessler has put it, much of the input to the new natural philosophy might be regarded "as essentially an attempt to integrate new physical experience and knowledge by transforming Aristotelian natural philosophy in accordance with Neoplatonic metaphysical principles" (Kessler 1990: 143–44). This, indeed, was the tradition to which Leibniz belonged, and that would be relevant to understanding the thought of later idealists as well—a tradition that, in its appeal to synthetic forms of Platonism and Aristotelianism, stood in contrast to the nominalistic and voluntaristic forms of thought *also* reflected in complex ways in the emerging natural sciences.

Thus, while Leibniz was intent on absorbing modern mechanistic forms of explanation into his philosophy, he conceived of such *physical* understanding as working only at a superficial level of analysis. This physical level of analysis must be underpinned, he thought, by a different, more rational and consistent *metaphysical* account. And without this deeper metaphysical account, grounded in the metaphysics of Plato and Aristotle, modern physical science could not be reconciled with religious belief and would ultimately lead to a Godless conception of the world. Hence Leibniz's metaphysical views were meant to show how modern science and Christian dogma could coexist.[5] Here as elsewhere, his thought was in the service of a type of *reconciliation* of what could otherwise seem to be antagonistic views.

In the emerging mechanistic view of the world, which Leibniz accepted at a *physical level*, the universe was ultimately made up of causally interacting extended material bodies. Leibniz rejected this as an *ultimate* account of the world: such mechanically interacting material bodies were, at a deeper level, to be understood as monadic, elementary units. Monads, according to Leibniz, are themselves without extension. Nor do they actually interact with each other, the way that Aristotelian substances were typically conceived as interacting. (If a monad's states were causally affected by other monads it could not be independent.) In fact, monads behave in the way they do because they are driven by their own "appetitions", conceived as *somehow like* desires or drives. Besides appetitions monads have "representations" of the states of all other monads in the universe—characteristic (g) above. In this sense monads have the features of "minds" or "souls", and Leibniz's philosophy involved a type of *spiritualism*, although not the "immaterialist" form of Bishop Berkeley. In contrast to Berkeley's immaterialism, Leibniz's idealism, in using the Aristotelian form–matter distinction, had more in common with the idealism of Kant and the post-Kantians.[6]

Relations existing between the behaviours of the different monads are not random but law-like, and this is why we *mistakenly* think of the bodies that are ultimately constituted by monads as causally interacting. That is, when we see one billiard ball strike another, apparently "causing" the second ball to move, the movement of the second ball is not *really* due to the impact of the first. It is actually due to a harmony among the "appetitions" of its constitutive monads.[7] Our everyday way of thinking of things causally affecting each other in space and time is simply a result of the limitations of our way of conceiving of them. When we think of causal relations in this way, as among the interactions of extended things in space, we conceive of their elements in terms of the "indistinct" and "confused" ideas resulting from perception. Like Plato, Leibniz was deeply sceptical of the type of "knowledge" that perception supplies.[8] In reality, the changing states of the monads constituting the two balls are simply coordinated with each other in the universal harmony among the states of all things, as indicated above in characteristic (g) (although from the perspective of an even deeper level of analysis, the "harmony" involved is not so much among the "external" behaviours of the constituent monads as among the *representations* constituting the monads "experiencing" the interactions). The metaphysical reality underlying the appearance is something we will come to understand when we *cognise* all this "clearly and distinctly", rather than relying solely on perception.

To capture the distinction between the limitedness of the knowledge possessed by finite minds and the infiniteness of God's knowledge, Leibniz on occasions appealed to the metaphor of "perspective". Thus, while a finite monad neither exists "in" space nor has extension, it nevertheless represents the universe as if from a *point of view* "rather as the same town is differently represented according to the different situations of the person who looks at it" (DM: §9). The difference between the apparent spatial "locations" involved here is cashed out in the specific relations among representations contributing to the states of each monad. In contrast, he distinguishes the "view" of God from that of each finite monad in the following way:

> God, so to speak, turns on all sides and considers in all ways the general system of phenomena which he has found it good to produce in order to manifest his glory. And as he considers all the faces of the world in all possible ways—for there is no aspect which escapes his omniscience—the result of each view of the universe, as looked at from a certain position, is, if God finds it good to actualise his thoughts and to produce it, a substance which expresses the universe in conformity with that view.
>
> (Ibid.: §14)[9]

Each perspectival finite monad is thus like a "mirror of God" in this regard, this being a familiar Christian Platonist trope found in Eckhart and Cusa to capture the relation of human and divine intellects. The underlying idea of the orderly harmonisation of individual perspectives in the mind of God seems to come from the Herborn Encyclopaedist, Bisterfeld (Antognazza 1999; Rutherford 1995: 36–40); however, the idea is at the heart of Nicholas of Cusa's Neoplatonic image of "infinite sphere".[10] It is a form in which we shall see the issue return in Kant's transcendental idealism.

One explanatory advantage of Leibniz's idea that all monads contain "representations" and "appetitions" is that it avoids the traditional mind–body or "subject–object" problem. It also explains how certain types of monads—human beings—are capable of *knowing* (having true representations of) the nature of the universe and of acting on their desires, because it makes this just a particular instance of a much more general feature of *all* monads. The cost of this, of course, is the peculiar idea that everything is somehow living and ensouled – the position of "pananimism".

2.3 Leibniz's conception of the *moral* order

Leibniz would appeal to universal laws not only in the explanation of physical phenomena but also in his conception of social life. The disastrous effects of the Thirty Years War on life in the German-speaking regions of

Europe prompted many thinkers of Leibniz's generation to reconsider the way society should be organised and structured so as to minimise the possibilities of conflict. Leibniz's solution runs counter to the developing, basically secular accounts of political relations found in thinkers such as Hobbes and Locke, for example, by Leibniz's grounding these relations in his strongly Platonistic and theocentric metaphysics.

As we have seen, Leibniz's monadological world is one in which there is no *actual* interaction between monads: instead there exists a "pre-established harmony" among the monads (that is, among the perceptions and appetitions characterising all the monads) that has been instituted by God. Not only is God responsible for the orderliness or harmony of the world, *this* world is actually the *best* (i.e., most harmonious) *possible* world. This follows from the perfection of God: since he is perfect, his kingdom (the world) must be the best possible object, as a perfect will wills only what is *good*. (This realm cannot *be* perfect, however, as only God himself is perfect.) Leibniz thinks this can effectively be discerned from the *concept* of God, as can the fact of God's *existence*.[11] Humans, with their less than perfect, perspectivally perception-tied understanding may not see that theirs *is* the "best of all possible worlds", but as a person's understanding comes closer to being perfect (as that person's ideas become clearer and more distinct, and *less* tied to the particularity of their perspective) they will grasp how all the apparent imperfections in the world actually contribute to its overall status as the best one possible.

This does not sound like a particularly fruitful starting point for moral and political thought (Leibniz was to be satirised in the eighteenth century by Voltaire, as Dr Pangloss in the novel *Candide*), but Leibniz, nevertheless, had a well worked out political philosophy, grounded in this theocentric metaphysics, and he applied this thought in many practical contexts. The "universal jurisprudence" governing the human realm is, like the universal physical laws describing the physical universe, grounded in the mind of God, and God, as perfectly rational and good, can only want the *best* laws— those that are the most just, the most orderly and harmonious—governing the universe. In turn these laws can be discovered and understood by humans to the extent that they learn to think rationally. Thus in an early work, Leibniz could describe theology as "a certain species of jurisprudence (the latter being taken universally), for it deals with the [system of] Justice and Laws obtaining in the Republic, or rather Kingdom, of God over human beings".[12]

Leibniz's idea that God's laws could be understood from the use of *reason* had distinct implications for his attitude to religion and implied that humans were not simply tied to what was revealed in the Bible or to what had to be accepted on faith. In this way, he thought, reason could be applied so as to reconcile such doctrinal differences as those between Catholicism and Protestantism that had rent the social fabric of Europe during the Thirty Years War.[13] Moreover, it also gave a distinct character to *God* as Leibniz conceived of him—a feature that set Leibniz's theology in opposition to those of the more voluntaristic Christian thinkers at the time. He thus opposed the idea that God, by an act of his all-powerful will, simply *defined* what was "the best" for the world. *That* view gave a certain contingent character to the laws governing the world—both natural and social laws—as it was thought that those laws *could have been otherwise* had God *willed them to be otherwise*.

In the seventeenth century, the voluntaristic position could be seen clearly in Descartes' claim that there are *no truths* antecedent to God's will. Moreover, similar remnants of such a voluntaristic theology were even contained in the otherwise predominantly naturalistic approach to political thought found in Hobbes. Hobbes is most well known for introducing the idea that political legitimacy is founded on the *agreement* of the will of those ruled, an agreement struck in a kind of "compact" or "social contract". Nevertheless, underlying Hobbes's account in *Leviathan* of political legitimacy as arising out of the agreement of those ruled was the idea that it was the "irresistible power" of God that was the underlying source of his *absolute* right of dominion—what Hobbes calls, "the right of nature":

> The right of nature whereby God reigneth over men, and punisheth those that break his laws, is to be derived, not from his creating them (as if he required obedience, as of gratitude for his benefits), but from his *irresistible power*.
>
> (L: ch. 31, §5)

Commenting on this passage, Yves Charles Zarka notes how it shows clearly that "Hobbes belongs to the tradition of theological voluntarism and that his natural and political philosophy depend on it" (Zarka 1996: 79).[14] *Irresistible* power, Hobbes thinks, is in fact not found in the political realm—hence the central role there of contract. However, he makes it clear that this is due to contingent features of power in the political realm: were a human to have irresistible power, this would be the ultimate justification of political authority. "Power irresistible justifieth all action really and properly, *in whomsoever it is found*" (HEW: vol. 5, 114–16, emphasis added).

Leibniz, like the Cambridge Platonist Ralph Cudworth, was explicit in his opposition to Hobbes' combination of nominalism and voluntarism, and such opposition would have important consequences for later idealist thought, not least in influencing the idealist conception of the *will*.[15] As has often been pointed out, it is difficult to see how Hobbes's contractarian idea can appeal to the grounding of authority on the *free*-willing of subjects, given his naturalistic account of the will.[16] Hobbes effectively identifies the will with an empirical bodily appetite or aversion: "In *deliberation*, the last appetite, or aversion, immediately adhering to the action, or to the omission thereof, is that we call the WILL; the act, not the faculty, of willing" (L: ch.

6, §53). In distancing himself from the *faculty* of willing, Hobbes was setting himself against the scholastic view going back to Aristotle of the faculty of the will—*voluntas*—as a type of rational power *causing* the action (L: ch. 46, §28). Instead, Hobbes introduces appetite and aversion as quasi-mechanically acting affective states, causally brought about by perceptual interaction with the world, and manifesting themselves in particular actions. This means that freedom for Hobbes *cannot* be identified with any notion of a *rationally self-determining* will, presupposed by the Christian Platonist tradition. A man can no more "determine his will than any other appetite, that is, more than he can determine when he shall be hungry or not" (HEW: vol. 5, 34). Rather than consisting of the will determining *itself*, freedom consists in doing "what the will is determined unto" (ibid.: 35). In psychology, just as in *theology*, voluntarism makes rationality consequent upon a concept of willing outside the scope of any reasoning. The content of the will is simply something *given*.

In his opposition to voluntarism in its theological and secular forms, Leibniz appealed to Aristotelian and Platonist considerations, but here as elsewhere this was done in a way that attempted to reconcile this mode of thought with the type of thought that was characteristically modern. These attempts were not without their problems, and in many ways Kant's later approach to the will with its similar opposition to psychological voluntarism of the Hobbesian variety appears to have been an attempt to get beyond those problems. But what characterises Kant in this regard is a commitment to the same broadly Aristotelian considerations that marked Leibniz's stance against the secularised version of the nominalist–voluntarist orientation of his antagonist, Hobbes.

2.4 The monadological conception of the soul and its capacities

As Leibniz's idea of a "monad" represents a modern version of the ancient Aristotelian idea of individual substance, we should think of the mind-like monads in terms of *Aristotle's* ancient conception of the "psyche", the "mind" or "soul", rather than any modern idea of the mind as found, say, in Descartes or Berkeley. For Aristotle, there are three types of soul found in the living world—plant souls, animal souls and human, rational souls— and here "soul" means something like the principle of something's activity and movement (DA: bks 2 and 3). Thus the Aristotelian "soul" was not particularly connected with the phenomenon of consciousness, as is the modern notion of the "mind", nor did it name a *type* of immaterial substance by contrast to the material nature of bodies.[17] Rather, Aristotle describes the soul as the *form* of the body—all substances being ultimately "formed matter". Moreover, the form of a substance is its explanatory principle, and so an attempt to explain the movement of a plant—that it grows *upwards*, for example—will appeal to the distinct characteristics of the plant "soul".

Plant souls are effectively nutritive, being evoked in the explanation of how a plant stays alive. In contrast, animals are mobile and hence need sense perception of their environment. The human soul has these characteristics and further ones as well. In explaining human action, one does not simply appeal to nutritive needs and the capacity to perceive surroundings, but also to the capacity to *reason*. Aristotle had understood this as involving the capacity, not only to perceive particular objects in the world (as an animal can), but also to take into the mind the *form* of those objects. It was this that enables humans to reason about, and not merely to respond to, objects in their world.

This difference between animal and human cognition is reflected in Leibniz's distinction between *obscure* and *confused* ideas, on the one hand, and *clear and distinct* knowledge, on the other. I have obscure (or unclear) ideas, like *my* idea "oak tree", when I cannot recognise instances of those ideas. Conversely, I have clear ideas, like my idea "gum tree", when I *can* recognise instances of those ideas. Or to put it another way, I have an obscure knowledge of oaks, but a clear knowledge of gums. But further, clear knowledge can be *distinct* or *confused* (or indistinct). "When I can recognize one thing among others without being able to say what its differences or properties consist in", says Leibniz in the *Discourse on Metaphysics*, "my knowledge is *confused*" (DM: §24). To illustrate clear but confused knowledge, Leibniz appeals to an example, the resonance of which we will see in Kant: *aesthetic judgment*. "In this way we sometimes know *clearly*, without being in any way in doubt, whether a poem or a painting is good or bad, because there is a certain *je ne sais quoi* which pleases or offends us" (ibid.). Distinct knowledge, on the other hand, involves the capacity to "explain the evidence I am using" in my making of some judgment. "An assayer's knowledge is like this; he can distinguish true from false gold by means of certain tests or marks which make up the definition of gold" (ibid.). This is crucial. Distinctness comes in degrees because it may be the case that my knowledge of the *evidence* I adduce in a distinct judgment is *itself* clear but confused. For example, I might give as evidence for my belief that this metal is gold, that it is yellow, shiny metal, but be unable to say anything further, as my ideas of "shiny", "yellow", and so on, are "confused": I can just pick out yellow, shiny things in the way that I can pick out a good painting or poem. The assayer doesn't stop at such confused ideas, however, but can do further tests. But the assayer *too* will stop somewhere in the giving of evidence, as there is only one being with knowledge whose distinctness goes "all the way down", as it were: God. It is the point at which one's distinct ideas give way to the confused ones of perception that defines, as it were, the "perspective" or "point of view" from which one understands the world.

Leibniz's distinction between beings capable of forming clear and distinct ideas, like ourselves, and beings unable to get beyond clear but confused ideas seems to be a modification of Aristotle's distinction between the type of perceptions capable by humans and nonhuman animals. Aristotle thought that while animals just perceive things as the *singular* things they are, we humans are capable of recognising objects as instances of kinds—as *this such*s. I see *this* thing in front of me *as* a tree, *that* thing *as* a car. In Aristotle's terminology, I perceive its *form*. In Leibniz's account, it is this ability that is linked to the capacity to give reasons ("evidence") for the claim. To be capable of the perception of "form", or what Leibniz describes as being capable of "apperception", is to be able to give reasons for the *as* of the perception.

As Robert Brandom has pointed out (Brandom 2000: 46) this understanding seems to mark off the approach to the idea of "representation" of the classical rationalists, like Leibniz and Spinoza, from that of Descartes and, following him, the British *empiricists*. While the rationalists

> accepted the central role of the concept of representation in explaining human cognitive activity ... they were not prepared to accept Descartes's strategy of treating the possession of representational content [i.e., certain knowledge of a merely *clear* idea] as an unexplained explainer. ... They were explicitly concerned, as Descartes was not, to be able to explain what it is for something to be understood, taken, treated, or employed *as* a representing *by* the subject: what it is for it to be a representing *to* or *for* that subject. ... Their idea was that the way in which representings point beyond themselves to something represented is to be understood in terms of *inferential* relations among representings. States and acts acquire content by being caught up in inferences, as premises and conclusions.
>
> (Ibid.)[18]

For Leibniz, nature has provided nonhuman animals "with organs which bring together a number of rays of light or of undulations in the air, this making them more effective by combining them" (M: §25), and combined with memory they are thereby capable of "a kind of *sequencing* which mimics reason, but which must be distinguished from it" (ibid.: §26). Humans too can operate in this way, by a type of association of ideas, for example "when we expect there will be daylight tomorrow on the grounds that it has always been like that up to now", but this is a different type of expectation to that found in an *astronomer* who, having a theory to explain the regularity of the transitions from night to day, "believes it on the basis of reason" (ibid.: §28).

It is the fact that the distinctness of knowledge is scalar that explains how for Leibniz the empirical knowledge provided by the sciences can be distinct from, and need the underlay of, metaphysical knowledge. It is "the knowledge of necessary and eternal truths" that is what "distinguishes us from mere animals and gives us *reason* and science, raising us to the knowledge of ourselves and of God" (M: §29). But, as we have seen, for finite monads like ourselves, reasons will run out *somewhere* in a type of knowledge that, although clear, will be confused and perspectival. Empirical science is like this to the extent that modern mechanistic physics still appeals to something *given* in perception. Only God's knowledge, located at the top of the scale of distinctness, will grasp *everything* in a way that is necessary and in the form of truths that are eternal.

In genuine *metaphysical* knowledge of the world, in which we aspire to bring all our ideas to the highest level of clarity and distinctness, we will grasp, for example, that the time and space within which such local inter-actions are meant to occur are not, in fact, *real*, as Newton supposed time and space to be.[19] That is, according to Leibniz, when we think about time and space clearly and distinctly, we will grasp that they refer, not to *substances* (i.e., to that which is ultimately real), but merely to *relations* of simultaneity and succession between the representations occurring within monads. For example, when I experience one billiard ball striking another and *causing* it to move, what I am experiencing is a certain succession of my sensory representations. Other monads may perceive the "same" event of one ball striking another, not because they are perceiving some *independent* "real" event as it is conventionally assumed, but only because God has harmonised the changes in all the representations in all the monads, thus the changes in the sensory states of humans. To "explain" this in terms of the "reality" of the event perceived would be to appeal to a form of understanding limited to the unclear and indistinct ideas of perception.

This view of the relation of perception to knowledge might be seen as involving a radical extension of changes in the conception of knowledge accompanying the new physics. To a degree, Leibniz was here simply agreeing with the view of Galileo and others who thought of the world as revealed by science to be quite different to that of everyday perception or common sense. For example, while for common sense the colours we see are real non-relational properties of external things, Galileo thought of col-ours as subjective effects produced *in us* by objects in the external world which were *not*, in the familiar sense, coloured. From a modern scientific point of view, certain features of the space and time of the perceived world seem "subjective", or limited to our point of view—for example, any naïve directional distinction between "up" and "down" or, less obviously, the directionality of "before" and "after". In everyday life, we have an intuitive sense of these directions and might, prior to *reflection*, think of them as "objective", rather than as occurring relative to our position.

As we have seen, in the Aristotelian cosmology, in which the earth is pictured as being at the centre of the cosmos, "up" and "down" acquire a less confused sense than they would have to a "flat-earther", say—as "up" would be thought of as something like the direction of a line drawn from the centre of the cosmos to *any* point on its circumference. From the perspective of modern cosmology and physics, however, "up" will be related to the gravitational field of any massive body. If I'm on the surface of the earth, "up" will be in a direction pointing away from the centre of gravity of the earth; if I'm on the moon, it will be in a direction pointing away from the centre of gravity of the moon—and so on.[20] Indeed, from the point of view of modern physics, it can be argued that time *itself* is symmetrical and that the apparent directionality of time from the past to the future is a function of the fact that the time so conceived is that of the point of view of a being located "in" time.[21] The possibility that, from the viewpoint of physics, the intuitive conception of time with its directionality is *illusory* helps make sense of Leibniz's "relational" account of time, and of his attribution of *appetitions* to monads. We tend to think of conscious beings like ourselves as having desires that are *forward pointing*, because they are connected with actions which *bring about* states of affairs in the future. Conversely, we think that we are unable to *change the past*. But this asymmetry is, of course, for Leibniz an illusion, because it is a feature of time which, to the extent that it is regarded as substantial, is *itself* an illusion. When thinking "clearly and distinctly" then, the radical difference between process of efficient causation and goal-directed action will disappear, an idea that would be exploited by Kant in his moral philosophy, and that would recur in Nietzsche's odd thought of "eternal recurrence".

Again, Leibniz's approach to time can be related to the Neoplatonic tradition. After Iamblicus, and most explicitly in Proclus, "imparticipable", or "monadic", time came to be distinguished from "participated", that is, empirical or physical time. Imparticipable time was "resting" time, as it was itself conceived as exempt from change, whereas participated or physical time was conceived as "suspended" within it. As Siorvanes explains,

> this timeless suspension contains all the sequences of events that will "unfold" once time becomes flowing. Monadic time encompasses what will constitute past, present, and future. ... In passing from imparticipable to participated time, we pass from metaphysical relations to empirical. Causal connexions between beings and between grades of being come to be seen in temporal sequences, and our time-bound language makes us associate and confuse temporal history with metaphysical priority.
>
> (Siorvanes 1996: 135)

2.5 Leibniz and mystico-religious Neoplatonism

The Neoplatonic strain of Christian thought that had influenced Leibniz had consequences for ways of conceiving of the relation between God and the world. While the orthodox view on creation, stemming from St Augustine, had God creating the world out of nothing ("ex nihilo"), the view of mystics like Eckhart was closer to that of the early pagan Neoplatonists, for whom the world was an "emanation" of God, a concept in terms of which they interpreted the doctrine of the Trinity. For orthodox Christians, the more Neoplatonic view came dangerously close to the heresy of "pantheism", which *identified* the world and an extended material God.[22]

The major representative of such a pantheistic world view in the seventeenth century was, of course, Baruch Spinoza. As we have seen, Newton in *his* natural philosophy and theology thought of the extended world itself as an attribute of God, but Newton had thought of the matter *inhabiting it* as created *ex nihilo* by God. Spinoza, influenced too by the ancient kabbalistic and Neoplatonic writings that had influenced Henry More, had effectively made the entire extended material world itself into an attribute of God, an idea to which More reacted with horror. For Spinoza, the ultimate substance making up the world had the attributes of thought and extension, and so considered *as* extended, God was simply identical to the world grasped in its entirety or as "one".[23]

Leibniz, whose conception of the relation of God and world had elements of this Neoplatonist emanationism,[24] was clearly influenced by Spinoza and interested in his ideas, but at the same time did much to cover up this interest.[25] Perhaps the strength with which Leibniz resisted pantheism was proportional to the perceived need to distinguish his own views from this clear heresy. Leibniz's monadological view gave to the material world and its parts something of the quality of a living thing, an idea prominent in the thought of Cudworth. While for Newton the world was made up of "dead" matter, passively moved around by the will of an omnipresent God acting at every single point in the universe, the bodies making up Leibniz's world *acted*, but not *on* anything other than themselves.[26] Nevertheless, Leibniz opposed the Spinozist view which made God *entirely* "immanent" to the extended world. From Leibniz's point of view, Spinoza, like Hobbes, had sacrificed any and every conception of individuals as freely self-determining, by subjecting them to natural laws conceived as absolutely determining in the same way as the voluntarists' all-powerful God. These metaphysical issues concerning God's relation to nature and to the human community and the individuals in it would later dominate German idealism in the post-Kantian period when the views of Spinoza and the Neoplatonists were revived and popularised.

Leibniz's interest in Neoplatonism was, however, not simply manifested in his metaphysical conception of the universe, which combines elements of the Platonic and Aristotelian traditions with those of the emerging new physics, or contemporary ways of conceiving the social order. He also seems to have been attracted to, and interested in, mystical *experience* such as that of the medieval Christian mystics. According to Jean Baruzi, Leibniz was "nourished on mystic literature. He was familiar with Jacob Böhme, [John of] Ruysbroeck, John of the Cross, [Valantin] Weigel and [Johann Angelus] Silesius, as well as Saint Térèse and Angela of Foligno" (Baruzi 1907: 436n1). Here too, however, Leibniz's attitude was reconciliationist. Mystical "contemplation" was, for him, neither supra- nor irrational, and he opposed the "quietism" of those who, like the Catholic bishop François Fénelon (1651–1715), advocated an abandonment of discursive reason ("meditation") and intentional action in pursuit of an entirely passive union with God. "The contemplation of mystics, he affirmed, 'was nothing other than a very clear view of an infinitely perfect Being'. And the thought that raised itself to God is meditative and contemplative at the same time" (ibid.: 437).[27] The modern investigation of nature, which Leibniz recognised as a fundamentally communicative, social activity, was itself a route to the appreciation of "God's glory", and Leibniz saw scientific activities as equally appropriate for religious orders as for scientific academies. "Social action", notes Baruzi, "is no stranger to the metaphysics of Leibniz: it is, one could say, the *ultimate reality of the Leibnizian universe*" (ibid.: 456).[28]

But if Leibniz did not see mystical states in irrational ways, others did, and his ideas later came to be linked with those of Emmanuel Swedenborg, the Swedish scientist and purported clairvoyant who believed he could communicate with the spirits of the dead and prophesy future events. Swedenborg's brother-in-law and mentor, Eric Benzilius, had met Leibniz in 1697, as Benzilius and Swedenborg had wanted to set up a Swedish Academy of the Sciences, modelled on the scientific academies with which Leibniz had been involved (Scuchard 1998). Swedenborg's basic interests, however, were as much in mystico-religious experience as in science itself. In a bizarre episode, Swedenborg later came to play a crucial role in Kant's break with his own early attempts to synthesise Leibniz and Newton and his turn towards his transcendental philosophy. In 1766, Kant published a book, *Dreams of the Spirit-Seer*, in which he satirised the popular interest in Swedenborg's prophetic visions. This book seems to have come at a turning point in Kant's own philosophy in which he criticised the more Leibnizian views he had held up to that time. According to recent interpreters (Laywine 1993: 57; Schönfeld 2000: 237–44), Kant there treats Swedenborg as a type of *reductio ad absurdum* of *his own* earlier metaphysical answer to the mind–body problem.

In his earliest work, Kant had held to a type of monadological conception of the world, although, *contra* Leibniz, it was one allowing *actual* causal interaction between monads. In Kant's version of the monadology, monads, considered as point-like, did not *occupy* a space conceived (as with Newton) as a type of absolute pre-existing "container". In another sense, however, they could be conceived as *in space*. Because they interacted by means of positive and negative forces, the idea of the space that they were "in" could be understood as, in some way, *a product of* that interaction. Kant had believed that with these background ideas, one could solve the problem of how material and nonmaterial monads (the mind and the body) could interact.

Kant's reflections on Swedenborg's implausible claims about seeing and communicating with nonmaterial monads (souls departed from their bodies after death) raised the question of how material and nonmaterial monads (bodies and souls) could interact in life. If a soul could have a causal effect on a body in life (the body of the person whose soul it is), why couldn't disembodied souls (souls after death) continue to have causal effects on *other bodies*—e.g., causal effects on their sense organs? Why couldn't we *all see* spirits as natural occurrences, as Swedenborg claimed to do? Kant seems to have answered this question by appealing to something like a "category mistake"—the soul is the proper object of a distinct *kind* of cognition and knowledge, one based on concepts alone, and we should not confuse this type of knowledge with that gained from sensory experience. Rather than try to work out how souls interact with bodies, we should regard them as objects of distinct *types of knowledge* (Kant's version of "cognitive pluralism") related to distinct *kinds of things*, which he came to distinguish as "phenomena" and "noumena".

Traditional philosophy, Kant thought, made the same mistake seen in Swedenborg's "spirits"—confusing objects properly belonging to different kinds of knowledge. The way forward in metaphysics was to pose the question of "transcendental reflection": Which particular kind (or source) of knowledge did a claim belong to? To confuse different types (or sources) of knowledge was to fall into a distinct type of error that he first called the error of "subreption" and later, the "transcendental illusion".

The influence of Swedenborg might be taken as a touchstone for the issue of the limits to any *irrationalist* dimension to post-Kantian directions in German philosophy. Undoubtedly, the German idealism flourishing after Kant enthusiastically took up elements from a heterodox mystical tradition that included many irrationalist elements. This is particularly true of Schelling, who is said to have become interested in Swedenborg after the death of Schelling's wife in 1811. At the same time it is clear that this popular tradition could be thought of as giving "symbolic" expression to truths, rather than as presenting some literal account of the world. This seems to have been Hegel's more rationalist orientation to this tradition, and it is more than likely that he maintained no belief in a personal God or in the afterlife, and seems instead to have accepted Kant's position on the non-separability of the individual mind from the body.

3

KANT'S DEVELOPMENT FROM *PHYSICAL* TO *MORAL* MONADOLOGIST

Immanuel Kant (1724–1804), one of the most influential philosophers in the modern world, was born in Königsberg (then part of Prussia, now called Kaliningrad and part of the Russian Federation) and lived and taught there for his entire life. He is most well known as the author of three "Critiques"— the *Critique of Pure Reason* (of 1781 and 1787), the *Critique of Practical Reason* (of 1788), which followed another work on moral philosophy, *Groundwork of the Metaphysics of Morals* (1785), and the *Critique of Judgment* (1791)— throughout which he developed his so-called "transcendental idealism".

In his earlier "pre-critical" philosophy, Kant put forward a type of natural philosophy which combined elements of Leibniz's metaphysics (transmitted mainly through the influence of Christian Wolff, the most influential of Leibniz's German followers) with elements of a natural philosophy associated with Newton (again, transmitted through the influence of earlier German philosophers). During this time Kant put forward a cosmological hypothesis explaining the structure of the universe from physical principles (later called the Kant–Laplace hypothesis). In the mid-1760s a series of reflections on the structure of space and time in which he pointed to problems in Leibniz's critique of the Newtonian account led to the fundamental thesis of Kant's later transcendental idealism, the thesis of the "transcendental ideality" of space and time. According to this thesis, what we experience as the basic features of space (its tri-dimensionality) and of time (its "one-way" directionality from past to future) are *not* features of what space and time are like "in themselves", but rather result from the way that the mind "represents" objects and events in its experience.

The thesis of transcendental idealism was developed in the *Critique of Pure Reason* into a general theory of the way in which coherent thought about and experience of the world depends upon the mind's own cognitive "architectonic". In the *Groundwork of the Metaphysics of Morals* and the *Critique of Practical Reason*, Kant linked such aspects of the mind's theoretical functioning to what he took to be the most important feature of human existence, the human capacity for *freedom* as it is manifested in moral action. In later work, including the "third Critique", the *Critique of Judgment* which was concerned with the role of judgment in *aesthetics* and (effectively) *biology*, Kant tried to unify the pictures of theoretical and practical reason—and, by implication, the account of humans as knowers *of* the world, and free agents *in* the world—found in the first two Critiques. This attempt to unify these two *divergent* pictures of ourselves was, in turn, central to the work of the subsequent German "idealists" that followed Kant.

3.1 Kant's pre-critical physical monadology and the mind–body problem

In the early eighteenth century Leibniz's influence in Germany was mainly transmitted via the writings of Christian Wolff, and Kant's early work was conceived broadly within such a Leibniz–Wolff framework. In his pre-critical philosophy Kant pursued a "monadology" which was, like Leibniz's, based upon a modification of Aristotelian *substances*. However, Kant rejected a central feature of Leibniz's monadology—the idea that the law-like harmony existing between monads—the type of harmony expressed in Newton's laws, for example—was *pre-established* by God in such a way that denied any *local* causal interaction between them. That is, he objected to Leibniz's conception of monads as "windowless", and wanted to reaffirm the idea of local causal interaction or "influence".[1]

For the early Kant, the *physical* monads that constituted the physical world *actually* interacted, and they did so in such a way that the "force" constituting the active core of any one monad could act on and bring about changes within the properties of other such monads within its sphere of influence. Moreover, as in accordance with Newton's Third Law, of the equality of action and reaction, this interaction was symmetrical. In the same interaction in which monad A brought about changes in the inessential properties of monad B, in virtue of the action of A's active forces, the active forces of B brought about changes in the inessential properties of A. One might therefore say that for Kant, the "harmony" of the totality of monads was not "pre-established" but *achieved*: it was a product of the *real* interactions among the physical monads themselves. But while Kant thought of the fact of the changes in any one monad as brought about by the real action of another, he considered the *regularities* of such changes as owing to the existence of a "schema" in the mind of God. Kant's physical monadology thus combined elements of Leibniz's monadology with the natural philosophy of British thinkers like Newton and Locke, an amalgam that Kant was to find to be very unstable.[2]

One of the central elements of the dispute between Newton and Leibniz had concerned their different conceptions of space and time. While Newton thought of space as a type of infinite container existing independently of the things in it because it was an attribute of God,[3] Leibniz held a so-called *relational* theory of space and time in which Newton's supposed empty but absolute infinite magnitude was to be explained through relations existing among the monads themselves. Monads, then, could not be conceived as existing *in* space and time, because this latter conception *presupposes* the independent existence of the spatiotemporal framework that the monads are "in". As with his general theory, Kant here too combined elements of Leibniz's and Newton's respective positions in what ultimately proved to be an unstable combination. For Newton, material bodies *occupied* space, but Kant thought of physical monads themselves as simple, indivisible and without the extension needed *to be* space occupying. Physical monads *seemed* to occupy some particular space at any particular time only because of the forces they could exert on other monads, specifically their *repulsive* forces.[4] This idea that a point-like monad *indirectly* occupied space in virtue of the "sphere of action" of its repulsive forces thus gave Kant an explanation of the apparent phenomenon that two bodies cannot occupy the same space at the same time, while avoiding the assumption of their being composed of a "matter", the primitive properties of which included being space occupying.

Kant seemed to think that his transformed monadology solved one of the unsolved problems of early-modern philosophy—the "mind–body problem". Descartes had conceived of mind and body as different substances: while the body was spatiotemporal, the mind was not. But this raised the problem of how a non-spatiotemporal substance could possibly interact with a spatiotemporal one. Leibniz had to introduce his elaborate idea of the pre-established harmony between monads. One difficulty with this idea, however, was seeing how it could be easily reconciled with another idea that Leibniz's conception of the monad was meant to secure—the idea of human monads as freely *self-determining*. If a monad's history in the world was already pre-established by God, was not the idea of its free self-determination an illusion, as, for example, Hobbes and Spinoza maintained?

Kant seemed to believe that his variant on Leibniz's monadological position could explain how these problems centring around the thorny issue of the mind's relation to the body could be overcome. "Mental monads", as extensionless, were not space-occupying. Nevertheless, they were *in* space in that they could be conceived as located *at* some particular spatiotemporal points. It would seem, then, that a mental monad might at any one time somehow coexist in space with physical monads because neither were *directly* space occupying.

Moreover, if physical monads were centres of force able to affect the nonessential states of other essentially force-like monads, then perhaps mental monads themselves could be conceived as exerting forces on other physical ones and as having *their own* nonessential states similarly affected.

Kant believed that we have direct experience of our own capacity *as* minds to affect physical bodies when we act voluntarily. I resolve to move this pen on the table in front of me, and, via the intermediary of my body, the pen moves. Similarly, *as* minds we experience changes in our own inessential states, such as our own *sensory* states, in ways that we can think of as being brought about by the influence of other *physical* monads. I touch the pen and have the sensation of its solidity; I look at it and have the sensation of its colour—and so on. Physical and mental monads thus seem to interact, and thinking of mental monads as essentially *force-like* gives us a way to understand this. Kant thus thought his modification of Leibniz's monadology promised a solution to one of the most intractable problems facing eighteenth-century thought.

3.2 The role of Swedenborg in the transformation of Kant's pre-critical thought

Historians of Kant's intellectual development in the period leading up to his "transcendental turn" have standardly referred to the influence of two intellectual giants of the mid-eighteenth century, David Hume and Jean-Jacques Rousseau. Less commonly, some point to the influence of a much more questionable figure, Immanuel Swedenborg, about whom Kant published a small book in 1766, *Dreams of a Spirit-Seer Elucidated by Dreams of Metaphysics*. Recently, however, a number of studies have stressed how crucial this figure was for Kant (Laywine 1993; Shell 1996). This influence was a negative rather than positive one, however. Swedenborg effectively provided Kant with a *reductio ad absurdum* of some of his own key early beliefs.

Swedenborg, a "visionary", had found in Leibniz's monadology an explanation of his own purported capacity to prophesy future events. After all, if it *were* the case that a monad contained its entire future history as implicit within its own internal representational states, and if in its representations a monad implicitly represented the state of the entire universe of monads from its own point of view, then presumably the capacity to prophesy the future would not be entirely ruled out on *metaphysical* grounds. That the mental monad was pregnant with its own future states was a view *not* shared by Kant; so what Kant seems to have taken as the sheer irrationality of ideas of prophesy was not threatening to his own system. But he *did* share certain views with Swedenborg that seemed to be equally connected with Swedenborg's extravagant claims, and this did seem to give Kant cause for concern.

Swedenborg claimed to have not only visions of future events but the capacity to see and speak to the *immaterial souls* of the dead—he claimed to have had conversations with the ghost of Aristotle, for example. Not only was the world made up of a community of bodies, it was made up of a community of immaterial immortal souls as well—individual spirits extended in space and time somewhat like those conceived by Henry More a century earlier. Kant seems to have realised that the obvious problems afflicting Swedenborg's beliefs pointed up the same problems in his own conception of the mental monad. For Kant, the mind was effectively *coextensive* with the body, an idea allowed by the notion that the point-like monads were themselves extensionless, together with the idea that mental monads lacked the repulsive force which gave physical monads their apparent space-occupying character. But repulsive force was that whereby physical monads interacted among themselves, and *without* repulsive force it became unclear how mental monads *could* act upon each other, or upon *physical* monads. These were the problems that were made glaringly obvious by Swedenborg's extravagant claims: if Swedenborg could in fact see and hear, say, the ghost of Aristotle, then Aristotle's soul must be capable of interacting with Swedenborg's *body*—it must have some repulsive force (Laywine 1993: 77). But if that were the case, how then could Aristotle's soul have occupied the same space as his own body for those years that it did so when Aristotle was alive?

3.3 The role of Leibniz in the transformation of Kant's pre-critical thought

Kant's attempted satire on the "spirit-seer", Swedenborg, was one of a group of works written in the 1760s, at the heart of which was a diagnosis of a philosophical error Kant saw as pervading not only his own work but all philosophy up to that time. The error concerned what now might be called a "category mistake", and for Kant it consisted in the "subreptive" conflation of different *forms of representation*. While Kant himself tended to dismiss all these works and declare his first "critical" work to be the work commonly known as the Inaugural Dissertation of 1770, it is clear that the ideas first made explicit in this work had been coming into focus in those earlier works.

This separation between two different faculties involved in knowledge—sense perception and conceptual thought—was to be at the heart of Kant's transcendental turn, but it effectively came in two versions. Version 1 is found in the first work of his "critical" or "transcendental" philosophy, "On the Form and Principles of the Sensible and Intelligible World", a lecture given in August 1770 upon his appointment to the position of Ordinary Professor of Logic and Metaphysics at the University of Königsberg in 1770, and popularly known as the Inaugural Dissertation. Version 2 is found in his great work, published eleven years after, the *Critique of Pure Reason*. As we will see, Kant considered the philosophical move resulting in the mature "transcendental philosophy" as a breakthrough in philosophy as significant as the Copernican breakthrough in cosmology which led to the modern physical sciences. Furthermore he saw certain analogies between these two revolutions in thought. Clearly, a complex tangle of factors was at work in Kant's turn to his transcendental philosophy towards the end of the 1760s. One of the strands of thought going through this tangle concerned his continuing struggle with Leibniz's philosophy, particularly Leibniz's theory of space and time.

In Kant's early Newtonian or "physical" monadology, the synthesis he had tried to achieve between Newtonian and Leibnizian natural philosophy was reflected in his account of space and time. Like Leibniz, Kant was critical of Newton's "substantialist" concepts of space and time, the account which presupposed something like More's spiritualistic conception of space as a property of an infinite immaterial substance—God. This critical orientation to what Kant would consider Newton's "transcendentally realist" account of time and space would continue to be central to the critical philosophy. But Kant had never accepted the whole of Leibniz's "relationalist" interpretation of space and time, and had tried instead to preserve *something* of Newton's "absolute" conception of space as independent of the actual things in it.[5] It was from Kant's ongoing attempts to wrestle with these issues that one of the central features of his transcendental idealism would emerge. This was his representational *dualism*—the thesis that in the mind's representational activity it employed two distinct types of representations, "intuitions" and "concepts".

The two basic elements of Newton's cosmology were space and time conceived as absolute void, on the one hand, and the space and time filling *matter* located "in" this void, on the other. On the basis of two of his most basic philosophical principles—the identity of indiscernibles and the principle of sufficient reason—Leibniz had argued against the coherence of the notion of empty space as real.[6] To think of space as real is to think of locations in space independently of any material things existing *at* those locations. But, claimed Leibniz, without reference to such bodies, we could never have any way of distinguishing between any two locations—as mere locations are, of course, entirely *featureless*. So, according to his principle of the identity of indiscernibles, if any two such locations could not be distinguished, then they were in reality *the same*.[7] Moreover, as we have seen, the thesis of the "real" void transgressed the principle of sufficient reason.

In the latter part of the 1760s, Kant experimented with various ways of differentiating his thought from Leibniz's approach to space and time. The resolution he settled on is the one most explicitly laid out in the opening sections of the Inaugural Dissertation and in the corresponding "Transcendental Aesthetic" of the *Critique of Pure Reason* of 1781, in which space and time are said to have a fundamentally *non-conceptual* form of representation, the form of "pure intuition". That Kant's distinction between intuitions and concepts is at the core of his transcendental idealism is uncontroversial. Nevertheless, when we dig a little deeper, it seems as though Kant runs together different ways of interpreting this dualism, or at best, that he in places gives misleading impressions on how to understand this distinction. What is often overlooked in Kant, however, is that *before* he alighted upon the dualism of human representation for his criticism of Leibniz's treatment of space and time, he had employed *slightly different ways* of making his point against Leibniz's treatment of space and time, and that these continued to play an important role in Kant's thought and were particularly important for his successors.

This is a topic to which we will return in examining Hegel's method of "determinate negation"; for the moment, however, it is important to see the reason why Kant was critical of Leibniz's "relational" conception of space. By conceiving of space "relationally" Leibniz could not explain a range of simple everyday facts that were easily accommodated by Newton's "absolute" conception of space—facts such as that one could not put one's right hand in the left-hand member of a pair of gloves. The difference between right- and left-hand gloves, or the difference between right- and left-hand screws[8]—differences between what he called "incongruent counterparts"— could not, Kant claimed, be explained by means of conceptualised relations among the spatial parts. *Newton's* absolute account of space was able to give an account of this difference, but Kant also believed that Newton's account provided no alternative. Kant's "transcendental idealist" solution, with its representational dualism between concepts and intuitions, was meant to rescue Leibniz's idealist account of space and time from the problem posed by incongruent counterparts, *without* lapsing back into the murky spiritualism of Newton's conception of the void.

Kant seems to have taken away an important lesson from all this. Swedenborg's absurdities had resulted from the mistake of thinking of minds as *something like* ghostly bodies, and Kant came increasingly to view this as rooted in a mistake that he thought endemic in philosophy, including his own, up to that time. This mistake he later called the fallacy of subreption, and it amounted to a confusion or conflation of what he came to distinguish as two different ways of knowing—the type of knowing that relied on the input of sensory data, on the one hand, and the type of knowing based purely in the exercise of conceptual capacities, on the other. Knowledge of the soul is not the sort of knowledge for which we rely on sensory data: it is the sort of thing understood by the use of concepts alone. It belongs to the "intelligible world". In contrast, our knowledge of the existence and behaviour of physical bodies relies on the input from our senses. Bodies thus populate a different, "sensible world".[9] The popular, Swedenborgian, conception of souls as ghostly bodies, extended in time and space, yet for the most part transparent and penetrable, was to conceive of them by running together the different conditions of our knowing about bodies and about souls. A much more *radical* conception was needed of what it is *to be* a soul or a mind. Using more recent terminology, Kant came to understand that what it was to attribute a "mind" or a "soul" to another was not to attribute to them some empirical state or property, let alone the possession of some kind of "thing". It was rather to adopt a particular *attitude* to them, an attitude of treating them differently to empirical bodies. It was to attribute to them a certain "normative status". The fruits of this discovery would be Kant's transcendental philosophical *displacement* of "metaphysics" into the realm of *practical* rather than theoretical philosophy, with his radical reconceptualisation of the foundations of *morality*, and this transformation seems to have resulted in part from what he had learnt from reading Rousseau.

3.4 The role of Rousseau in the transformation of Kant's pre-critical thought

Kant's separation, in the Inaugural Dissertation, of sensory and intellectual *worlds*, together with his stress on the need to keep conceptual knowledge free from the distorting influences of the senses had strong *Platonic* resonances that were to be important in the subsequent development of idealism after Kant. Similar Platonic characteristics had been detected in another thinker to whom Kant became attracted in the mid-1760s—the French-Swiss social philosopher, Jean-Jacques Rousseau.[10] In the highly influential work of political philosophy, *The Social Contract* (of 1762), Rousseau used the conception of a social contract to explain the legitimacy of political arrangements in a way which radically transformed the conception of the relation of an individual to society implicit in earlier "contractarian" views of society. For Rousseau, the social contract was not a device for the satisfaction of individual desires, as it was in Hobbes. Rather, it was a device for the formation and expression of a *general will*, a unified "will" which expressed the interest of the substantially conceived community considered as a whole—a general will that was not to be equated with the sum of its parts, the "will of all". The social contract was thus an answer to a *political* version of the ancient metaphysical problem of "the one" and "the many".

From Rousseau's point of view, it is only when individuals are conceived as dependent parts of this *totality* to which they belong that the proper conditions of their freedom can come into focus. In his words, the "fundamental problem of which the social contract provides the solution" was finding

> a form of association which will defend and protect with the whole common force the person and goods of each associate, and in which each, while uniting himself with all, may still obey himself alone, and remain as free as before.
>
> (SC: 174)

What such a contract demands is "the total alienation of each associate, together with all his rights, to the whole community; for, in the first place, as each gives himself absolutely, the conditions are the same for all." Total alienation of individual rights is required because each individual "in giving himself to all, gives himself to nobody" (ibid.). That is, one overcomes the evil of the *local* dependencies of individuals on particular others by making each equi-dependent on the whole. With this conception it is easy to see how Kant could have compared Rousseau to Newton. "Newton", Kant claimed, "was the first to see order and regularity bound up with great simplicity, where before him disorder and badly matched manifoldness were to be met with, whereas since then comets travel in geometric course. Rousseau was the first to discover under the manifoldness of the available shapes of mankind man's deeply hidden nature and the concealed law according to which providence through its observation is justified".[11]

Here, however, we must remember the particular relevance that Newton had for Kant in his attempted transformation of Leibniz's monadology. From this point, Kant seems to have grasped that the type of laws envisaged as regulating the *human* world must be conceived as discontinuous with, but analogous to, those regulating the *physical* world. As Kant was later to put it in the *Groundwork of the Metaphysics of Morals*, humans, in acting "in accordance with laws," act *"in accordance with the representation of laws"* (GMM: 4.412).[12] Or, put in another way, the laws which humans follow in their moral lives are *prescriptive* laws to which they *hold* their behaviour, not laws which merely *describe* their behaviour. From Rousseau, Kant acquired the idea that human freedom was to be thought in terms of the capacity to be the author of the laws that one follows. As Susan Shell has put the point, for Kant "[b]oth Newton and Rousseau bring rule-governed order and unity to a manifold formerly perceived as chaotic. But whereas the laws uncovered by Newton concern physical necessity, those uncovered by Rousseau concern principles of freedom" (Shell 1996: 83–84).

3.5 Kant's "semi-transcendental turn" in the Inaugural Dissertation of 1770

The full title of Kant's Inaugural Dissertation, "On the Form and Principles of the Sensible and Intelligible World", makes the issue at the heart of his Swedenborg critique clear. In conceiving of souls as ghostly analogues of bodies, Swedenborg was clearly confusing the "form and principles" pertaining to the sensible world (the world of bodies) with that pertaining to the "intelligible world" (the world of "souls"). But while Swedenborg's error was overt, the same confusion in other more reputable philosophers (including Leibniz and Kant's earlier self) was more subtle.

In the dissertation, Kant's separation of the "form and principles" governing the sensible and intelligible world takes the form of a distinction between two kinds of mental representations (*Vorstellungen*): concepts and intuitions. Manfred Kuehn, who refers to this separation as the "discontinuity thesis", makes it the first of the three major linked theses presented in the Inaugural Dissertation, the other two being *subjectivity* of space and time and the essentially *rational* nature of morality (Kuehn 2001: 191). These theses would form the central pillars of his transcendental idealism.

3.5.1 The representational duality of concepts and intuitions

For Kant, concepts are *general* representations—one concept can be applied to many separate individual things. The easiest way to think of this is to think of the concept expressed by certain types of words—especially common names or "sortals" like "chair" or "horse", on the one hand, or adjectives such as "blue" or "piebald", on the other.[13] Thus the concept "chair" applies to all chairs, the concept "horse" to all horses, "blue" to all blue things, and so on. This is true even when we use such concepts to pick out particular things, as when we say, for example, that *this* chair has a broken leg, we pick out that individual thing *as* a chair—that is, in terms of the *kind* of thing it is—and so in terms of the properties it will have in common with other chairs.[14] Kant's account implies that there are no "singular" concepts and so no properly singular *judgments*. Concepts cannot *in principle* apply to one object alone, as a proper name like "Julius Caesar", for example, is thought to apply to one person alone. Even if there were only one horse in the universe, the concept "horse" would apply to it *as* a general term which could be applied to other horses, were they to exist.

In contrast, intuitions are *singular representations*—that is, they present to the mind an individual thing and they present it *as* individual rather than as an instance of a kind. Kant's new representational species of *intuition* seemed to combine aspects of Leibniz's notion of a clear but confused idea with Locke's notion of a "sensory idea", but in contrast to both Leibniz and Locke, Kant insisted on there being two structurally distinct types of representation, where Leibniz and Locke both settled for a single type.[15] Kant's analogues of Locke's sensory ideas are "empirical" intuitions, because they have sensory content, but the space *within which* the chair is represented is also considered by Kant to be single and hence to be intuited. The empirical intuitions of spatiotemporal things, such as chairs, are sensory, but the intuitions of space and time themselves have no sensory content: they are "pure".

In the *Critique of Pure Reason*, Kant was to add another distinction, and to say that while intuitions are *immediate*, concepts are *mediated*. By this he seems to have meant that concepts never apply directly to objects themselves, but only apply to objects as they are presented by intuitions, or by other concepts. That is, concepts working alone are incapable of representing anything, an idea expressed in the first half of his well-known claim that "thoughts without content are empty, intuitions without concepts are blind" (A51/B75). I will call this thesis, which is central to the first Critique, the "mutual dependency thesis"—it holds that taken *alone* neither concepts *nor* intuitions can function as representations. Contentful representation requires both to be operative. But in the Inaugural Dissertation, Kant does not seem to have construed his representational dualism in this way, as *there* he seems to imply that concepts alone *can* function representationally, as he thinks of properly metaphysical knowledge in just this way. From conceptual thought alone by a process he calls "analysis", we can arrive at properly conceptual knowledge of "noumena", and this, in turn, seems to be a thesis abandoned in the first Critique, where he argues that we are incapable of knowledge of "things in themselves". Yet I will suggest in the following chapter that Kant's position in the *Critique of Pure Reason* is not in such obvious contrast with that of the Inaugural Dissertation.

There is no doubt that the *Critique of Pure Reason* is plagued by many apparent contradictions, contradictions from which Kant's followers attempted to free transcendental idealism. One of these apparent contradictions seems to be Kant's differing attitudes to the possibility of metaphysical knowledge. The parts of the first Critique that speak most directly to the modern philosophical reader are those apparently *epistemological* parts in which Kant attempts to give an account of the conditions of our knowledge. All we can know are things grasped *relative* to our finite mode of knowing, and this rules out a knowledge of things as they are independently of our sensuous apprehension, "things in themselves". Our relation to the world then is like that of Leibniz's viewers of the distant city—we can only know it from the particular "point of view" at which we are located. But Kant gets around a possible *relativist* reading of the conditionedness, by saying that there are *universal* epistemic conditions applying to *all* finite but rational beings. We are all "located", then, at *the same* place, and it is this that allows us to talk of our knowledge being "objective", *despite* its perspectivity. This is perhaps the most common view of what Kant's transcendental idealism is about, and it presents it as a doctrine that is *sceptical* at the prospect of "metaphysical" knowledge regarded as of things in themselves. I will call this stance "weak transcendental idealism" (weak TI).

There is another conception of transcendental idealism in the first Critique, however, that we occasionally glimpse, in stark contrast with the "sceptical" pessimistic approach. For example, in the Preface to the first edition, Kant says of metaphysics that it

> is the only one of all the sciences that may promise that little but unified effort ... will complete it. ... Nothing here can escape us, because what reason brings forth entirely out of itself cannot be hidden, but is brought to light by reason itself as soon as reason's common principle has been discovered.
>
> (CPuR: Axx)

This clearly reflects an approach to metaphysics that is anything *but* sceptical. Scientific metaphysics is possible and completable, and here nothing can escape reason because in metaphysics reason is concerned entirely with *its own products*. I will call this stance "strong transcendental idealism" (or strong TI). This passage, I think, brings out the source of the apparent contradiction concerning the having of metaphysical knowledge: "metaphysics" means something different in both cases.[16] In weak TI, "metaphysics" means what philosophers had traditionally taken it to mean (and mostly still do): a knowledge of how the world ultimately and "really" is, independently of our knowledge of it in empirical experience.[17] But *strong TI* urges us to think of metaphysics in a different way. Metaphysics should be thought of as the science of *what* reason produces out of its own activity. From this point of view, traditional "pre-scientific" metaphysicians had an erroneous conception of their own activity. This is the frame of mind reflected, for example, in Kant's claim to understand Plato—surely the paradigm of a metaphysician—*better than he understood himself* (CPuR: A314/B370). Kant's prevarication about the nature of metaphysics is central, I believe, for correctly understanding the relation of the post-Kantian idealists to Kant. In short, they pursue the project of strong TI, the first version of which, I will go on to suggest, being that of Fichte's so-called "doctrine of knowledge". But to glimpse how Kant might conceive of this project we need to know a little about the method he uses for attaining a theoretical knowledge of noumena in the Inaugural Dissertation, his "analytic method".

"Analysis" is standardly thought of as involving a breaking down of some whole into its constituent atomic parts, a connotation common in "analytic philosophy", for example, but this has not always been the case.[18] Kant's philosophical education was an Aristotelian one, and Kant's distinction between the "analytic" and "synthetic" methods seems in fact to go back to Aristotle's distinction between inference to "the fact" (*to hoti*) and inference to "the reason" (*to dioti*), as transmitted to German philosophy via the logic of the Renaissance Paduan logician, Jacobo Zabarella (Pozzo 2004: 176). Simply put, Aristotle's way of classifying things ontologically via the "species–genus" relation had suggested a type of diagrammatic form of representation, as given by the Neoplatonist philosopher Porphyry with his imagery of a tree-like hierarchy of sortal concepts (although it is easiest to think of the "tree" as in inverted one with the trunk above and the branches below) (Int: 109–10). The Linnaean classification of living things can be thought of as instantiating such a structure, although Porphyry thought of *all things*, not just biological ones, as belonging to a single tree, at the top of which is the most general concept, "being". As one "ascends" the tree, one thus moves from more specific to more general concepts, as one might move up the Linnaean tree from "species", to "genus", to "family", and so on, up to the uppermost category of "life" itself.

Aristotle's idea of inference to "the reason" that would explain a given fact seems to involve the idea of a type of "regression" up such a tree. To give the familiar banal example, I may *know* that Socrates is mortal (he *has* died!) and wonder what the explanation of this fact is. I postulate that it is his being human that explains his mortality, because it is one of the essential properties of humans that they are mortal. Here, that mortality is essential to humans can be seen by their place on the tree, as the subbranch of "humans" will ultimately be derived from one named something like "mortal living things", which, together with "*immortal* living things (gods)" is itself a branch of "living things". Porphyry's idea of a branching tree actually gives a formal representation to a way of thinking about conceptual hierarchies that goes back to Plato's method of "collection and division".

Kant's "analytic" method was basically meant to work in the same way. For any fact, one could attempt to find an explanation for it by regressing *up* the tree. Thus, it would seem, the ultimate explanation would be reached when one eventually reached the highest concept. Really, this was just another way of picturing Leibniz's interpretation of the project of making one's ideas clear and distinct. It will be remembered that, according to Leibniz, I have a confused idea of something when I can recognise the thing among others "*without* being able to say what its differences or properties consist in" (DM: §24, emphasis added). On the model of regression, saying what "its differences or properties consist in" is just what we are doing when we subsume the thing under a higher-order concept on the tree and thereby distinguish it from things belonging to the class it is divided from.

The "analytic method" of Kant's pre-critical philosophy is in fact continued in the *Critique of Pure Reason*, though not under this name. It is found in Kant's account in the "Transcendental Dialectic" of the way that Plato's paradigmatically metaphysical inquiry generated "ideas". It is here, however, that the strain between the different understandings of "metaphysics" in Kant—belonging to strong and weak construals of transcendental idealism, respectively—will become most visible.

3.5.2 The subjectivity of space and time

The representational dualism of Kant's transcendental idealism is in turn related to his own solution to the debate between Leibniz and Newton over the nature of space and time.

After the transcendental turn started with the Inaugural Dissertation, Kant still agreed with Leibniz's rejection of Newton's idea of the "reality" of space, but he now rejected any realism about space for different reasons. (This part of the Inaugural Dissertation is largely the same as his treatment of space and time in the *Critique of Pure Reason*.) Kant's idea is that when we experience individual objects in the world, we do so on the basis of their causing us to have certain sensations, but perceptual experience involves more than just the *having of sensations*. When I look at a tomato, for example, I don't just have "sensations" of redness and "roundness", and so on—I see a tomato *as* an enduring object *in* space and time (a "spatio-temporal continuant"). Part of my representation of the tomato is, then, *as* a material thing which exists in this spatiotemporal medium. However, Kant thinks that there is no way that I could have *learnt about* the nature of space and time themselves *from* experience. Experience is of things *as in* space and time and must then *presuppose* the representation of space and time as given *a priori*. I must already have the capacity to represent space and time "in me" as a condition of any perceptual experience at all.[19]

But this *Leibnizian* aspect of Kant's thought is countered by a certain "Newtonian" aspect. Kant's idea that space is represented by a specifically *non-conceptual* form of representation (intuition) provided him with a way of restoring something of Newton's idea of the *independence* of the empty space filled by objects from the objects filling it. But now this independence was secured by the idea that our representation of the space *filled by* an object was of a different nature to the type employed to represent the object *filling it*. Crudely, Kant's basic point might be put this way. Think of a brick, say, and think of the actual space filled by the brick. Bricks are the sorts of things about which we can make statements in sentences with subject–predicate form. I might say, for example, that "this brick is red". But I have no equivalent way to refer to the space occupied or otherwise demarcated by objects other than by referring to those objects. Space *itself* is devoid of properties like colour, shape and so on. But this only goes to show that the sentential is the *wrong type of representation* to use when trying to represent the space directly. Not all representations are sentences, after all. A painting or a photograph of a brick can be said to be a representation of it, and it is not clear that these are to be thought of in terms of the subject–predicate structure of sentences. Might not some other form of representation be relevant here?

Kant thus thought that his idea of the non-conceptual nature of spatial representation maintained something of Leibniz's idea of the "ideality" of space, without the adverse consequences of Leibniz's *conceptual* formulation of this point. But if space and time are "ideal", and if the things appearing in space and time (that is, things with *spatiotemporal* "properties") are thus only things *as they appear to us*, rather than things *as they are* "in themselves", what can we say about things "in themselves"? That is, what can we say about the traditional objects of metaphysics? In both the Inaugural Dissertation and the *Critique of Pure Reason*, Kant answers that we must not employ intuition as a form of representation of things in themselves. But while in the Inaugural Dissertation he still seemed to hold to the idea that we can come to know things in themselves (by reasoning from pure concepts alone, with the analytic method), in the *Critique of Pure Reason* he asserted that reasoning from concepts alone can result in no substantial knowledge at all. It is in this sense that it *is* a "critique" of "pure reason" (reasoning from concepts alone).

In line with weak TI, Kant mostly contextualises this discussion within the framework of an epistemological account of why we *cannot* reach the top of Porphyry's tree. Nevertheless, in both versions of his transcendental idealism, the thesis of the intuitive unity of space and time provided a model for the unreachable ideal unity of a subject's knowledge. At the same time, the unreachability of such a unified knowledge prompted him to reinterpret the project of metaphysical inquiry away from its traditional *theoretical* form to within that of *practical reason*. It is this reinterpretation that grew out of the third distinguishing feature of the Inaugural Dissertation on Kuehn's account, Kant's belief in the *rational nature of morality*.

3.5.3 The rational nature of morality

Metaphysics is (purported) knowledge about the *intelligible*, not the *sensible*, world. In the Inaugural Dissertation Kant holds that one should reason about and come to know purely intelligible entities (such as the soul) with concepts alone: sensory intuitions should play no part in their representation. To employ sensory intuitions here—to try to *picture* the soul as a type of "thing" in space and time—is what had led Swedenborg to picture souls as ghostly types of bodies. Swedenborg's errors were obvious, but they were only obvious forms of the *same* type of mistake that Kant had thought of himself as making in his early work, where he had fallen prey to this subreptive fallacy.

But there is another way in which we commonly make this mistake. When we think of our moral actions, we can picture them *as* physical events unfolding in the spatiotemporal realm of physical interaction, and from this perspective it becomes mysterious how they can be thought of as free actions, originating in our own "wills". But this is to commit yet another version of Swedenborg's mistake. The "soul" is an *intelligible*, not a *sensible* entity, and we must think of its operations and effects under pure concepts alone. That is, morality is grounded in *rational*, not *sensible*, processes. In this moral perspective, then, Kant retains much of Leibniz's monadological perspective from which the monad is thought of as containing within itself the grounds of its own actions and its independence from local causal influence.

Within the framework of the Inaugural Dissertation, Kant still understood this truth about the essentially rational nature of morality within a framework of traditional metaphysics as a theoretical endeavour. In his fully developed version of transcendental idealism, found in his "critical philosophy" of the 1780s and 1790s, however, he dropped the idea of such "metaphysical" knowledge as a branch of theoretical philosophy. What remained intact from transcendental idealism's first version was the thesis of the essentially rational nature of morality. But it was now turned into one about the equally "moral", that is, *practical*, nature of *rationality*. That is, what Kant had done was to essentially displace "metaphysics" from its traditional ground of theoretical philosophy to its new ground in *moral* philosophy. What Kant had done, I suggest, was to fully abandon his original project of a *Newtonian* version of Leibniz's monadology and replaced it with a *moral* monadology.

4

KANT AND THE "COPERNICAN" CONCEPTION OF TRANSCENDENTAL PHILOSOPHY

On its first appearance in 1781, the *Critique of Pure Reason* was met with considerable incomprehension, criticism and, Kant thought, misunderstanding. Six years later he published a second ("B") edition with numerous additions and changes. In particular, he added a new preface, in which he attempted to explain his approach. In it is contained what at first seems to be an odd claim about the method of metaphysics.

> Up to now it has been assumed that all our cognition must conform to the objects; but all attempts to find out something about them *a priori* through concepts that would extend our cognition have, on this presupposition, come to nothing. Hence let us once try whether we do not get farther *with the problems of metaphysics* by assuming that the objects must conform to our cognition, which would agree better with the requested possibility of an *a priori* cognition of them, which is to establish something about objects before they are given to us.
>
> (CPuR: Bxvi, emphasis added)

On first reading this, we might object. Surely Kant has got the relation of mind to world back-to-front. In the project of coming to *know* the world, we are surely meant to bring our beliefs into conformity *with* the world. To talk of the world ("objects") as conforming to our *knowledge* seems to suggest that it is the fact of our knowing something to be so that simply *makes it so*. This must be wrong!

However, it is crucial to note here that Kant is *not* at this point talking of the objects of empirical knowledge, but the "objects" investigated by *metaphysics*—that is, timeless objects purportedly known independently of experience and by pure reason alone in the way that Leibniz claimed we could know monads. Kant is *not* saying that in relation to my knowledge that, say, the tomato before me is red, we should think of the tomato as

52

somehow necessarily conforming to my *state of mind* rather than vice versa. For such empirical claims about the world, Kant took himself to be a *realist*.[1] The reality for which he was advocating an "idealist" orientation was the purported underlying "metaphysical" reality to which early-modern philosophers such as Leibniz had appealed—the reality that was thought in some sense to underlie or support the world as known in empirical experience. Crucially, for Leibniz it was the distinction between the world as described by mechanical science and the underlying metaphysical world that reconciled the new world of science with some version of the traditional Christian worldview. In an analogously reconciliationist way, Kant thought that the only *way* to be a realist about the empirical world was to be an "idealist" about that "metaphysical" one.[2] Given that in early-modern philosophy this metaphysical world was, to all intents and purposes, identifiable with God, this move would have profound consequences for the idealists' conception of orthodox religion.

We must remember that Kant stresses the mind's *activity* in bringing about empirical knowledge; in particular, he conceives of the mind as actively contributing *form* to the objects we come to know. But it *only* contributes form. The world contributes something too; it contributes the *matter* which is so "formed": "I call that in the appearance which corresponds to sensation its *matter*, but that which allows the manifold of appearance to be intuited as ordered in certain relations I call the *form* of appearance" (CPuR: A20/B34). In empirical knowledge—my knowledge that the tomato is red, for example—some aspect of the world (the tomato) contributes the "matter" of sensation involved in my knowing it to be red rather than, say, green. But even with respect to such simple examples of empirical knowledge, this knowledge has a logical form—if I know that this tomato is red, and that a tomato is a fruit, then I know that there is a *fruit* that is red. It is the relations between the concepts involved here, the relations between the concepts "tomato" and "fruit", that allow us to make such inferences. Such logical structure contributing to the *form* of our knowledge is, like the forms of intuition of space and time on Kant's account, contributed by the *knower*, rather than by the known. We only have to remember that the father of metaphysics, Plato, thought of knowledge as being ultimately directed to what he called "forms", and that after him Aristotle had made the forms inseparable from "matter", to see something of what is behind Kant's idea that we should think of what is known in *metaphysics* as conforming to the mind rather than vice versa.[3]

We might get some assistance in understanding Kant's relation to the respective points of view of Plato and Aristotle by examining the analogy Kant draws between his own revolutionary "change in perspective" in metaphysics and the change in perspective found in Copernican cosmology in the early period of modern natural science.

4.1 The Copernican reversal of perspective and its consequences for metaphysics

In the second (or "B") edition Preface to the *Critique of Pure Reason*, Kant links the approach of the first modern astronomer, Copernicus, to this reversal of the mind–world relation. Thus he continues the passage quoted earlier:

> This would be just like the first thoughts of Copernicus, who, when he did not make good progress in the explanation of the celestial motions if he assumed that the entire celestial host revolves around the observer, tried to see if he might not have greater success if he made the observer revolve and left the stars at rest. Now in metaphysics we can try in a similar way regarding the *intuition* of objects. If intuition has to conform to the constitution of the objects, then I do not see how we can know anything of them *a priori*; but if the object (as an object of the senses) conforms to the constitution of our faculty of intuition, then I can very well represent this possibility to myself.
>
> (CPuR: Bxvi–xvii)

In the pre-Copernican cosmos of Ptolemy and Aristotle, a feature of the world as purportedly known (the movement of the sun and the stars) was, as we have come to understand after Copernicus, a movement properly belonging to *ourselves*, in that unbeknownst to ourselves, we always observed the sun and the stars from a *moving* earth. Copernicus' thought experiment had been to conceive of the cosmos from some point of view other than that of his actual place on earth, and from this point of view to imagine the earth as just another planet spinning on its own axis and orbiting the sun. From such an imagined point of view—already prepared by Nicholas of Cusa's new way of conceptualising space—we could then reflect on how things *would* look to observers on a hypothetically rotating earth, and this leads us to realise that things would look just as they actually *do* look.

Kant now generalises this way of thinking from the *particular* spatio-temporal properties of objects (e.g., whether they are moving or at rest) to their possession of the *spatiotemporal form* itself. The very possession of such "form" is now regarded as an effect of the observer's own "move-ment"—that is, as an effect of the observer's own representing activity—and not a function of how such objects actually are "in themselves".[4] Next, in line with his *representational dualism*, Kant now conceives of the mind as contributing an independent level of form to its objects—*conceptual* form. The argument to the subjectivity of *conceptual* form will be parallel to that concerning the object's intuitive form. First, Kant appeals to the idea that sensory intuition alone is insufficient for knowledge. It must be supplemented by our *conceptually* determining what is *given* in intuition. "I cannot stop with these intuitions, if they are to become cognitions, [I] must refer them as representations to something as their object and determine this object through them" (CPuR: Bxvii). That is, they need to be expressed in judgments, where something is said *of* the object. As Kant later puts it in an oft-quoted passage, "Without sensibility no object would be given to us, and without understanding none would be thought. Thoughts without content are empty, intuitions without concepts are blind" (ibid.: A51/B75). Given the necessity of concepts for cognition, Kant now poses the same question for *these concepts* as he posed for intuitions.

> I can assume either that the concepts through which I bring about this determination also conform to the objects, and then I am once again in the same difficulty about how I could know anything about them *a priori*, or else I assume that the objects, or what is the same thing, the *experience* in which alone they can be cognised (as given objects) conforms to those concepts, in which case I immediately see an easier way out of the difficulty, since experience itself is a kind of cognition requiring the understanding, whose rule I have to presuppose in myself before any object is given to me, hence *a priori*, which rule is expressed in concepts *a priori*, to which all objects of experience must therefore necessarily conform, and with which they must agree.[5]
>
> (Ibid.: Bxvii–xviii)

We might be aided in understanding core issues in Kant's endeavour if we develop this suggested parallel between intuitive and conceptual form.

The idea of an object's *intuited* form, let's say its spatial form, initially seems relatively straightforward. After all, if we talk about an object's "form", it is probably its shape that first comes to mind. But as we have seen from the early-modern dispute about the nature of space, how to think of space itself (and by implication, spatial "form") is far from simple. The early alternatives had been Descartes' nullibilist identification of extension as a fundamental property of matter, Newton's substantialisation of space itself (as an attribute of God), and Leibniz's relationalist account of space. Kant's answer to this dispute was to think of the properties of space and time as morphological features of a *non-conceptual* form of representation that presents us with a body as defined by its external relations to other bodies. A body's spatial form, then, is grasped as the determinate chunk of space it carves out from this infinite homogeneous and unified space within which other bodies exist.[6] But what are we to make of the idea of the *conceptual* form of an object?

I suggest here that we are meant to think of a thing's conceptual form analogously, as a "location" within a type of *conceptual* "space". The "space"-occupying entity here is not the spatiotemporal object of intuition, but something more like the proper content of a judgment—what we think of as a "fact" or "state of affairs". A "fact", such as the fact that "this tomato is red", is more an abstract entity than a spatiotemporal thing, like the tomato itself. It is something *knowable* (rather than, like the intuitable tomato, throwable) and its proper relations are relations to *other* knowable facts. The "space" within which it exists is one between knowables, the space we traverse, as it were, in reasoning, a space articulated by the complex relations among purported facts, determined by their truth or falsity.

Think, for example, of witnessing a thrown rock smash a windowpane at a certain time *t*. Here, the fact learnt will be one that stands in what are now called "truth-functional" relations to other actual or possible facts. To know that the rock smashed the window at time *t*, is to know that the window will at a time later than *t*, but not before time *t*, be broken. Moreover, it is to know that had the rock *not* been thrown, then, all other things being equal, the window would still be *intact*.[7] So, just as we might think of a tomato in a bowl of tomatoes as standing in certain spatial relations to its surrounding tomatoes, we can analogously think of the "fact" of the rock smashing the window as standing in truth functional relations to "surrounding" facts. The mind traverses this type of "logical space" when making inferences.

It is this type of picture, I suggest, that is implicit in Kant's thoughts about conceptual form, a picture more clearly discerned in Ludwig Wittgenstein's later idea that it is "the possibility of its occurring, in a state of affairs" that constitutes "the form of an object" (Wittgenstein 1922: §2.0141).[8] Wittgenstein's interpretation of the idea that objects have a conceptual form was accompanied by a quite specific, and in some way counterintuitive, reinterpretation of the notion of the "world". In short, Wittgenstein declared the world to be a totality of "facts" or "states of affairs" (*Tatsachen*), rather than a totality of "things" (*Dinge*) (ibid.: §§1–1.1). Moreover, the world was not simply a collection of "facts", but rather facts *in logical space*: "The facts in logical space are the world" (§1.13). Kant, I suggest, had a picture something like this in mind when, in his infamously difficult "transcendental deduction of the categories", he alludes to concepts as depending upon "functions": "All intuitions, as sensible, rest on affections, concepts therefore on functions" (CPuR: A68/B93).[9]

"By a function", Kant says, "I understand the unity of the action of ordering different representations under a common one" (ibid.). The "ordering" of representations he seems to have in mind is the sort that allows the unification of experience that is brought about by subordinating some concepts to others, for example, when concepts like "red", "green", "blue", etc., are unified by being brought under the concept "colour". Kant seems to be saying that while the identity conditions for intuitions are given from the bottom up (they "rest on" affections), the identities of *concepts* are derived from the top down by the division of their superordinate concepts. It is this relation that allows us to identify concepts with "rules". The role of concepts is to be applied in judgments, and in such application the judging subject is constrained by rules, the rules, we might say, articulating "logical space". In judging a tomato to be (uniformly) red, for example, I am committed to denying that it is simultaneously (uniformly) green. That I cannot say that it is both (uniformly) red and green has something to do with the logical relations between (the rules connecting the use of) the concepts "red" and "green" themselves. In contrast, the concepts "red" and "round" are *not* connected in that way: in judging a thing to be red, I am not excluding the possibility of judging it to be round in the way that I am excluding the possibility of its being green.[10] These constraints on judgment have to do with the "logical space" of the world, a space articulated by the relations between concepts like "red", "green", "round" and so on.

Kant, as we have seen, insists that the *subject* of knowledge is the one contributing the logical form of the world, its "logical space". Kant's transcendental or "formal" idealism, then, can be understood as one possible way to interpret the Wittgensteinian idea that the world *has* a logical space. The contrary ontological interpretation of logical space would be the formal *realist* position that the world simply *is* made up of knowable units—"states of affairs" or "facts". It is Kant's idealist reading of this conception, however, that is presented in his difficult notion of the "transcendental unity of apperception". Kant again draws on the analogy of this *logical* space with *physical* space:

> There is only *one* experience, in which all perceptions are represented as in thoroughgoing and lawlike connection, just as there is only one space and time, in which all forms of appearance and all relation of being or non-being take place.
>
> (CPuR: A110)

Kant's stress here on the *unity* of experience—there is "only *one* [nur *eine*]" experience, just as there is one space and time—brings out the underlying *Platonic* references of his approach.

As Dieter Henrich (2003: 85–86) has pointed out, Platonism can be contrasted with Aristotelianism in as much as it identifies "unity" rather than "being" as the central concept from which all reasoning begins. Platonism is, as he says, a "henology" (from the Greek *to hen*, the one) as opposed to an Aristotelian "ontology".[11] As we will see, Kant's relation to both Plato and the Platonist tradition was complex. In contrast to Plato himself, Kant was not a *realist* about the form that brings all appearances via their "relation of being or non-being", that is, via the relations that hang on their truth or falsity, into a unity. Therefore he would, in line with the *weakly* transcendental idealist dimension of critical philosophy, deny that there is available to philosophy any *knowledge* of such a unified cosmological whole. But taking it as a "transcendental scepticism" is not the only way of taking the critical philosophy here, and Kant could be understood as repeating a claim that is familiar within the *Neoplatonist* tradition—the claim found in Plotinus and Proclus that the cosmos itself, grasped as a unity, cannot be thought in terms of the determinate concepts that apply to the "many", the particulars, making it up, not even the concept of "being". Thus Plotinus, for example, said of the "One" or "Absolute" which is the principle and source of all particular things that "its nature is that nothing can be affirmed of it – not existence, not essence, not life – since it is That which transcends all these" (Enn: Ennead III, treatise 8, ch. 10), while Proclus had *criticised Plato himself* for implicitly attributing "being" to "the one".[12] Moreover, Kant maintains his broadly Platonist "henological" credentials where he affirms that nevertheless reason must work with, in the sense of being *regulated by*, the idea of the ultimate unity of the world.

All this, I suggest, is at least implicit within Kant's "Copernican" answer to the paradox with which all later Continental idealists would grapple— that implicit in the thesis first explicitly raised by Leibniz of the *perspectivity* of knowledge. In short, if we are *conscious* of the perspectivity of our knowledge, do we not *understand* that condition from a point of view *free* of that perspectivity? In Platonist fashion, Kant links the achievement of an aperspectival "God's-eye view" with conceptual thought. This had been most apparent in his "semi-transcendental position" of the Inaugural Dissertation, in which, freed from the input of sensory knowledge, the "analytic method" was thought to result in knowledge of the "intelligible world".

In this work, the "analytic method" effectively instantiated what Plato alluded to with the myth of the human soul as being, in virtue of its conceptual capacities, capable of a type of "flight" in the heavens, and so of transcending its specific bodily bound location in time and space. This notion of *indifference* to spatiotemporal location had been a staple of the Platonic tradition and is reflected in the view of the Christian Neoplatonist Meister Eckhart that "in the head of the soul, in the intellect, I am as close to a point located a thousand miles beyond the sea as I am to the place where I am presently standing" (SW: 114).[13] A similar idea would later be expressed by Wittgenstein's claim that the "metaphysical subject" conceived of as the subject of logical thought "does not belong to the world but it is a limit of the world" (Wittgenstein 1922: §5.632).[14] That is, the mind is free from the body not in the sense that it can "fly" free of it in the way spiritualists such as Swedenborg suggested, but rather in the way that conceptual thought seems to free the thinker from the effects of perspective— the distant, is, as it were, to be taken as of equal significance to the near.

Capturing the idea expressed in the biblical injunction to be "in the world" but not "of it", Eckhart had interpreted living according to Christian values as a form of life in which a person's "knowing is one with God's knowing, their activity with God's activity and their understanding with God's understanding" (SW: 149). As we will see, with his idea of a *fully conceptualised* "pure *practical* reason", Kant would effectively *secularise* the idea that leading a moral life would be one in which personal activity merged with "God's activity". For the moment, however, we can start to see how, with Kant's Copernican revolution, these metaphors could be cashed out. Separating out intuitive and conceptual forms of representation, Kant could identify the influence of spatiotemporal location with the contribution of sensory intuition. I can perceive the tomato's redness because it is "here", "now". But to the extent that the content of thought is *conceptual*, its content is neither spatial nor temporal—*the fact that* that particular tomato is red is *not* located in actual space and time but in "logical" space. This facet of logical space is reflected in the idea that if a proposition is true, it is *eternally* true—genuine propositional contents must be free from tethering to any particular place and time. But for the Kant of the *Critique of Pure Reason*, *purely* conceptual knowledge must be "empty". In line with weak TI, we can never *reach* a unified knowledge of the world "as it is in itself", but must nevertheless continually attempt to unify our empirical knowledge by finding increasingly general explanations for particular facts. Such "bottom–up" inquiry into the totality of the world will never go beyond a grasp of the "distributive unity" of empirical facts about the world, and can never achieve a grasp of the world as a "collective unity"—a grasp that could only be available to a omniscient God.

4.2 The aporia of traditional metaphysics

Somewhere between the time of giving his Inaugural Dissertation and the appearance of the *Critique of Pure Reason*, Kant had given up his Platonist optimism that if the philosopher kept the influence of the sensible world at bay, and kept the forms of intuitive and conceptual representation carefully distinct, then pure conceptual thought could result in such properly divine knowledge of the world as it is in itself. Plato's imagery of a divine intellectual view of the "ideas" to which philosophy aspired was now thought of as revealing a *misunderstanding* of the very nature of the ideas and our relation to them, as it involved a conflation of the generality of concepts and the singularity of intuitions. For Kant, ideas are types of concepts and concepts are, of course, not *intuitions* with their singular empirical content, nor representations of some reality in itself. As concepts, ideas must be thought of as something more like *rules* to which empirical subjects can subject themselves. To mix intuitive elements into purely conceptual thought gives rise to a fallacy—a fallacy, recall, that Kant first referred to as the subreptive fallacy—operative within traditional metaphysical speculation. Under the spell of the subreptive fallacy, philosophers had attributed to concepts the singularity of intuitions and regarded them as capable of working in isolation, so as to present the mind with the singular objects of metaphysical speculation. In the Transcendental Dialectic of the *Critique of Pure Reason* Kant now diagnoses the ways this fallacy, now called the "transcendental illusion", generates the problems besetting metaphysical thought, especially in its investigation of the ultimate singularities: the self, the cosmos considered as a whole, and God.

The knower *as* knowing subject is not a spatiotemporal unity like the body, but this is not because it is a strange kind of alternative thing, like Descartes' non-locatable mental substances or Swedenborg's transparent ghostly presences. The subject is not a spatiotemporally locatable substance, because it is a mistake to think of it as a substance *at all*. However, under the influence of the subreptive fallacy or transcendental illusion, this is just how the subject was treated within the perspective of Wolffian "rational psychology". Among the consequences of this was that rational psychology became entangled in a type of sophistical inference that Kant calls a "transcendental paralogism"—an inference deriving from the proposition "I think", the conclusion that there is a thing, an entity, a substance, that "thinks".[15]

The paralogisms—in which the transcendental idea of the thinking subject is substantialised—result from the misinterpretation of the role of categorical syllogisms (syllogisms whose major premise is a categorical judgment). A similar problem affects the misapplication of *hypothetical* syllogisms, in which empirical phenomena are unified under universal laws. The sophistic extension of this explanatory process results in the positing of the cosmos itself as a unified *being*, the problematic nature of which is manifest in the "antinomies" resulting when one attempts to say anything determinate about the cosmos as a whole that is *more than* the sum of its constitutive factual parts. For example, if one tries to answer the question as to whether the world has an origin at some point in time, one finds that equally plausible arguments can be found to support the contrary claims that the world had a first point in time or that it has existed eternally. Such antinomies recall the irresolvably opposed contrary views that ancient sceptics saw ensnaring philosophical inquiry,[16] but Kant now believed he had the key to the resolution of these inquiry-stopping dilemmas: they have their source in the unchecked transcendental illusion in which reasoning is illegitimately stretched beyond its proper limits.

Under the influence of the transcendental illusion we do not limit our reasoning to the postulation of the cosmos as an *actual* empirical totality, but inquire further as to the "ground" of all things within that totality—for example, we think of the totality of empirical existence as itself existing as *one* reality within a more encompassing "whole of possibility [gesamte Möglichkeit]" (CPuR: A572/B600), a conception found in Leibniz's *Theodicy*.[17] Kant here reveals assumptions that will be crucial for Hegel's later critique. Of the possible empirical predicates applicable to an object, some, for example, "red" or "square", will be affirmative, and others, for example, "unhappy" or "ignorant", will be negative or "privative". Semantically, Kant assumes that negative predicates presuppose their contrary positive ones, but not vice versa.[18] The completely determinate concept of a thing, then, will include reference to those properties the thing *lacks*, as referred to by its privative predicates, as well as reference to the properties it actually possesses. This means that our concept of the totality of empirical existences depends upon a representation of a "transcendental substratum, which contains as it were the entire storehouse of material from which all possible predicates of things can be taken" (CPuR: A575/B603), an idea of all reality Kant calls the *omnitudo realitatis*, and in turn this requires the representation of an individual being, an *ens realissimum*, in which the totality of positive properties inhere. The "ideal of reason" is this representation, and it is responsible for the genesis of the notion of God. But it is a representation, an idea, however, and without independent empirical content, can be afforded no objective reality, and thus Kant subjects traditional proofs of the existence of God to critique, seeing them as generated by the transcendental illusion.

The error underlying all these misguided forms of metaphysical reasoning—the paralogisms, the antinomies, and the ideal of reason—is the transcendental illusion, in which intuition is conflated with concept, and all repeat in some way the tendency of reason exemplified by Plato's misunderstanding of ideas as archetypes. But Plato, albeit unconsciously, also showed the way out of this illusion, since, as Kant points out, he took all his *examples* of ideas from the realm of *practical* rather than *theoretical* reason. With this, then, Kant signals the direction of his critical philosophy. The metaphysical project is not to be understood as primarily a "theoretical" endeavour. "Pure reason" (without empirical content) cannot aim at knowledge understood as a kind of *theory* of entities like the soul, the cosmos, and God. Pure reason is primarily *practical*. The philosophical project is not ultimately about knowledge of the world, it is about the attainment of *freedom*. This is a theme taken up in *Groundwork of the Metaphysics of Morals* and the *Critique of Practical Reason*. Before moving on to those works, however, it is necessary to explore further the question of Kant's relation to ancient philosophy and the thought of those who, for him, were its greatest figures, Plato and Aristotle.

4.3 Kant's modernism

Kant's image of the Copernican reversal of perspective is clearly meant to convey the sense of a transition between ancient and modern modes of thought, involving a radical reinterpretation of what it means to be a knower of the world. Indeed, Wittgenstein's opening claim in the *Tractatus Logico-Philosophicus*, that the world is one of "facts" rather than "objects" might also be read as contrasting the modern "world" that is coordinate with the transcendental unity of apperception with the classically Aristotelian world as one of "substances". To capture the distinction between the modern "fact world" and the ancient "object world" it might be helpful to appeal to another more recent distinction between a "world [Welt]" and an "environs [Umwelt]".

We generally think of cats and dogs as aware of objects in their immediate vicinity and of events unfolding around them—objects and events of their surrounding *environs* (Gadamer 1992: 443–45). It is difficult, however, to think of a creature without language or conceptual thought as having any kind of notion of what might go on in parts of the world *outside* its environs. The "world" of a nonhuman perceiving creature, we might say, must just *be* its environs, that is, that egocentric space and time radiating out from its particular location at any one time towards some limiting "horizon". In contrast, beings with the capacity for conceptual thought, it might be said, have the resources for representing objects and events existing beyond the horizon of perceptual awareness, because it is only by *reasoning to* such representations that we could extend the range of thought in this way, and only *concepts*, it might be thought, could provide an agent with the means for such inferential reasoning. Thus, for example, humans can make inferences about parts of the world of which they have no experience, as when they infer what things might be like at a subatomic level or in some distant part of the universe, on the basis of evidence to which they *do* have perceptual access.

But when we reflect back on the nature of the ancient Aristotelian "cosmos", it looks decidedly more like a representation of an "environs" than a "world". It has humans at its centre, and it ends at a distant encircling horizon, just as an environs so ends. The Copernican reversal, however, radically alters our conception of the world that we inhabit and our own relation to it. The knower is now no longer unreflectively at the centre of such an environing cosmos; rather, as reflected upon, the knower sees him- or herself as contingently occupying some place within a homogeneous universe, and as the *reflecting* subject, being nowhere in particular within it. This is the split, in Kant, between the psychological or "empirical" subject, on the one hand, and the "transcendental" subject, on the other. With a conception of oneself as transcendental subject, it is clear that the *perceptual* model of knowledge as a type of "seeing" of objects is no longer appropriate. If the world of the transcendental subject is now conceived, as I have suggested, as a totality of logically related "facts", then the "facts" making it up are not the sort of entities one *can* think of on the model of perceivable objects. *Worldly* "facts", unlike environing "things" are not entities that *can* be located at any point of time or at any point in space, and not the sort of entities one can be *closer* to, or *further away* from. To aspire to a knowledge of the world as a totality of facts is to aspire to transcend the particularity of space and time, not in the sense of attaining a point of view from the heavens, but in that of detaching oneself from any particular "point of view" whatsoever.

But if Kant's "Copernican turn" is paradigmatic of the turn to the *modern world* from the *ancient*, it nevertheless employs means for doing this equally from the ancient world. As we have seen, the "Copernican turn" is in *one way* anticipated by the fifteenth-century Christian Neoplatonist Nicholas of Cusa; and indeed, Neoplatonic ideas had long been invoked to capture the infinity of space, as opposed to the Aristotelian conception of space as the totality of finite cosmic "places". Kant's transcendental idealism therefore exhibits a complex use of conceptions from both the Aristotelian and Platonic traditions to effect its modern "Copernican" revolution.

4.4 Kant on Aristotle's "categories" and Plato's "ideas"

Kant's idea that we project a conceptual form *onto* perceivable objects, rather than intuit any form that exists *in them*, fits with his reinterpretation in the *Critique of Pure Reason* of Aristotle's theory of the "categories". In the work *Categories*, Aristotle had attempted to list those basic features of objects reflected in the ways we talk about them. Reflecting on the idea that in making assertions we typically say something of, or "predicate" some characteristic or property *of*, something, Aristotle attempted to capture the ways things must be such that we are able to do this. The independent things *of* which we can assert some characteristic are what he called "substances", and he distinguished the category of substance from those concerning the possible ways such substances might *be*. In saying that Socrates is in the marketplace, then, I designate the substance *Socrates*, and say *of* Socrates, *where* he is, and Aristotle takes this verbal distinction to reflect an ontological distinction between the category of *substance* itself and the category of *the being somewhere* of such substances.[19]

In the Transcendental Analytic, Kant provides his own account of the categories; but while Aristotle seemed to consider the categories as telling us something about things (primary substances) "in themselves", from Kant's reversed *Copernican* point of view, these categories reflect the logical structure of our cognition of things—their fundamental *conceptual form*. That is, while Aristotle thinks our talk and thought realistically reflect the form objects actually have,[20] Kant thinks of the form as projected onto the objects in our judging of them (Thompson 1983). For the main, much of what Kant calls the Transcendental Analytic is concerned with this reversal of Aristotle's approach to the categories. The basic idea seems to be that we bring the categorical structure of the understanding to the objects we perceive in the same way as we do the "pure intuitions" of space and time to those objects. The focus here is on the form of objects we encounter and make judgments about in perceptual experience. In contrast, the metaphysician presupposed in the second half of the book, the Transcendental Dialectic, is *Plato*, because there Kant is interested, not in isolated judgments about perceptual objects, but in our capacity to reason inferentially and *unify* the judgments we make about such objects—the capacity that for Plato releases us in thought from our terrestrial limitations and allows thought to soar freely in the heavens. This more "Platonic" theme seems linked to a further set of remarks regarding Copernicus which suggest an extension of the Copernican analogy *beyond* the range of the categories.

In the third of a series of footnotes in which Kant attempts to spell out the parallels between his new approach to metaphysics and Copernicus' way of doing cosmology, Kant points out that if Copernicus had not been able to adopt his new "point of view" (which takes the movement of the sun to be an illusion brought about by the movement of the earth), the subsequent discoveries of Galileo and Newton (the role of the force of gravity in explaining motion) would not have been possible.

> [T]he central laws of the motion of the heavenly bodies established with certainty what Copernicus assumed at the beginning only as a hypothesis, and at the same time they proved the invisible force (of Newtonian attraction) that binds the universe, which would have remained forever undiscovered if Copernicus had not ventured, in a manner contradictory to the senses yet true, to seek for the observed movements not in the objects of the heavens but in their observer.
>
> (CPuR: Bxxii, note)

Copernicus' move had broken the grip of the unreflectively egocentric *environing* picture of the Aristotelian cosmos and thereby undermined the idea of segmenting the cosmos into supra- and sublunar precincts. By moving towards a conception of space as infinite and homogeneous, rather than as finite, egocentric and stratified, Copernicus and Bruno provided Galileo with the resources to take the next important step of unifying the mechanical principles explaining movement on earth and the circular movement of the planets, including now the earth itself. In turn, Galileo's advance enabled *Newton's* hypothesis of the force of gravity as the force which "holds the universe together".

In these footnotes Kant goes on to compare the method he employs in the Preface (but not in the text of the *Critique of Pure Reason* itself) to Copernicus' hypothetical adoption of the new point of view,[21] and, I suggest, he conceives of his own metaphysical "hypothesis" as itself leading to a discovery *similar* to that of the post-Copernican discovery of the "invisible force … which holds the universe together". On this interpretation, what Kant's hypothesis leads to is what he regards as the *truth* of Plato's "forms" or "ideas", in that Kant comes to see Plato's ideas as playing a role analogous to that played by gravity in "holding the universe together". But while Newton's forces hold the actual objects together, for Kant, Plato's ideas hold *our representations* of the universe together, because they are effectively what underlie our capacity to make inferences, and it is the capacity to reason inferentially that allows us to know the universe as a world of facts rather than as an assembly of environing objects and events. While the Transcendental Analytic had involved an idealistic reinterpretation of Aristotelian *ontology*, we might say that the Transcendental Dialectic involves a similar transformation of Platonist "henology".

As we have seen, historians of the rise of the new world view in the early-modern period have pointed out the important role played by the Renaissance revival of Platonism in the modern overcoming or transformation of the more traditionally "Aristotelian" cosmology of the Middle Ages.[22] The role of Plato in this type of revolution in thought is at least implicitly present in Kant's variant of it. In the Transcendental Dialectic, he comments on Plato's notion of "idea":

> Plato made use of the expression *idea* in such a way that we can readily see that he understood by it something that not only could never be borrowed from the senses, but that even goes far beyond the concepts of the understanding (with which Aristotle occupied himself), since nothing encountered in experience could ever be congruent to it. Ideas for him are archetypes of things themselves, and not, like the categories, merely the key to possible experiences. In his opinion they flowed from the highest reason, through which human reason partakes in them; our reason, however, now no longer finds itself in its original state, but must call back with toil the old, now very obscure ideas through a recollection (which is called philosophy).
>
> (CPuR: A313/B370)

In the scientific extension of experience we go beyond knowledge of isolated individual things, and link up different areas of our experience in systematic ways, as did Galileo when he linked up the movement of objects on earth to the "eternal" circular movement of objects in the heavens—types of movement that Aristotle thought were of a different *kind*. But as we have seen, this requires going beyond the immediate evidences of the senses, as Copernicus had done in reinterpreting the apparent movement of the sun around the earth. Elsewhere Kant appeals to a type of hypothetico-deductive reasoning, in which one conjectures some hypothetical state of affairs as a possible explanation of some observable fact.[23] What would count as possible explanation here is that from the hypothesised *truth* of the conjecture one could infer the truth of the perceived state of affairs, and here Kant relies on the types of *syllogistic* inferences of ancient logic to capture such reasoning. But Aristotle's syllogistic was itself a form of reasoning which went together with a conception of things as organised into hierarchical patterns of natural kinds, a conception effectively derived from Plato's "top–down" method of "collection and division". In this way, then, the Platonic goal for a conception of the cosmos as a unified whole underlies this form of explanation. As Kant says of Plato early in the Transcendental Dialectic, "only the whole of its combination in the totality of a world is fully adequate to its idea" (CPuR: A318/B374–75). Plato had thought of his "ideas" as archetypes for things in themselves, but for Kant, Plato's ideas are rightly understood as *demands for the unification of the understanding*, and so play for him a role *analogous* to the role played by Newtonian gravity: they hold together the contents of all our *judgments*. Once more, Kant's move is that of an *idealist* reinterpretation of another's *realism*, in this case, Plato's realistic understanding of the ideas.

I have suggested that it is from the vantage point of this type of inferential reasoning, an outlook of thinking of the world as a totality of "facts" rather than of objects, that we might think of Platonic "ideas" as playing a role analogous to Newtonian forces. That all our beliefs (in Kant's language, our "representations") are *consistent* seems to be the requirement implicit in the type of unification of belief that Kant understands as the "transcendental unity of apperception".[24] This represents the degree of logical coherence among the "facts" constituting the empirical world that is demanded by the understanding and that characterises the "distributive unity" between judgments considered from the point of view of the transcendental analytic. Understood from the perspective of "weak TI", this idea takes the form that we can never go beyond such a theoretical conception as a "distributive unity" of empirical facts. No holistic knowledge would be possible of the world as a "collective unity". But the post-Kantians would go on to read this in line with the perspective of *strong* TI. The proper object of metaphysics is what "reason brings forth entirely out of itself", and so it has nothing in it in principle incapable of being known. And, I suggest, part of their efforts to read transcendental idealism in such a way will be consequent upon a different take on the Platonic ideas.

4.5 Kant's "Plato"

The significance of Plato for Kant, while generally recognised, is easy to underestimate or misconstrue. From the perspective of the generally empiricist or naturalist orientation of recent English-speaking philosophy—the orientation informing weak TI—Kant's criticism of the theoretical claims of "pure reason" appears as part of a more general turn in modernity against the idea of a purely conceptual inquiry into a supersensible realm. Kant's relation to Plato, however, is far more nuanced than this.[25] As will be developed in the next chapter, rather than appearing to dismiss

Platonism in the way characteristic of much standard modern philosophy, Kant is better seen as transposing the Platonist henological approach from the realm of theoretical to that of *practical* philosophy, at the same time as asserting the *primacy* of practical reason. Rather than abandon Platonism, Kant claims to retrieve a *truth* about the nature of it that even *Plato* had misunderstood. But to understand correctly Kant's complex position here, it is important to keep in mind the doctrines that he himself took to constitute Plato's philosophy. In fact, from the perspective of current understandings of Plato, Kant makes a number of telling *mistakes* which conflate Plato's own views with those of later Platonist thought. Knowing of these mistakes is significant for understanding the relation to Kant of post-Kantian idealists such as Schiller, Schelling and Hegel.

In his account of Plato's ideas in the first book of the Transcendental Dialectic, "On the Concepts of Pure Reason", Kant, in describing how Plato's ideas were "archetypes of things themselves", adds that in the opinion of Plato, these ideas "flowed from the highest reason, through which human reason partakes in them" (CPuR: A 313/B 370; see also A 318/B 374). Later, in the section of the Transcendental Dialectic treating the "Ideals of Pure Reason", Kant again attributes to Plato the notion of a "divine mind" within which the "ideas" exist. An "ideal", Kant says, "was to *Plato*, an *idea in the divine understanding*" (ibid.: A568/B596). But as the editors of a recent English edition of Kant's *Critique of Pure Reason* point out, the idea of a divine mind as *container* of the ideas did not originate until the "syncretistic Platonism from the period of the Middle Academy" and "was later adopted by Platonists as diverse as Philo of Alexandria, Plotinus, and St. Augustine, and became fundamental to later Christian interpretations of Platonism".[26] Moreover, even with Plotinus and Proclus, it is contestable that "the One" that is the object of pagan Neoplatonic philosophy and theology should be equated with what we normally regard as a "mind".[27] And importantly, such a "mind" would have in no real sense a *will*.

It was only with Augustine's adding of a will to the Neoplatonic "One", taken as a divine understanding, that the more familiar anthropomorphic idea of "the mind of God" took shape,[28] and it did so in conjunction with a conception that separated orthodox Christian belief from the Neoplatonic thought that had otherwise so influenced the early church fathers—the idea of the creation of the world "*ex nihilo*" and occurring in time, the idea we have seen as present in the thought of Newton. The ideas in the mind of Augustine's God are creative in that it is in virtue of these ideas that the material world comes into existence. And *what* God wills is conceived as that which initially exists *in* his mind *as* ideas. Here it seems that Augustine had borrowed the model of the mind's creative ideas from Cicero's account of Phidias' creation of his *sculptures* (Panofsky 1968).[29] The tension between Augustine's voluntaristic idea of God as creator of the world *ex nihilo* and the Neoplatonic conception of the "emanation" of the world would therefore return in the form of the dispute between the voluntarism of medieval nominalists such as Ockham and the Neoplatonic opponents of voluntarism who thereby courted the accusation of a pantheist heresy. We can see the successor of this same dispute emerge in the context of Kant's idealist reshaping of philosophy at the end of the eighteenth century.

We should not be surprised at Kant's interpretative distortion of Plato. As Frederick Beiser has pointed out, in the first part of the century "Plato was almost forgotten, having been eclipsed by the Aristotelian scholasticism of the universities" (Beiser 2003: 68). Consistent with this, Kant's early philosophical education had been fundamentally *Aristotelian* (Tonelli 1975). Vieillard-Baron attributes Kant's first reference to Plato, which apparently occurs in the Inaugural Dissertation, to an intense interest in Platonism, stimulated by his first in-depth engagement with the philosophy of Leibniz in 1768 (Vieillard-Baron 1979: 58). And while Kant was working out the details of his transcendental philosophy in the "silent decade" between this work and the publication of the *Critique of Pure Reason* in 1781, "it was not until the 1780s that the Platonic renaissance truly began" (Beiser 2003: 69).[30] It is not known how much Plato Kant had read, but like others of his generation Kant was clearly influenced by the interpretation of Plato given by Johann Jakob Brucker in his widely read *Historia Critica Philosophiae*.[31] Kant disagreed with Brucker's generally negative assessment of Plato,[32] but otherwise he seems to have followed Brucker, especially in his account of Plato's ideas.

One of the earliest critical historians of philosophy, Brucker consciously tried to separate the views of Plato, himself, from what had come down from the interpretations of Neoplatonists such as Plotinus and Proclus, and that had been revived in the Renaissance and represented most recently by Cudworth. Indeed, Brucker regarded the pagan Neoplatonic "monism" of Plotinus and Proclus as a forerunner to Spinoza's atheistic materialism (Franz 2003: 20). But in doing this, he attributed to Plato a *substance dualism* which separated the material world and the divine mind, and although aware that it was impossible to find the Christian idea of creation *ex nihilo* in Plato, Brucker had still regarded the divine mind of the *Timeaus* as the creator of the ideas:

> [Plato] taught that there is an Intelligent Cause, which is the origin of all spiritual being, and the former of the material world ... God, according to Plato, is the Supreme Intelligence, incorporeal, without beginning, end, or change, and capable of being perceived only by mind.
>
> (Brucker 2001: 130–31)

According to Vieillard-Baron, it was this, together with the influence of Malebranche's synthesis of Augustine and Descartes, that underlay Kant's distinctively Augustinian interpretation of Plato (Vieillard-Baron 1979: 35–36).

One later especially vehement critic of the submerged orthodox Christian assumptions of Kant's supposedly *non-religiously based* philosophy was Nietzsche, but as we will see, similar objections were to be found more immediately in the attitudes to Kant of Schelling and Hegel. Often, the point of departure was not Kant's theoretical as much as his moral philosophy, to which we will next turn. And importantly, the critique of the version of Platonism that survived in Kant's moral philosophy was often made in the name of *another* form of Platonism, one that regarded the pagan Neoplatonists as true inheritors of Plato and that avoided Augustine's voluntaristic synthesis of Neoplatonic thought with an anthropomorphised creative God. Moreover, it was indeed the case that such a form of Neoplatonism had the features that Brucker had denounced, features that made it approximate to what orthodox Christians regarded as Spinoza's "atheistic materialism". But as will be seen (in Chapter 6), elements of this critique were also to be found within one of Kant's earliest *immanent* critics—Kant himself!

5
THE MORAL FRAMEWORK OF METAPHYSICS

Kant's Copernican method was to have negative and positive consequences for metaphysics. The negative consequences seem obvious. Metaphysics had been conceived as the rational inquiry about "things in themselves", using the faculty of inferential reasoning alone, and the "critique of pure reason" had undermined the idea of such inquiry—it tells us what we *cannot* know. We cannot know things in themselves, we can only know things in relation to our own knowing faculties, i.e., "appearances". The paralogisms and antinomies bear witness to the limits of the human intellect when it attempts to stretch its reasoning beyond the regions of sensibility. In this respect Kant's philosophy often appears as a form of scepticism—as it is sometimes put, a "transcendental" form of scepticism—the position of weak TI.

However, Kant conceived of his project as having a positive aspect as well:

> when we become aware that the principles with which speculative reason ventures beyond its boundaries do not in fact result in *extending* our use of reason, but rather ... inevitably result in *narrowing* it by threatening to extend the boundaries of sensibility, to which these principles really belong, beyond everything, and so even to dislodge the use of pure (practical) reason.
>
> (CPuR: Bxxiv–xxv)

If theoretical reason were to give us comprehensive knowledge of "things in themselves" it would be impossible to see how free action, and hence morality, would be possible, as all action would seem determined by the nature of things.

> Now if we were to assume that the distinction between things as objects of experience and the very same things as things in themselves, which our critique has made necessary, were not made at all, then the principle of causality, and hence the mechanism of

nature in determining causality, would be valid of all things in general as efficient causes. I would not be able to say of one and the same thing, e.g., the human soul, that its will is free and yet that it is simultaneously subject to natural necessity, i.e., that it is not free, without falling into an obvious contradiction.

(CPuR: Bxxvii)

But if the deterministic world of theoretical knowledge *is* the world of appearance and not that of things in themselves, then we can maintain the notion of a free will without contradiction:

But if the critique has not erred in teaching that the object should be taken in *a twofold meaning*, namely as appearance or as thing in itself; if its deduction of the pure concepts of the understanding is correct, and hence the principle of causality applies only to things taken in the first sense, namely insofar as they are objects of experience, while things in the second meaning are not subject to it; then just the same will is thought of in the appearance (in visible actions) as necessarily subject to the law of nature and to this extent *not free*, while yet on the other hand it is thought of as belonging to a thing in itself as not subject to that law, and hence *free*, without any contradiction hereby occurring.

(Ibid.: xxvii–xxviii)

Moreover, not only did the critique of pure *theoretical* reason protect the idea of a noumenal free will from the problems of determinism, it helped save religion from the criticisms of a modern scientific view of the world. Empirical science could only tell us about "appearances" and not "things in themselves". The critique of pure theoretical reason undermined the traditional metaphysical proofs for the existence of God, but at the same time protected the existence of God from the ravages of scientific criticism. It made the world of pious believers, like Kant's servant Lampe, safe from the type of Enlightenment critique of religion that had grown throughout the second half of the eighteenth century.

The picture of Kant just sketched, the "transcendental sceptic" of weak TI is faithful to a picture of Kant as seen by many subsequent philosophers, among whom we can count Hegel. However, *contemporary* interpreters of Kant have engaged in a deep dispute over exactly what he had in mind by this distinction between appearances and things in themselves, and how to interpret his transcendental idealism in general. Indeed, some still hold to the traditional view of him as a transcendental sceptic, who regards appearances and things in themselves as the denizens of two different *worlds*, one spatiotemporal and sensible, the other non-spatiotemporal but intelligible (for example, Van Cleve 1999). For them, the former is a type of construction out of mental representations, while the latter is what Kant posits as a genuine but *unknowable* reality. Others, however, in opposition to the "two-worlds" view, see appearances and things in themselves more as two different "aspects" of the *one* reality: those, on the one hand, that come into view when one engages with objects *as* empirically knowable in space and time, and those aspects, on the other, that are *understood* (although never known) from the "point of view" of a type of *pure*, conceptually articulated thought.[1]

From the former point of view, it is as if Kant's move between the Inaugural Dissertation and the *Critique of Pure Reason* had involved a change of attitude towards our capacity for purely conceptual knowledge of things in themselves. On this sceptical view, whereas Kant had initially thought we could have knowledge about such a realm, he later came to change his mind and to regard its objects as unknowable. On the "two-aspect" view the change is more radical, involving something more like a shift in the fundamental *stance* appropriate to objects in the world. According to this interpretation, Kant is saying something like we shouldn't think that *knowledge* is the ultimate orientation to the world, on which all our other ways of relating to the world depend. Rather, there is a purely conceptually articulated stance not reducible to one of knowing.[2] Kant finds the prototypical expression of this stance in human *morality* which, he thinks, proceeds from purely conceptual considerations and does not ultimately rest on knowledge. Metaphysics is reconceived from within a *practical* point of view. Metaphysical knowledge is indeed possible, but something quite different is meant by "metaphysics". This is the root of the interpretation I call strong TI.

For our part, it is unnecessary to decide which of these two interpretations represents Kant's "real" view, as textual evidence from the *Critique of Pure Reason* can be adduced for each. To acknowledge this is to acknowledge a certain tension running through the formulation of transcendental idealism as articulated in the *Critique of Pure Reason*, allowing subsequent writers, *including Kant himself*, to play off some aspects of the doctrine against others. Moreover, it is clear that Kant himself did not rest content with his views as expressed in the first *Critique*. First, reacting against certain criticisms and construals of his ideas there, he rewrote significant parts for its second edition which in general can be seen as veering away from the phenomenalistic, two-worlds interpretation.[3] Moreover, when Kant shifted his focus away from the theoretical framework of the first to the practical framework of the second Critique, and beyond that, to the aesthetic and teleological considerations of the *third* Critique, different aspects and possibilities for interpretation came into view as Kant responded to problems peculiar to those realms. Here, it seems safe to say that the *general trajectory* of Kant's journey through various areas of his transcendental idealism was towards conceptions that are more like the two-aspects than the two-worlds interpretation, and that are closer in spirit to the type of idealism developed by those coming after him, such as Fichte, Schelling and Hegel. To this extent, we might even count Kant himself among his post-Kantian idealist critics. For the moment, however, it is important to grasp how the philosophy given expression in the *Critique of Pure Reason* could *lead into* the conception of practical reason found in Kant's paradigmatic works of transcendental practical philosophy, *Groundwork of the Metaphysics of Morals* (1785) and the *Critique of Practical Reason* (1788).

We have seen how in the *Critique of Pure Reason* Plato's "ideas" play a crucial role in Kant's account of how we come to understand the world scientifically, as the idea of the world as a unified whole encourages us to search for greater and greater unity among our empirical judgments, necessitating the subsumption of entities under more and more general concepts that articulate a generally *nomological* understanding of reality. Here our capacity to hypothesise about how the world *might be* at least momentarily frees us from the constraint of our purported knowledge of how the world *is*, even if we have to return to the realm of sense experience to evaluate whether these hypotheses are in fact true to the world. When we hypothesise, we ask after the consequences of the hypothesised "fact", and regard the "conditional" form of thought involved, "if *p* then *q*", as holding independently of the *actual* truth of *p*.[4] But while reasoning is loosened from knowledge in hypothesising, in properly *moral* reasoning, Kant seems to suggest, it is distinctly *detached*.[5] Practical reason, in contrast to theoretical reason, can be "pure", and it is this that allows Kant to *displace* the project of metaphysics from a theoretical outlook to a *moral* one. Kant's idea of this, however, is considerably more nuanced than it is commonly taken to be, and itself creates problems that Kant tried to resolve in his later philosophy.

5.1 The primacy of practical reason in Kant's critical philosophy

Theoretical reason is concerned with true beliefs—determinations of knowledge. Analogously, practical reason is concerned with determinations of what Kant calls "the will". But how are we to think of the act of willing or the capacity underlying this activity, "the will"? And how are we to think of the relation of willing to *knowing*?

It is tempting to think of voluntary action as ultimately motivated by desire or aversion, and to think of such desires and aversions as ultimately grounded in our bodily natures.[6] This is the typical assumption behind approaches to "practical reasoning" found, for example, in Hobbes, for whom reason will operate practically just in case it is brought to bear on the sorts of action needed to satisfy such desires. In fact, this type of "instrumental reason" seems constitutive of *reason per se*, for Hobbes. Or, to put his project in another way, Hobbes seems to reduce all forms of normativity to that of instrumental reasoning—the *only* sense in which reasoning is "rational" is in that of helping an agent satisfy desires and avoid pain. (As we will see, in his account of the foundations of political obligation, Hobbes has been criticised for seemingly attempting to ground the "normative" role of the will in an entirely "naturalistic" account of the will as bodily based appetite.) From a Kantian point of view, however, Hobbes's naturalistic thesis of the will as appetite undermines his attempt to capture *even instrumental reason* as a normative process. Thus Hobbes describes the will as the "last appetite" in a process of deliberation, but says little about what this deliberative process itself might be like. Kant, by focusing on the process of practical reasoning itself, attempts to show how the will *cannot* be identified with any naturalistically conceived appetite or inclination.

Henry Allison has characterised Kant's account of a "minimally rational agent" as of one "who forms interests on the basis of some kind of reflective evaluation of inclination and adopts policies on the basis of these interests" (Allison 1990: 89). The idea is that such a reflective evaluation would seem to be a minimal requirement for even instrumental reasoning. For example, while something like felt hunger might be a candidate for a Hobbesian "last appetite" immediately before eating dinner, it is unlikely that it was *that state as such* that had steered me through the deliberative network that led me to, say, buy the ingredients for and then prepare the meal with which I was ultimately to satisfy my hunger. Some sort of "practical syllogism" would seem to be involved in any such bit of deliberation that exploits the conceptual links between concepts like "hunger", "eating" and "food". Kant alludes to the implicit "syllogisms" of practical reasoning with his idea of the role of "maxims" in such instrumental reasoning (Beck 1960: 81), maxims that Allison characterises as having the general form "when in S-type situations, perform A-type actions" (Allison 1990: 89–90). For the implicit reasoning behind my purchasing of the ingredients for tonight's dinner, one might think of the relevant maxim involved as something like "when in *food-needing* situations, perform *food-procuring* actions", and all this suggests that for me *qua* deliberator it is not simply my *being* hungry that is the relevant state for instrumental reasoning, but rather my *being aware* that I am the kind of being who *will be* hungry, *and* my being aware that being hungry is being in a *food-needing* state. Kant expresses this point with the claim that an incentive cannot determine the will to an action "*except so far as the human being has incorporated it into his maxim* (has made it into a universal rule for himself, according to which he wills to conduct himself)" (Rel: 6.24).

With this "incorporation thesis", as Allison calls Kant's central notion, Kant had radically altered assumptions about the role of given inclinations and aversions in the behaviour of beings with the capacity to reason.[7] Rather than, like Hobbes and Hume, seeing inclinations and aversions as contents *naturally* given to reason and as determining the content of "the will", Kant considered them as having to be "incorporated" into a "maxim"— that is, as having to be given some sort of conceptual and thereby *general* form of expression, so they could be *reasoned about* and *acted upon* by an agent. Reason *itself* acquired thereby a role in *shaping* or *determining* the will, and this seemed to suggest a source of normativity deeper than that of instrumental reason conceived in the Hobbesian way. In turn, this suggested a possible source of *moral* normativity. It was the idea of the self-determination of "reason", rather than any instrumental status that would be assigned to it, as with Hume's "slave to the passions" (THN: 415), that was at the basis of Kant's critical moral philosophy.

In his early *pre*-critical attempts to unite Leibniz's monadological position with something like Newtonian causal explanations and the idea of *actual* interaction, Kant had thought of specifically *moral* behaviour as being grounded in some particular type of disinterested but otherwise *natural* inclinations and aversions which would bring about actions to harmonise rather than conflict with the interests of others. From the seventeenth and eighteenth centuries, models had been available for such a response to Hobbes's egoistic psychology, and they were commonly of a *Platonist* kind. Rousseau, for example, had posited a type of natural aversion to the suffering of others, *pity*, as a source of morality, and others had invoked the role of love against Hobbes's mechanistic account of motivation. A quasi-aesthetic version of disinterested moral motivation was to be found in the English Platonist thinker, the Third Earl of Shaftesbury, and after him, Francis Hutcheson, who especially strongly influenced Kant's early moral thought.

Kant, however, felt the need to abandon this approach with the "transcendental turn" that established the philosophical position of his Critiques. From the critical position, Kant would criticise *any* idea of *natural* determination of the will, be it either Hobbesian or Rousseauian, as an illegitimate conflation of phenomenal and noumenal standpoints. With this point of view, his *new* conception of moral reason came to be, in some respects, a return to a more *Leibnizian* position, with the rational agent's monadic self-determination having absolute priority. In morality, the will was to have no "external" determination, even if this determination were such that it led to actions directed to the good of others. The will had to be *self*-determining, and such self-determination Kant came to see as *the* characteristic of reason. The autonomy Leibniz posited in the monad as a type of ultimate independent substance became for Kant the autonomy of the faculty of reason itself in its self-determination. To posit some underlying *thing* knowable by theoretical reason would be just to fall into the trap of traditional metaphysics. The positive side of the *critique* of such metaphysics (the metaphysics of pure *theoretical* reason) was just to grasp that the Leibnizian goal of individual self-sufficiency did not need this theoretical infrastructure. It was to be delivered by the idea of a pure *practical* reason.

We might see practical reasoning as giving a degree of autonomy to the practical subject *analogous* to the autonomy the theoretical subject has with respect to any "given" perceptual beliefs, an autonomy that comes from the capacity to reason inferentially. Thus a "Copernican turn" developed from the point of view of practical reason, analogous to that of theoretical reason. In theoretical reason, it is the capacity to link up beliefs in inferential patterns, together with the demand that so linked they form a coherent set of beliefs about *one world*, that suggests the possibility of correcting certain "given" observation statements, even if we have no ultimate goal of a total and comprehensive knowledge of the world "in itself". Thus *the sun's* movement is reinterpreted by the Copernican, for example, in terms of the movement of *the earth*. And as we have seen, this depends on our conceiving of the world as one of *facts* rather than as merely one of *things*. It is only when the world is so conceived, that it is a fit subject for the sort of inferential reasoning needed for us to pursue nomological explanations of particular facts.

Similarly, at the level of *practical* reason, Kant sees reasoning as bearing on the ways inclinations can be differently responded to, depending on how they are incorporated into some *maxim*—a generalisation acting as the practical equivalent of a theoretical *explanation*. Thus, to use one of Kant's examples, someone who felt *compelled* to satisfy an irresistible lust might feel somewhat *less* compelled after realising that some particularly nasty consequence would follow—that he or she would be immediately hanged, for example (CPrR: 5.30).[8] Even instrumental reasoning thus liberates the will from determination by such seemingly given, fixed desires, just as hypothetical reasoning might liberate beliefs from given, fixed perceptual contents. But Kant thinks that in the realm of practical reason the *moral laws* defining what we *must* do cannot have a basis in reason relying on empirical content to even this degree: "all practical principles that presuppose an *object* (matter) of the faculty of desire as the determining ground of the will are, without exception, empirical and can furnish no practical laws" (CPrR: 5.21).[9] Moral reasoning must be something like *metaphysical* reasoning, as it had been conceived in the Inaugural Dissertation: it must be kept free from the distorting influence of sensibility and from intuitive forms of presentation. It must be *pure* intellectual or conceptual reasoning.

5.2 The object of "pure practical reason"—the moral law—can only be grounded in the *form*, rather than in the empirical *content*, of the will

Hypothetical (instrumental) reason cannot provide the form of morality, because appeal to any given content of the will (inclination) would fail to produce the *necessity* required of a *law*. Trying to urge someone to work hard, for example, by appealing to the conditional, "if you want to become wealthy, you should work hard", will always be subject to the possible reply, "but I don't want to be wealthy"! Such is the dilemma for an account of practical reason that, as in Hume's understanding, puts desire outside the scope of reasoning.

Kant's solution is to argue that rather than being grounded in a specific type of content or object—some good or happiness, say—the objectivity of the moral law must rely on its logical *form*. The fundamental law of the pure practical reason will be, as Kant famously puts it in the first form of the "categorical imperative": "Act so that the maxim of your will can always at the same time hold good as a principle of universal legislation" (GMM: 4.421). That is, it is the very capacity of a maxim to be "universalised" that will determine its objectivity. This provides a criterion, the "categorical imperative", which can be invoked in our reflecting on the possible objectivity of moral maxims. The general idea is that *if* you can coherently will that your maxim *be a law* for all rational beings, then it is objective.[10]

There is a definite parallel here with our capacity to achieve knowledge. There we had to adopt the stance of holding ourselves to the rule structure of concepts governing inferences. If I believe that p is the case, and if the conceptual form of the belief that p is such that it implies that it is *not the case* that q, then it is necessary for me to believe that it is *not the case* that q. These sorts of logical relations are relied upon in hypothetical reasoning; they are necessary for us, *regardless* of what we learn about the world—that is, regardless of what the content of our beliefs turn out to be. Logical laws are those to which we *unconditionally* subject ourselves in order to be knowing agents in the first place. We might express these in the form of an imperative: determine your beliefs in such a way that the appropriate logical relations exist among all their contents. This is just the norm represented by the "transcendental unity of apperception". And such an imperative would be unconditional or "categorical". If we conceive of believing as a type of mental action, then the laws of logic would define something like a "morality" of knowing. In this sense, then, we might think of Kant's *moral* categorical imperative, as just a generalisation of this unconditional norm of reasoning applied specifically to the self-determinacy of the will.

The avoidance of contradiction will be the basic idea behind the operation of the categorical imperative in its testing of maxims, as in one of Kant's examples, the contradictoriness of attempting to universalise a maxim to make a deceitful promise whenever it would be to one's advantage. We are meant to imagine a world in which this maxim has become a type of universal law of behaviour: in this world, everyone will make promises they don't intend to keep in situations where they can get away with it. There is, of course, no formal breach of the law of non-contradiction involved in behaving this way, but we are meant to grasp how such a world would be one where the *instrumental* benefit from falsely promising in this way would be lost. So to make a false promise, and simultaneously *have it* that the maxim of false-promising become a natural law, is an act having a type of contradiction at its heart.

In the *Groundwork of the Metaphysics of Morals* Kant famously distinguishes three different formulations, or groups of formulations, of the categorical imperative. The first is the one referred to above: "act only in accordance with that maxim through which you can at the same time will that it become a universal law" (GMM: 4.421)—the formulation most closely tied to the "logic" at the heart of the issue. In the second formulation, the categorical imperative demands that you "[so] act that you use humanity, whether in your own person or in the person of any other, always at the same time as an end, never merely as a means" (ibid.: 4.429), while the third, at least in one of its sub-variants, runs, "every rational being must act as if he were by his maxims at all times a lawgiving member of the universal kingdom of ends" (ibid.: 4.438). The formal principle of these maxims is to act as if your maxims were to serve, at the same time, as a universal law (for all rational beings). The third formulation—with its appeal to a *legislating* for a "kingdom of ends", a moral realm whose law-governed regularity is analogous to that of nature except that here the laws are self-imposed[11]—shows the obvious influence of Rousseau's account of the formation of the common will through a "social contract". Kant insists that these three different formulations are nevertheless formulations of the "very same law, and any one of them of itself unites the other two in it" (ibid.: 4.436), and we might see in these various versions something of those traditional metaphysical themes that had been ejected from the theoretical reason in the first Critique. That is, now the objects of rational psychology, cosmology and theology appear to have been transposed into the framework of practical reason.

For Kant, the "paralogisms" of the first Critique signalled the project of rational psychology, that is, the aspiration to a *theoretical knowledge* of the nature of free rationally self-determining monads, overstepped the bounds of theoretical inquiry. But in the second formulation of the categorical imperative we find that we must *act* in such a way towards others as to essentially *treat them* as free, rationally self-determining monads. Similarly, the antinomies demonstrated that theoretical reason cannot attempt to know the universe as an integrated whole rather than as a mere distributive unity of empirically judgeable facts. But the third formulation of the categorical imperative demands that we act in a way as if we were *legislating* such a moral universe into existence—Kant even paraphrases "kingdom of ends" with *mundus intelligibilis* (GMM: 4.438), the "intelligible world" of the Inaugural Dissertation. Finally, the categorical imperative is clearly connected with the traditional idea of God, it having been standardly assumed that the moral law to which we must unconditionally subject ourselves is legislated by God himself. But Kant, as we have seen in the *Critique of Pure Reason*, reverses the relation between our rational capacities and the idea of God. In the "Transcendental Ideal", the idea of God had been shown to be generated out of the logical structures of reason itself, and this reversal will be at the heart of Kant's developed account of religion. In his practical philosophy, Kant first establishes the objectivity of the moral law via the categorical imperative, then reconstrues the idea of God as a "postulate" that becomes a necessary subjective condition for acting according to the moral law (CPrR: 5.124–25).

As we have seen, the Copernican turn involves a change of our *stance* towards the world in which it is no longer simply conceived as an environs of objects and events radiating out from us, but as a totality of "uncentred" facts. To the extent that we aspire to the role of such a "transcendental" subject of this world, we aim at a cognitive existence as no longer located somewhere in particular *in* the world, and so as closer to some objects and events than others. To a subject considered ideally as pure knower, there are no facts "closer" than others: facts are not just the sorts of "things" that exist in time and space. The reflective subject seems to be able to think about the fact world effectively from no *particular* place within it (Nagel 1986), and this seems to give him or her a peculiar freedom *from it*, the type of freedom that Plato expressed in the image of the "winged soul", or that Eckhart did, in the idea of being as close to a point located a thousand miles away as to where I am now. To have this freedom from the world, the rational subject is compelled to adopt certain attitudes towards the fact world and to itself. First, the *world* must be considered as a unity in the way thematised in the Platonic and Neoplatonic tradition, and the *self* must be considered, analogously, to have a unity in the sense of that of all its constitutive representations. But the *type* of unity involved here cannot be the one relevant to particular objects of empirical knowledge, because those objects involve an intuitive form of spatiotemporal location.

Kant's account of morality, while attracting many adherents, has also attracted many critics, and deep divisions between interpretations exist here, just as they do for Kant's theoretical philosophy. Moreover, while the generally favourable interpretations of Kant's moral philosophy show no strict overlap, they tend to take a tack similar to the defence of the "two-aspects" account of the noumenon–phenomenon distinction. Thus, consonant with the two-aspects view, some readers of Kant's practical philosophy have stressed the *stance* or *standpoint* he advocates with respect to others.[12] One can adopt a theoretical stance, as when, for example, one looks for explanations for another's behaviour, but this is not the same as, nor is it presupposed by, the *moral* stance. Effectively, to adopt a moral stance to another is to treat that person as a moral monad—as a self-sufficient being, a "substance" whose future states are expressions of its own internal states, rather than the effects of the local actions of other substances.[13] This, in turn, dictates the shape of one's relation to that person's future states. While from the theoretical point of view it makes sense to talk of *predicting* their future actions, from a moral point of view it makes more sense to talk about *holding them* to certain considerations, and *holding oneself* to certain considerations where they are involved. The easiest model here is the stance one adopts to another on one's giving or receiving a promise. To promise to another to do such and such is not to offer a *prediction* to them, that one will do such and such, but rather to *undertake* to do it and to simultaneously give the other the right to hold one *to* one's promise.[14]

5.3 Kant's political theory

In his two classic works on practical reason, the *Groundwork of the Metaphysics of Morals* and the *Critique of Practical Reason*, Kant attempted to show the *objective* foundations of the moral law. Once founded, the law could then be applied in a theory of politics and law (*Recht*) and a theory of personal morality or virtue (*Tugend*), and this he attempted to do in the work from 1797–98, the *Metaphysics of Morals*.[15] Kant's political theory is commonly discussed in relation to two overlapping early-modern approaches to political authority—those of the natural law and the social contract traditions—and Kant is commonly seen as transforming both of these approaches to politics. Understandably, it is his transcendental separation of the phenomenal and noumenal that is taken to allow him to develop a unique approach to political legitimacy combining elements of both traditions.

Again, looking at Kant's transcendental philosophy as growing out of his failed earlier attempts to combine Leibniz and Newton might help us understand something about his political thought. Leibniz, it will be recalled, accounted for the order and "harmony" found in the world by its having been preordained by God, as the condition of the best of all possible worlds. Such harmony is discoverable at the physical level in the modern natural sciences where explanatory unification of the phenomenal realm is achieved by bringing the disparate phenomena of the world under the purview of a few universally applicable laws. Here Galileo's unification of what had been understood as different sub- and superlunar physics would be an exemplar of the disclosure of such "harmony". At the social level, harmony was similarly conceived as requiring that God had created the best of all possible worlds, the "Republic, or rather Kingdom, of God over human beings".[16]

The idea of a "natural law" regulating human existence can be traced back to the ancient philosophy of the Stoics, but the medieval idea of natural law conceived as issuing from God's command derived largely from the work of Thomas Aquinas. In the early-modern period, the notion became transformed by Hugo Grotius (1583–1645), who saw natural law as arising from human nature itself, and in particular, from mankind's natural rationality and sociableness. While still holding that the natural law derives from the "author of nature", God, Grotius suggested that it would still have a *kind* of validity even if there were no God—a validity derived, as it were, from its mere *rationality* alone (CLPB: 13).

In its political application the idea of natural law was meant to provide some sort of foundation to enable us to either justify or criticise the coercive, positive laws of the state. In contrast, the understanding of political legitimacy which invoked the notion of a *social contract*, and which stemmed from the revolutionary approach of Thomas Hobbes, saw the grounds of an individual's obligation to positive law as resting in that individual's own voluntary *consent* to the law—a consent which, for Hobbes, derived from the individual's rational self-interest. Thus, whereas Grotius saw humans as *naturally* sociable, Hobbes saw them as naturally isolated and egoistic, with their fragile sociability as artificial, and as consequent upon their willingness to *leave* their natural state. In Hobbes's account, the explanation of social behaviour was much like the type of explanation found in Galilean physics. No teleology was needed, as the movements of any of the isolated parts— the egoistic individuals—could be described in terms of the basic properties of the parts, on the one hand (basic, naturally given inclinations and aversions, together with a capacity for calculation) and the fact of their interaction, on the other. Paradoxically, as we have seen (section 2.3), Hobbes's seemingly materialist and "atheist" approach can also be viewed as a development of the nominalist outlook emerging from the late Middle Ages, as a consequence of *theological* "voluntarism". For its part, while the natural law tradition seemed superficially more theocentric, *its* idea of a law, which might be rational *even if* not ordained by God, testified to elements of the influence of the pagan philosophy of Plato and Aristotle, an influence the voluntarists found questionable within Christian culture.

It will be recalled that in his early natural philosophy, Kant had wanted to preserve *some* sense in which the harmony among physical monads, rather than being "pre-established", could be viewed as an outcome of their individual interactions. At the same time, he saw the law-like harmonious nature of these interactions still with reference to a conformity to a Godly decree and as a consequence of a schema in the mind of God. We might imagine that, transposed to the question of social or political existence, what would result would be something combining elements of the natural law tradition *and* the contractarian one, and this is what we indeed find. However, it was Kant's "critical" separation of the phenomenal and noumenal orders that allowed him to combine these elements and to answer some of the problems within existing approaches to political legitimacy.

Like Grotius, Kant saw the legitimacy of the laws of particular states as established by a universal law found in the inner being of humankind, and not reliant on the simple idea of God's command. However, *like* the model of divine legislation, Kant conceived of the law as issuing from a *command* and having the form of an *imperative*. But his account of the origin of the law displaced itself from the earlier theocentric approaches to natural law, even more than that of Grotius. For Kant, what was at play was the moral law as expressed in the categorical imperative, the objectivity of which was established in the *Groundwork of the Metaphysics of Morals* and the *Critique of Practical Reason*.[17] As J. B. Schneewind expresses it, for Kant, "the agent's own rational will thus performs the task for which the natural lawyers ... brought in the will of God. It enacts the law that we have compelling justification to obey, regardless of our own contingent ends" (Schneewind 1998: 521).

Only with the writings of the 1790s did the application of Kant's transcendental approach to practical reason to politics become clear, and most explicitly with the "Metaphysical Foundations of the Doctrine of Right", the first section of the *Metaphysics of Morals* (1797). The fundamental principle of practical reason can be applied to human existence at two levels. Applied at the level of personal morality, or "ethics", the relevant object will be the good will, the topic of the second half of the book, headed the "Metaphysical Foundations of the Doctrine of Virtue". As one would expect, here the relevant level of analysis is not so much the concrete action of an agent as the character-expressing "maxim" behind it.[18] In contrast, the political and legal considerations of an action explored in the first half of the book pertain more to the concrete action itself, not its motivation. The legality of an action is indifferent to *why* it was performed, particularly whether it was performed out of respect for the moral law or out of egoistic motivations. The positive laws of a state, therefore, must be based on considerations indifferent to the actual propensity of the population to virtuous behaviour.[19] Fundamentally, it is the threat of punishment that is meant to secure fidelity to the law, and only prudential motivations on the parts of agents need be assumed. From this *phenomenal* point of view, Kant seems to presuppose nothing more than a *Hobbesian* conception of individual psychology and behaviour.[20] However, this does not make the principles underlying the legal framework something other than moral ones. It is the moral law, not issues of prudence, that ultimately justifies the coercive but just positive laws of a state.

This combination of their applying to egoistic individuals and being grounded in moral rather than prudential considerations accounts for the ambiguity of the relationship of Kant's account to the Hobbesian "social-contract" theory of political legitimacy. For Kant, the social contract has a different type of normativity than it has for Hobbes. For Hobbes, it is prudent for an individual to accept life in a community ordered by external coercive laws because *any* orderliness will be better than the chaos of the "state of nature". For Kant, however, one has a *duty* to enter into the social contract, as one thereby enters into a state to remove impediments to allowing self-interested individuals to act from moral considerations alone.[21] Clearly, as mentioned earlier, Kant has a greater affinity with Rousseau on the issue of the nature of the social contract than with Hobbes. Rousseau, it will be remembered, had conceived of the social unity achieved in the social contract as a "universal will", not to be equated with the "will of all", that is, with some outcome of the interaction of empirical wills of egoistic individuals, as in Hobbes,[22] and the analogy of Rousseau's self-legislating community to Kant's self-legislating moral individual has often been pointed out (e.g., Kelly 1969). Nevertheless, despite the influence of Rousseau, Kant's philosophical interpretation of the social contract is different to that of Rousseau. For Rousseau, who is more overtly Platonist in the sense of Platonism of which Kant is critical, the general will has a type of objective, *metaphysical reality*, and the social contract is effectively a device for *discovering* the nature of its content. For Kant, by contrast, it is an "Idea", the primary relevance of which is for practical, not theoretical reason, and to mistake it for a type of existing reality would be to fall prey to the transcendental illusion. Kant's attitude to Rousseau here would thus be effectively the same as to Plato in the *Critique of Pure Reason*.[23]

5.4 Concerns with Kant's practical philosophy

The "German idealists", philosophers coming after Kant with whom we will be concerned, were influenced by Kant's Copernican "revolution" in philosophy, yet unsatisfied with the state in which Kant had left it. Seeing in Kant's noumenon–phenomenon distinction something more like that recently described as the "two-world" interpretation, they were unsatisfied with Kant's resolution of the problem of human freedom, in which he assigned it to the "noumenal world", as opposed to the "phenomenal world". That is, Kant's solution to the problem of freedom in a world of natural necessity seemed to imply that we had to live in *two separate worlds*.

Moreover, while Kant's critique of pure *theoretical* reason had allowed him a response to the implicitly nihilistic and anti-religious implications of a philosophy where the practical depends upon an autonomous theoretical reason, such a radical uncoupling of practical from theoretical reason left a chain of problems in its wake. By restricting theoretical knowledge to "appearances", the fundamental thesis of weak TI, Kant not only deprived humans of a comprehensive knowledge of the actual world they lived in, but also created problems for any moral-psychological reflection concerning acting *in the world*. What Kant believed he had established with respect to practical reason was to show how, given the deterministic picture of science and without appeal to the commands of God, there could *be* morality and an objective moral law. This had, however, as critics like Schiller and Hegel were to later argue, all the problems of an entirely *formal* solution. The categorical imperative might instruct us to treat ourselves and others as "ends in themselves", but this abstract conception conflicts with what we can know or experience of ourselves or others *as* worldly beings, given the moral indifference of the world, as we experience and know it.

This morally indifferent nature of empirical humanity for Kant is revealed in a passage in the *Groundwork of the Metaphysics of Morals* where he discusses the actions of generally beneficent individuals whose souls are "so sympathetically attuned that, without any other motive of vanity or self-interest they find an inner satisfaction in spreading joy around them and can take delight in the satisfaction of others" (GMM: 4.398). Such individuals, we would surely say, are morally exemplary. However, Kant states that

> in such a case an action of this kind, however it may conform with duty and however amiable it may be, has nevertheless no true moral worth but is on the same footing with other inclinations, for example, the inclination to honor, which, if it fortunately lights upon what is in fact in the common interest and in conformity with duty and hence honorable, deserves praise and encouragement but not esteem; for the maxim lacks moral content, namely that of doing such actions not from inclination but *from duty.*
>
> (Ibid.)[24]

One early influential and otherwise sympathetic critic who articulated the worries of many idealists to follow was Friedrich Schiller (1759–1805).

Schiller had been induced to the exciting intellectual community of the University of Jena by Johann Wolfgang Goethe, who had been appointed the privy councillor of the Duchy of Weimar. On taking up the chair of history, Schiller was introduced to Kant's philosophy by Karl Leonard Reinhold, who was establishing Jena as a centre of Kantianism. While clearly attracted to transcendental idealism, Schiller was critical of what he took to be the antagonistic relation within Kant's moral philosophy between rational duty, on the one hand, and sentiment and inclination, on the other. Clearly this did not fit Schiller's more anti-dualistic and corporeally humanistic outlook. Not only had Schiller been trained in medicine;[25] he had been influenced by the heterodox Swabian version of Protestant pietism of his native Württemberg. As a variety of commentators have pointed out, the religious culture that flourished in the Swabian Duchy of Württemberg had distinctly unorthodox characteristics.[26] Swabian pietism has been described as an anti-authoritarian and practically oriented, eschatological variant of Lutheran pietism, within which the "kingdom of God" was regarded as achievable on earth. It thus annexed religion to politics, rather than seeing it in relation to some other-worldly beyond, as in the Augustinian tradition.[27] Moreover, it was regarded by many as being aligned with, rather than opposed to, the "Enlightenment" (Dickey 1987: 12). In particular, the mid-eighteenth-century preacher and writer F. C. Oetinger,[28] had propagated the teachings of Jacob Böhme—a thinker whom Hegel, a Swabian like Schiller, was to treat in his *Lectures on the History of Philosophy* as of significance equal to that of Francis Bacon for the eruption of modern philosophy.[29] It was from this perspective of a socially *engaged* worldly ethical outlook that Schiller was to describe Kant's moral point of view as "Carthusian"—the Carthusians being the strictest of the Catholic monastic orders, its adherents living out their silent lives in seclusion from society.[30]

The complaints that Schiller aired in On Grace and Dignity (of 1793) against Kant's polarisation of duty and inclination, a polarisation amounting to an "oppression" of mankind's sensuous nature by reason, were further developed in On the Aesthetic Education of Man (of 1794–95). To be a "member of the tribunal of reason", he notes, involves raising oneself "from an individual into a representative of the species" (AE: letter 2, para. 4),[31] thereby speaking and acting as that "ideal man, the archetype of a human being" that each individual carries within himself (ibid.: letter 4, para. 2), rather than as the actual "empirical" or "psychological" being that one is. But reason and morality as conceived by Kant may not just be indifferent to the individual corporeal human being; they may be antagonistic. Appealing to the actual life led by subjects, both individually and collectively, and with clear reference to the course of revolutionary events unfolding in France, Schiller warned of the dangers of the external imposition of reason on a living body.

> This Natural State (as we may term any political body whose organisation derives originally from forces and not from laws) is, it is true, at variance with man as moral being, for whom the only Law should be to act in conformity with law. But it will just suffice for man as physical being; for he only gives himself laws in order to come to terms with forces. But physical man does in fact exist, whereas the existence of moral man is as yet problematic. If, then, Reason does away with the Natural State (as she of necessity must if she would put her own in its place), she jeopardises the physical man who actually exists for the sake of a moral man who is as yet problematic.
>
> (AE: letter 3, para. 3)

Seemingly drawing on the idea of the "formative drives" shaping biological phenomena, from the contemporary biologist J. F. Blumenbach, Schiller transposed Kant's concept–intuition distinction into one between two drives: the sensuous and the formal drive.[32] The sensuous drive proceeds from mankind's natural, sensuous nature and "its business is to set him within the limits of time, and to turn him into matter" (AE: letter 12, para. 1). The formal drive proceeds from the "absolute existence of man, or from his rational nature, and is intent on giving him the freedom to bring harmony into the diversity of his manifestations" (ibid.: letter 12, para. 4). While, under the influence of the sensuous drive, mankind is "swept along by the flux of time" (letter 12, para. 2), under that of the formal drive, one wants the "eternal and the necessary to be real", and hence it "annuls time" (letter 12, para. 4). These drives can be at war: when the sensuous sub-ordinates the formal drive, the condition of "the savage" results, and when the formal subordinates the sensuous drive, the result is the "barbarian". It is important that Schiller was critical of Kant from a position that he thought of as that of the spirit, if not the letter, of the Kantian system,[33] and that the solution to the problem of *harmonising* the drives was to be taken from Kant himself—Kant's conception of *aesthetic* judgment in the *Critique of Judgment*. In Schiller's terms, it involved a mediation of the sensuous and formal drives by the "play drive" (letter 14, para. 3), by which a *reciprocity* between the sensuous and formal drives could be sustained. Nevertheless, there was a genuine difference here, one that might perhaps be most easily caught in *theological* terms. I have suggested, in Chapter 4, that Kant's understanding of Plato is, in fact, coloured by assumptions coming from a third party, St Augustine. In Kant's moral philosophy too, what Schiller found objectionable might be described in a similar way.

In his *Lectures on the History of Moral Philosophy*, John Rawls describes Kant's moral psychology as having distinctly "Augustinian" features.[34] In particular, for Kant:

> moral failures of all kinds, from the lesser ones of fragility and impur-ity to the worst extremes of wickedness and perversity of which we are capable, must all arise, not from the desires of our physical and social nature, but solely from our exercise of our free power of choice.
>
> (Rawls 2000: 294)

Similarly, that Kant's practical philosophy is strongly Augustinian has been argued by Frederick Beiser in the context of his examination of Kant's doctrine of the "highest good" in the *Critique of Practical Reason*, which "reaffirms the traditional Christian view". Beiser points out that

> in crucial respects, the precedent for Kant's argument is Augustine. ... Pivotal to Kant's argument is a conception fundamental to Augus-tine but alien to Epicureanism, Stoicism, and the entire Enlight-enment tradition: the concept of sin. In going back to Augustine in all these respects, Kant proves to be deeply loyal to the Reforma-tion, whose founding fathers, Luther and Calvin, found their inspiration in the same Augustinian doctrines.
>
> (Beiser 2006: 594)[35]

What Kant shares with Augustine, the exclusive focus on the human *will* in matters of morality, is expressed clearly at the start of the *Groundwork of the Metaphysics of Morals*: "It is impossible to think of anything at all in the world, or indeed even beyond it, that could be considered good without limitation except a *good will*" (GMM: 4.393).[36]

We have seen how Augustine, having added a *will* to the Neoplatonic divine mind, the "One",[37] had conceived of a God who had created the world *ex nihilo* from ideas contained in his own mind. Moreover, Augustine's voluntaristic stress on the *inscrutable nature* of God's justice—as he puts in it one of his sermons, "God's inscrutable justice is beyond justice"[38]—was to be taken up and emphasised in the late medieval period by voluntarists such as Ockham. With the doctrine of humans made in the image of God, the will becomes central also to the anthropological dimension of such a theology, and this relation will be preserved regardless of whether humans are seen as made in the likeness of God, as with the orthodox Christian view, or, as with Kant, the idea of God is regarded as generated from the structures of an autonomous human morality.[39] And yet from the time of the first fathers of the church there had always existed a rival picture of the Christian God to that of Augustine, one that pictured the relation of God to the world in a way that relied more on Plotinus and Proclus' idea of the world as "emanation" of God rather than his temporal creation. It was this theology that had informed the heterodox Christian thinkers from the later medieval period, such as Eckhart and Cusa, and seventeenth-century critics of Calvinist voluntarism, such as Cudworth and Leibniz.

This anti-voluntarist tradition also informed Schiller's objections to Kant's moral philosophy, objections which were still made from a generally Kantian standpoint. Much the same picture would begin to be seen in the approaches of other post-Kantians as well, including Schelling, Hegel and, perhaps, Nietzsche. The relation of these thinkers to Kant and to the earlier part of the tradition of Continental idealism, however, can only be appreciated in light of the attempt to sharpen Kant's philosophical position, an attempt undertaken in the first instance by Reinhold and Fichte. Before turning to these thinkers, however, it is important to chart some of the changes that were occurring within the approach of Kant himself as he moved away from the classically transcendental picture and in a direction that, in some ways, paralleled later developments among the post-Kantians.

6

THE LATER KANT AS A "POST-KANTIAN" PHILOSOPHER?

The Kant who is most familiar to an English-speaking philosophical audience is the epistemological critic of the extravagant claims of early-modern metaphysics, found in the *Critique of Pure Reason*,[1] and the "deontological" moral philosopher found in his two works of moral philosophy from the 1780s, the *Groundwork of the Metaphysics of Morals* and the *Critique of Practical Reason*. It is probably not unjustified to say that for much of the twentieth century, for analytically trained anglophone readers of Kant, these texts present the "essential Kant", the exponent of what I have described as weak TI.

A somewhat different Kant emerges, however, if one focuses, not on the works of the 1780s, but on those commencing with *Critique of Judgment* from 1790 and ending with Kant's final manuscripts, published only in the twentieth century, as the *Opus Postumum*. Indeed, from the perspective of later idealists such as Schelling and Hegel, it was in the *Critique of Judgment*, with its treatment of the operations of judgment in the realms of aesthetics and biology, that was to be found key to a Kantian move beyond the problems of the paradigmatic works of the 1780s, represented by those issues identified by Schiller (Pippin 1997: 129–53). When read with an eye to the potential for Kant's transcendental philosophy to get beyond the problems of its initial formulations, a somewhat different "essential Kant" takes shape, one that prefigures some of the solutions offered by the post-Kantian "German idealists" themselves. It is this other aspect of Kant that is the topic of this chapter.[2]

6.1 From empirical to transcendental accounts of Hutchesonian moral sense

As a student at Karlsschule, in Stuttgart, Schiller had been introduced to the attempts by British moral-sense theorists, Shaftesbury and Hutcheson, to marry feeling and morality in a way appearing in stark contrast to Kant's transcendental approach. The *aesthetic* focus of these works, together with the particular organic or quasi-vitalistic point of view on the world, reflected the influence of Platonism, as found in the anti-voluntaristic thought of the Cambridge Platonists, importantly Cudworth. And yet, in Kant's own pre-critical period, he *too* had largely aligned his own moral philosophy with Hutcheson's. Thus in his "Prize essay" of 1764 he praised Hutcheson and other moral-sense theorists who had "under the name of moral feeling [des moralischen Gefühls], provided us with a starting point from which to develop some excellent observations" (TP: 2.300), and his lectures on moral philosophy from around the same time show the same sympathetic attitude.[3] But the Platonistic approach of Shaftesbury and Hutcheson could not survive the transcendental turn, after which, as we have seen, Kant came to ground the moral law on the conceptual *form* of the will itself. This marginalised the role of feeling, and hence actions that flowed from benevolent feelings came to be regarded as morally neutral,[4] resulting in just the type of attitude Schiller found objectionable. And yet, throughout his critical period Kant maintained a favourable attitude to Hutcheson's moral-sense theory, despite the overt dogmatic metaphysics underpinning it, and in the *Critique of Judgment* we see the obvious effort to accommodate Hutchesonian ideas within the framework of transcendental philosophy.

Hutcheson had found in the appreciation of beauty a type of egoless disinterestedness that he took to be a model for the objective moral judgment of the actions of others and one's self. With this, he was clearly drawing on the aesthetic focus of the revived Platonism of the Renaissance, together with the English Platonist revival, as interpreted by Anthony Ashley Cooper, the Third Earl of Shaftesbury. But Hutcheson, a Protestant minister, was far more orthodox in his religious beliefs than his predecessors. Shaftesbury had been influenced by Cudworth, who, in his *The True Intellectual System of the Universe* (of 1678), had incorporated from Renaissance Platonism the idea of an animating world soul—a "life or plastic nature ... which runs through the whole corporeal universe" (TISU: bk 1, ch. 3, §37.3). Cudworth distinguished his views from those of atheists, who *substitute* the plastic life of nature for "the true Omnipotent Deity, which is a perfect mind or consciously understanding nature, presiding over the universe" (ibid.: bk 1, ch. 3, §37.26), but the suspicion of pantheism would clearly have been aroused. Pantheist ideas had indeed been common among the most radical of the protestant sects active during the English civil wars of 1642 to 1651 (Jacob 2006), and the term itself had been coined by the shadowy figure of John Toland (1670–1722), an associate of Shaftesbury, correspondent of Leibniz, and editor of an English edition of the works of Giordano Bruno.

Hutcheson used the disinterestedness of our aesthetic responses as a refutation of the claims of Hobbes and Mandeville as to the egoistic nature of all motivation, and explained the particularly *moral* salience of our bodily reactions in terms of the idea that God created us so that our natural responses would conform to the dictates of his will.[5] This allowed him to distance himself from the more pantheist features of Shaftesbury's treatment of moral sense, as well as from the rationalism of Cudworth's approach to morality.[6] Hutcheson was widely read in Germany in the 1760s, having been translated by no less a figure than Lessing, and Hutcheson's views on the bodily nature of the aesthetic–moral responses were ripe for retranslation back into the more pantheistic version of moral-sense theory, given the simmering Spinozist culture of intellectual life in the later decades of eighteenth-century Germany. While with the transcendental turn, Kant abandoned the idea that morality could be grounded in some quasi-natural response to the world, he was never to dismiss the idea of an aestheticised moral-sense theory as *irrelevant* to morality.

Even in the *Groundwork of the Metaphysics of Morals* Kant avoided reducing Hutchesonian moral feeling to the status of any simple inclination, even when criticising any attempt to find in feeling "a uniform standard of good and evil" and a ground for the judgment of the actions of others. It is still the case, he asserts, that moral feeling

> remains closer to morality and its dignity inasmuch as it shows virtue the honour of ascribing to her *immediately* the delight and esteem we have for her and does not, as it were, tell her to her face that it is not her beauty but only our advantage that attaches us to her.
>
> (GMM: 4.442–43)

Kant's critical turn had, of course, left room for various sorts of teleological and theological ideas to play a *regulative role* in cognitive life. Thus, while not entering into the consideration of the *objective* conditions of morality, such teleological notions were exactly the sort of ideas that played a crucial role within the *subjective* conditions of morality, and so were relevant from the point of view of "moral anthropology" (Louden 2000). In particular, in the *Critique of Practical Reason* Kant attempted to give an account of the role of *respect* (*Achtung*) qua *moral feeling*, as part of what has been described as a "theory of moral sensibility", having something akin to the role played by the Transcendental Aesthetic in the *Critique of Pure Reason* (Reath 1989).[7] After the second Critique, this type of "moral sensibility" came to play a more central role in Kant's moral anthropology as he sought ways to accommodate aesthetic judgment into the critical framework.[8]

6.2 The ethical infrastructure of aesthetic judgment in the *Critique of Judgment*

In the *Critique of Judgment* Kant agrees with the modern reflective outlook, denying that beauty can be an objective property of empirical objects or situations—for Kant, the world of appearance, it must be remembered, is effectively the world as described by Newtonian science. However, Kant still attempts to find a way of considering judgments of aesthetic taste *in some sense* objective. Thus, following Hutcheson's account of disinterestedness, he points to a difference between the "beautiful" and that which *merely* gratifies a subjective desire—the "agreeable". This distinction, then, allows him to think that while aesthetic judgment is grounded in pleasure and, as such, is "subjective", the pleasure involved is nevertheless *not* one consequent upon the satisfaction of some bodily need or appetite. Since our interests and needs are individualised by our separate embodiments, they typically divide and oppose us. The *disinterestedness* of aesthetic pleasures thus promised a type of sensuous motive that is otherwise shareable, and free from the discord that follows upon our acting on egoistic motivations. It hence promised a type of sensuous motivation that could lead to social harmony rather than to discord, the very thing that had so attracted Shaftesbury.

Hutcheson's idea of *disinterested* pleasures motivating our correct evaluations of the world can be traced back to Plato's idea of *pure* or *true* pleasures—pleasures "unmixed" with the corresponding *displeasures* of need or desire. That pleasure can be conceived of and experienced *in abstraction* from its opposite, displeasure or pain, had been important from the Platonic perspective.[9] For Plato it meant that the quality that it responds to, beauty, can itself be grasped independently of any relation to its opposite, ugliness—hence the possibility of a pure or unmixed pleasure. This attitude is indeed present in Hutcheson, who seems to conceive of ugliness as the simple *lack of* beauty.[10] But such a Plato-derived conception of the pleasure taken in beauty in fact comes with considerable metaphysical baggage. For Plato, the locus of this experience was in the philosophical mind's final intuitive grasp of the world as a whole, a grasp with equally cognitive, moral and aesthetic dimensions.[11] In Aristotle, the pleasurable aesthetic dimension of this was reflected in the perfect unalloyed joy that *theos*—God—takes in his own thinking, a state which finite human beings can only ever approximate (Meta: bk 12, ch. 9). Indeed, it is possible to trace through Christian culture from the time of the church fathers onwards, a tradition of "theological aesthetics" that interpreted the appreciation of natural and artistic beauty in Platonistic terms of a type of mystical unification with God.[12]

Hutcheson's moral-sense theory was clearly grounded in his orthodox Christian metaphysics, based on the idea that we have been created by God in just such a way as to *make* our natural reactions respond appropriately to the morally salient aspects of the world. That is, for Hutcheson, God's will is the source both of the distinction between good and evil, and our otherwise *natural* tendency to react to good and evil in morally appropriate ways. Kant needed to translate such ideas into a form compatible with his own

critical philosophy that was meant to be free of all such metaphysical assumptions, and he therefore needed a new theory of beauty itself, a theory of the
nature and origin of the *pleasure* involved in its experience, and a theory of
how this is relevant to our moral, and not simply our aesthetic, judgments.

One of Kant's key innovations introduced in the *Critique of Judgment* is
that of the distinction between two forms of judgment—"determinative"
and "reflective". In the unpublished first introduction, Kant puts forward
the distinction in this way:

> Judgment can be regarded either as mere[ly] an ability to *reflect*, in
> terms of a certain principle, on a given presentation so as to [make]
> a concept possible, or as an ability to *determine* an underlying con-
> cept by means of a given empirical presentation. In the first case it
> is the *reflective*, in the second the *determinative*, *power of judgment*.
> To *reflect* (or consider [überlegen]) is to hold given representations
> up to, and compare them with, either other representations or
> one's cognitive power [itself], in reference to a concept that this
> [comparison] makes possible.
>
> (CJFI: 399–400)

The idea that one can compare a given representation to one's own cognitive power is perhaps clearest in the case of teleological judgments, the
subject matter of the second book of the *Critique of Judgment*, "The Critique of Teleological Judgment": it is because I *am* an agent capable of purposeful acting, that is, acting on the basis of a concept I have of the
intended goal, that I can judge organisms as exhibiting an analogous purposiveness. Thus the property of purposiveness expressed by an organism
is neither an objective property, like its mass, for example, nor a fictitious,
purely subjectively based one projected onto it, like something's "agree-
ableness". One understands an organism "as if" an end, purpose or design
is built into and manifest in its structure and processes because one can
recognise in it a purposiveness analogous to that of one's own free mental
acts. And the purposiveness of one's own cognitive capacity is both essential to one's own act of judgment and something one shares with other
rational creatures; it is not like an inclination or desire one merely happens
to have. It is just *this* that separates teleological from "merely" subjective
judgments. The situation in the context of aesthetic judgment is in ways
parallel, in ways different. It concerns a type of teleology that is subjective
and manifested in our feelings rather than one external to us, as perceived
in the functioning of organisms. It is as if our felt responses had been
designed to act favourably (as Hutcheson had actually believed) to bring us
into the right cognitive relation to an object in the world.

In the opening paragraphs of Part I of the *Critique of Judgment*, the "Critique of Aesthetic Judgment" (§§3, 4 and 5), Kant explores the logical

structure of judgments of beauty compared with the "interested" judgments of practical reason. By judgments of the "good", Kant has in mind the instrumental judgments of prudential reasoning, not *moral* judgments, and so he treats judgments of the "agreeable" and the "good" as both grounded in the satisfaction of some need or interest.[13] The agreeable is known through the immediate contents of intuition—"AGREEABLE *is what the senses like in sensation*" (CJ: §3)—and what is *good* is "what, by means of reason, we like through its mere concept" (ibid.: §4). But these are to be contrasted with judgments of the beautiful, which are *disinterested*. And yet, in a certain respect, a taste for the beautiful is *like* the taste for the agreeable—it is *immediate* and does not depend on some particular concept or knowledge concerning the nature of the object. But at the same time, the appreciation of beauty is more like a liking for the *good* in that it does *in some way* depend on "reflection"—the reflection involved in the contemplation of the *form* of the thing's presentation *in isolation from considerations of its existence*. So we might think of beauty as somehow bridging the gap between those judgments that are similarly beholden to the demands of the body and those that reflect the free operations of the mind.[14]

Kant draws an important consequence from the disinterestedness of aesthetic liking, a consequence that would become crucially relevant for Schiller: one is self-consciously *free* in one's disinterested attraction to *form*. Moreover, in the act in which we judge a presentation to be beautiful, we feel that our acknowledgment of the beauty of the presentation is *freely given*, and constrained neither by our given desires nor by our faculty of reason. In aesthetic judgment, "we are not compelled to give our approval by any interest, whether of sense or of reason" (CJ: §5). But if one recognises that no *private conditions or interests* lay behind one's own aesthetic liking, thinks Kant, then we can *expect* this of others. The attribution of beauty to a presentation thus contains an implicit acknowledgment that the judgments of others could also be freely given in this way (ibid.: §6).

In ordinary empirical judgments without any contribution of feeling, we think of the ground of our agreement as having to do with the objective content of the judgment. We *agree* that the meadow *is* green, and we grasp that it is the *being green of* the meadow itself that is the rational *ground* of our agreement. Here, judgment tracks properties in the empirical world.[15] However, in ordinary, *interested* judgments of taste, we think of the judgment as grounded in our subjective needs and desires. The idea is that if I find strawberry gelato "agreeable", while I do so because of actual sensuous properties that it has, the fact that these properties *count as* agreeable is nevertheless grounded in *my* desires. However, judgments of aesthetic taste are reducible to neither of these extremes. Neither is beauty an objective property of empirical things, nor, thinks Kant, is it a mere projection of subjective preferences. Kant's discussion in §6 suggests that the real ground of aesthetic judgment is, in fact, the nature of the interrelation *between* the judging subjects, in as much as they must mutually *recognise* each other *as* free in their judgments.

Kant notes that if an individual subject is aware that their liking for something is without interest, then they must regard the thing itself as containing the ground for its being universally liked. "[I]f someone likes something and is conscious that he himself does so without any interest, then he cannot help judging that it must contain a basis for being liked [that holds] for everyone" (CJ: §6). The idea that the object itself must contain the ground for my liking of it seems to come about by a type of disjunctive inference. Either my interest must be the ground of my liking, or this ground must be in the object itself. I am conscious that my interest is *not* involved, therefore it must be the object itself that is responsible.[16] But to take the object itself as the ground would seem to be to take something that, from an empirical point of view, appears as much a subjective or mind-dependent quality as an "objective" one. But then Kant shifts his position, and rather than appeal to the object *itself* to explain the subject's judgment, he appeals to the subject's own *freedom* as the ground of its capacity for disinterestedness. Moreover, this freedom, he claims, is something that can be presupposed in *others*. Thus,

> the judging (person) feels himself fully free in consideration of the pleasures which he devotes to the object: in this way then he can discover no private conditions as the grounds of liking on which he alone is dependent, and must regard it as grounded in something that he can presuppose in each other person.
>
> (Ibid., trans. modified)

Again, Kant has appealed to something about the *stance* of the judging subject, him or herself, to capture a distinction that one is *tempted* to think of in a "metaphysical" way.

We grasp, then, that it is the fact that a judging subject can recognise him- or herself *as* free, in the sense of being capable of overcoming his or her own narrowly egocentric point of view, that is the true "ground" of normative judgment. "Consequently [this judge] must believe he has grounds to demand a similar liking from everyone" (CJ: §6, trans. modified). On the analogy with Kant's moral philosophy, it might be said that in addressing my aesthetic judgment to another, I am addressing them as worthy of "respect" and am simultaneously offering my own judgment as an act that is *itself* worthy of respect. I claim for myself, and demand of the other, that the aesthetic claims that pass between us express a type of quasi-moral character, the character of a person whose actions are not determined by their own narrow interests.[17] Thus Kant appeals to a type of community of *sensus communis* or common sense (ibid.: §§20–22)—allowing us to make judgments that are "subjectively universal", in virtue of the fact that we can appeal to shared evaluative criteria and not just idiosyncratic preference.

While we can think of objects as objectively having or not having certain non-evaluative properties, with notions of value it is difficult to think of the value of objects or events as existing independently of the fact of anyone's valuing of them: a thing *has a value*, it would seem, only in as much as *someone* actually values it. Hutcheson could be an objectivist about evaluative properties like beauty and goodness because he saw those values as ultimately stemming from *God*'s valuing. We start to glimpse in Kant, however, a way around this role given to God. The shift from the theoretical to the practical stance concerns in the first instance the adoption of a stance towards others in which one treats each of them according to the "formula of humanity" of the *Groundwork of the Metaphysics of Morals*, as "an end, never merely as a means" (GMM: 4.429). While theists would have justified this on the basis that God decreed it, for Kant, as we have seen, this stance is thought of as immanent to the very structure of reason itself: it doesn't need to be understood as a decree issuing from God. From within this attitude to others, we will treat them as capable of making claims about the world as rational and free subjects, that is, as capable of *not* having their responses dictated by their personal interests. We treat them as *not* enslaved to their passions, but *as rational beings*, capable of rising above them, and we can appeal to the shared criteria of common sense. So from within this stance, we treat them (and ourselves) as capable of grasping *values* in a "disinterested" way, despite the fact that we do not see values as empirically real or independent of our evaluating activity. Thus the role ascribed to God in Hutcheson's moral sensibilism has now been made immanent to a feature of human communicability.[18]

6.3 The symbolic dimension of beauty

There is, of course, much more to Kant's account of aesthetic judgment than this, but it at least gives us something of the potential development of the programme of critical philosophy to be found in Kant's critique of aesthetic judgment. Aesthetic properties for Kant can in no way be thought of as "objective" in the sense of belonging to the world as it is in itself: they are prototypically subject relative or dependent. And while from the perspective of traditional metaphysics this would exclude them from having any "metaphysical reality", it does not do so from the perpsective of strong TI, in which reason is concerned with "its own products". What is significant is the *type* of subjectivity to which an entity or property is relative or dependent. And for Kant, aesthetic properties are relevant to the processes of *practical* reason, a theme introduced, somewhat unexpectedly in the closing pages of the critique, where Kant discusses beauty as a "symbol of morality" (CJ: §59).

In the *Critique of Practical Reason* he had identified a particular problem for the transcendental approach to morality having to do with the application of the moral law. There he notes some "special difficulties" facing pure practical reason and a crucial asymmetry between it and theoretical reason.[19] While the pure concepts of theoretical reason (the categories) have *schemata* by which they could be applied to the phenomenal world, "the morally good as an object is something supersensible, so that nothing corresponding to it can be found in any sensible intuition" and yet "a law of freedom is to [be] applied to actions as events that take place in the sensible world and so, to this extent, belong to nature" (CPrR: 5.68). In the *Critique of Pure Reason* Kant had introduced "schemata" to enable concepts to be applied to the contents of intuitions, but there was nothing equivalent to this for practical reason. Later, in the *Metaphysics of Morals*, he was still concerned with this problem, noting that:

> just as a passage from the metaphysics of nature to physics is needed – a transition having its own special rules – something similar is rightly required from the metaphysics of morals: a transition which, by applying the pure principles of duty to cases of experience, would *schematize* these principles, as it were, and present them as ready for morally practical use.
>
> (MM: 6.468)[20]

The idea of symbolic exhibition (*Darstellung*) or *hypotyposis* that Kant appeals to in explaining how beauty can be a symbol of morality is one of a set of similar devices that he repeatedly appealed to in his attempts to address this "special difficulty" facing pure practical reason.[21]

The problem is that of giving some form of intuitable, sensory presentation to an *idea*. While an empirical concept can be *exemplified* (one can give a phenomenal presentation of the concept "dog", for example, by pointing to *this actual dog*) and a pure concept *schematised* (one can give a phenomenal presentation to the concept "cause" by pointing to *this actual event of a ball smashing a window*) an idea can only be *symbolised*. By this, he is quick to point out, he does not mean the assigning of a merely arbitrary sign to the idea such as when a number is represented by a numeral: the symbolic relation works by analogy involving a complex relation between four terms. An intuitable object such as a machine—a hand mill, for example—can give a symbolic presentation to a despotic state because the mechanically efficient causality of the mill has something about it analogous to the processes of a state governed by the single will of a despot. In contrast, an organism can symbolise a constitutional state because the operations of an organism—that it works by a type of interaction among its parts—has something about it analogous to the operations of a state ruled according to constitutional laws. Kant's example is hardly perspicuous, but the point seems to be that the analogy works at the abstract level of a similarity between *two relations*. When Kant says that "there is no similarity between a despotic state and a hand mill" (CJ: §59) he presumably means that a state is not like a hand mill in the way another *machine*, a bicycle, say, is "like" a hand mill: a state and a hand mill do not belong to the same *genus*. An analogy, we might say, is a similarity that holds across differences of *type*.[22]

Similarly, beauty and moral goodness are not instances of the same *type* of goodness, but some similarity holds between them nevertheless, and the judgment that they are similar is *itself* a type of reflective judgment:

> Now I maintain that the beautiful is the symbol of the morally good; and only because we refer the beautiful to the morally good (we all do so naturally and require all others also to do so, as a duty) does our liking for it include a claim to everyone else's assent.
>
> (CJ: §59)

This, then, is the shape of Kant's reinterpretation of Hutcheson. For Hutcheson, our responses become reliable indicators of objective moral properties, courtesy of God's having created us in a way that brings our responses into line with his will. For Kant, these moral responses are not objective, but are rooted in subjectively universal aesthetic responses which in turn, by analogy, provide a sensuous presentation for moral ideas.

6.4 The teleology of the world considered as a whole

In Part II of the *Critique of Judgment*, the "Critique of Teleological Judgment", Kant returns to the Platonic theme of the ideas as touched upon in the Transcendental Dialectic of the *Critique of Pure Reason*. There he had noted that

> Plato was right to see clear proofs of an origin in ideas not only where human reason shows true causality, and where ideas become efficient causes (of actions and their objects), namely in morality, but also in regard to nature itself. A plant, an animal, the regular arrangement of the world's structure (presumably thus also the whole order of nature) – these show clearly that they are possible only according to ideas.
>
> (CPuR: A317–18/B374)

Kant had gone on in the "Transcendental Ideal" to show how this issue of the regularity and apparent purposefulness of structures found in organisms within nature, and then extended to nature itself considered as a whole, were at the heart of those "physico-theological" proofs for the existence of God that he subjected to critique. In general, such proofs fall prey to treating as "constitutive" the ideas that for our finite human cognition

97

can only be regulative. Thus in these "proofs", under the influence of the transcendental illusion we transgress the limits of human discursive thought for which intuitions can only ever be sensible.

In the critique of teleological judgment, the same territory is explored, not for presumed proofs of the existence of God, but for the question of how to think of our knowledge of organic nature without losing reference to teleology. When we reflect on phenomena such as the way positioning of the wings and tails of birds enable their flight, we are not helped by appealing simply to the efficient causation (*nexus effectivus*) that otherwise is the cornerstone of scientific explanation, since:

> considered as a mere mechanism, [the organism] could have structured itself differently in a thousand ways without hitting on precisely the unity in terms of a principle of purposes, and so we cannot hope to find a priori the slightest basis for that unity unless we seek it beyond the concept of nature rather than in it.
>
> (CJ: §61)

Rather, to capture such purposeful unity, we typically attribute to nature a type of causality we find directly in ourselves and that is manifest in intentional purposive action. But the lesson we should take away from the necessity of attributing such purpose to nature is not a lesson about nature itself—that such purpose is really found there—but one about the limits of our own cognitive capacities.

Kant's idea from the first Critique of the regulative rather than constitutive use of ideas had found a resonance in the work of Johann Friedrich Blumenbach, a professor of medicine at the University of Göttingen, who, in the same year as the appearance of Kant's first Critique, had intervened in the embryological dispute between "preformationists" and "epigeneticists", by effectively interpreting the epigeneticist idea of a "formative drive" used to explain the reproductive and self-generating properties of organisms as a *regulative principle* (Blumenbach 1781: 31–32; Müller-Sievers 1997: 41–45). In turn, in the critique of teleological judgment Kant appealed to Blumenbach's use of the formative drive to exemplify his own approach to the treatment of organisms as natural purposes. For a thing to be considered as having a natural purpose entails two requirements. First, "the possibility of its parts (as concerns both their existence and their form) must depend on their relation to the whole"; next, "the parts of the thing [must] combine into the unity of a whole because they are reciprocally cause and effect of their form" (CJ: §65). Such a reciprocal cause and effect among parts cannot be found in a mechanism such as a watch, as "one gear is not the efficient cause that produces another gear", nor does "one watch produce other watches": "a machine has only *motive* force. But an organized being has within it *formative* force, and a formative force that this being imparts to the kinds of matter that lack it (thereby organizing them)" (ibid.). Later, Kant appeals to Blumenbach as having established the right principles for applying this idea:

> he rightly declares it contrary to reason that crude matter on its own should have structured itself originally in terms of mechanical laws, that life could have sprung from the nature of what is lifeless, and that matter could have moulded itself on its own into the form of a self-preserving purposiveness. Yet by appealing to this principle of an original *organization*, a principle that is inscrutable to us, he leaves an indeterminable and yet unmistakable share to natural mechanism.
>
> (Ibid.: §81)[23]

Like aesthetic judgment, teleological judgment is, as we have seen, a species of "reflective judgment" in which we "hold given representations up to, and compare them with, either other representations or one's cognitive power [itself], in reference to a concept that this [comparison] makes possible" (CJFI: 399–400). Thus in my attempts to understand the anatomy of the bird, for example, I hold up its representation to, and compare it with, the type of purpose expressed in my own intentional actions, and on the basis of this analogy understand its organisation. It is *as if* the bird had been made by an intelligent designer such that its organisation served the purpose of flight. The teleology apparently grasped is thus a product of what we might call the "teleological stance" the knower has adopted towards it.[24]

This, of course, is another application of Kant's "Copernican" reversal of the attitude of the naïve realist. The organism's purpose, like the movement of the sun, is not real, but an artefact of the limited conditions under which we experience and know it. But Kant's idealist successors, especially Hegel, were attracted to Kant's treatment of teleology precisely because of the pressure that, they believed, it put on the classical transcendental framework itself, a pressure that was thought to be especially apparent in Kant's attempt to spell out the knowledge involved in the finite agent's self-conscious awareness of his or her own teleological stance. In fact such a paradox seems endemic to the type of "perspectivist" picture presupposed by the Copernican turn. Perspectival self-understanding is meant to reveal the *limit* of one's knowledge, but as Hegel was to quip, one can only *know* of the existence of a limit once one has moved beyond it and grasped it from the other side. Being aware of the nature of the limits of one's epistemic grasp on the world surely indicates one has in some sense freed oneself from them. And for Hegel, as for both Plato and Kant, it was the *conceptualised* nature of thought that allowed the transcendence of finite perspectivity.

In §§76 and 77 of Division II of the critique of teleological judgment, the "Dialectic of Teleological Judgment"—the latter section headed, "On the Peculiarity of the Human Understanding That Makes the Concept of a

Natural Purpose for Us"—Kant repeats the by now familiar claim that the "distinguishing feature of the idea of a natural purpose concerns a peculiarity of *our* (human) understanding in relation to the power of judgment and its reflection on things of nature". But if this is so, then

> we must here be presupposing the idea of some possible understanding different from the human one. ... Only by presupposing this idea can we say that because of the special character of our understanding *must we consider* certain natural products ... as having been produced intentionally and as purposes.
>
> (CJ: §77)

We must find in the relation of our understanding to judgment "a certain contingency in the character of our understanding, so that we can take note of this peculiarity as what distinguishes our understanding from other possible ones" (ibid.). But rather than make the idea of the contingency of our understanding particular by contrasting it with "other possible ones", he does it by contrasting it with a *particular* other possible one, the divine understanding, the proof of the existence of which had been the agenda of the physico-theological type of proof of God's existence.

In contrast to our discursive understanding, such a divine understanding would be *intuitive* in that it would proceed Platonistically "from the *synthetically universal* (the intuition as a whole) to the particular, i.e., from the whole to the parts" (CJ: §77), in somewhat the same way as we proceed from the whole to the parts in our determination of space.[25] Reminding us of his treatment of modality in the *Critique of Pure Reason*, Kant notes that even the distinction between possibility and actuality "holds merely subjectively for human understanding" and that "if our understanding were intuitive it would have no objects except actual" ones (CJ: §76). That is, for the divine understanding there would be no distinction between theoretical and practical reason: all the objects cognised by such an understanding would exist, simply from the fact of their *being* cognised.[26] In short, Kant seems to suggest that in order that I can be conscious of the limitations of my own understanding of organised bodies in the natural world, I must be able to contrast it with the type of creative divine intellect that we have seen erroneously attributed to Plato's account of the ideas in the *Critique of Pure Reason*—a divine mind something like that envisaged by Augustine and modelled on Cicero's account of Phideas' creative realisation of his own ideas. As Béatrice Longuenesse has commented, "[a]lthough he introduces the intuitive understanding as a merely negative notion, Kant nevertheless gives a vivid account of what the world might be like, as known by such an understanding" (Longuenesse 2007: 173). In fact, what this world *is* like is, not surprisingly, effectively that described in the section, "The Transcendental Ideal", of the first Critique, as the *ens realissimum*.

The *ens realissimum*, it will be remembered, is a "whole of possibility" forming a greater context within which what we discover in the empirical world is reflectively understood as a type of perspectivally available aspect of that greater whole. For us, this wider whole of possibility is necessarily thought of as required for the making determinate of what we know as empirical actuality. Thus in our empirical judgments we may come to know some object in terms of its privative properties, as when we come to know, say, that Carl is toothless, but such a determinate judgment will require that we understand that the corresponding *non-privative property*—here, that of being toothed—is a possibility. We then have to think of the actual world with toothless Carl as surrounded, as it were, by a penumbra of a possible world in which Carl is toothed; but we now reflectively know that this modal distinction is, in fact, subjective. Of course we can have no *knowledge* of either God's mind or the world as God knows it; these are simply *ideas* which we must entertain in a regulative way in coming to know what we can of the empirical world. But the paradox of Kant's position is that while he construes such ideas, as Longuenesse says, "negatively", and so as employed only to give a determinate shape to our knowledge *as limited*,[27] he seems to pack them with considerable content.

Hegel was to see Kant's account of the divine intellect here as pushing beyond the limitations of the *transcendentally sceptical* structure of Kant's official transcendental philosophy, the thesis of weak TI. But once again, such stress on what we *cannot* know seems at odds with that dimension of Kant's idealist approach to metaphysics that I have been calling strong TI. Kant's official position on the teleological conception of the world as a whole is that we should not think that it captures the way the world is "in itself", the way the world is "anyway", independently of the way *we* are as knowers, and this seems to suggest an underlying *realist* metaphysical orientation. Here, there is a way the world considered as a whole *really* is that makes the teleological conception *false*, and to have only an "as-if" status. But at the same time, Kant had taught in the first Critique that metaphysical "entities" such as God and the world considered as a collective totality should be approached "idealistically" rather than realistically, and be considered to be *constituted* by "reason", the very reason that is operative in a regulative way in our own thinking. If the mind of God is unknowable, then this must be because reason *constitutes* the mind of God in this way *as* unknowable, not because that mind is "in itself" unknowable. But why should we think reason constitutes the mind of God *in this way*?

Again we might most easily capture Hegel's criticism of Kant by moving to the theological register. Kant's theology, as we have seen, combined anti-voluntarist with voluntarist dimensions. His insistence that we cannot know the mind of God, nor the world as God knows it, together with his understanding of God as a productive will whose output is, from our point of view, an imperative moral law, would be consistent with the voluntarist tradition. But Kant's further understanding of that will as *rational*, and of the moral law as accessible to *reason*, fits more with the anti-voluntarist tradition. Stressing the limits of human reason, voluntarists had characteristically asserted that we are thereby reliant on revelation for understanding the content of God's will, but consistent with anti-voluntarism, Kant treated revealed religion as a symbolic presentation of a moral law equally capable of being known *through* reason; and the very idea of God, Kant showed in his discussion of the transcendental ideal, came about through our tendency to hypostatise and personify principles of human reason itself. From the transcendental standpoint, we should consider God not as a knowable reality but as an "idea". But if we discard the notion of God as a knowable reality, might we not also discard the notion of him as an unknowable reality *too*?

The positive account of God seeping though in §§76 and 77 of the critique of teleological judgment seemed to the likes of Hegel to suggest just that. From the perspective of the post-Kantians, Kant, in the *Critique of Judgment*, was going in just the direction they themselves were going, and this was not a reversion to dogmatic pre-critical metaphysics, but a realisation of the very project of a critical one. Moreover, there is now available further justification for such an assessment of the direction of Kant's philosophising after the *Critique of Judgment*. This comes in the form of Kant's final attempt at articulating the project of transcendental idealism, as revealed in manuscripts dating from his last years and not published until the 1930s, the so-called *Opus Postumum*.

Hegel's diagnosis of the implicit "post-Kantian" dimension opened up by the *Critique of Judgment* in Kant's own work has received support among some readers of the *Opus Postumum*.[28] The issues are far too labyrinthine and controversial to be more than alluded to here,[29] but among the peculiarities of the *Opus Postumum* are Kant's turn to the Fichte-like talk of the subject's necessary *Selbstsetzung* ("self-positing"); Kant's pursuit of what looks like a pre-critical Spinozistic metaphysics of material nature, together with references to Spinoza as a type of transcendental philosopher; Kant's apparent extension of the transcendental deduction of the critical philosophy from *formal* to *material* conditions of experience and knowledge; and his treatment of reason as *preceding* the understanding rather than vice versa. If one thing is clear from the *Opus Postumum*, it is that Kant never abandoned an interest in the *topic* of the type of interactionist version of Leibnizian monadology that had consumed much of his pre-critical writings, and that Kant had never rested content with the solutions provided by his earliest formulations of the critical philosophy, as found in works such as the *Critique of Pure Reason* and the *Groundwork of the Metaphysics of Morals*. But if, in the 1790s, Kant was moving beyond his "official" transcendental philosophy of the 1780s, many others were moving in this way as well.

7

JENA POST-KANTIANISM: REINHOLD AND FICHTE

In 1786 and 1787, Karl Leonhard Reinhold (1757–1823), a former Catholic monk turned Freemason, published a series of letters on the Kantian philosophy, which together constituted the first popular and influential account of Kant's critical philosophy. The success of these articles (later to be expanded into book form) led to Reinhold's appointment at the University of Jena to a chair in critical philosophy—the first such position to be established in the new philosophy emanating from Königsberg. Reinhold held this position until 1794, and under his influence Jena became a unique centre for the pursuit of the new style of intellectual inquiry.

It was, however, Reinhold's successor at Jena from 1794 to 1799, Johann Gottlieb Fichte (1762–1814), who was the first to establish this distinctively "German" form of idealism into a major force in philosophy. Claiming to be following the "spirit" if not the "letter" of Kant's philosophy, Fichte worked on building a *system* of philosophy that he named the *Wissenschaftslehre* (the "doctrine of science"). The initial direction of the series of attempts to construct the *Wissenschaftslehre* was set by Fichte's response to sceptical attacks on Reinhold's earlier project, especially that by the Humean G. E. Schulze, who wrote under the pseudonym of "Aenesidemus". During the later 1790s, Fichte extended his approach into a theory of rights and ethics, in the former introducing the notion of "recognition" (*Anerkennung*), which would later be a crucial concept for Hegel. Fichte left Jena in 1799, after having been forced to resign his university position because of accusations of "atheism", and he moved to Berlin. When the University of Berlin opened in 1810, Fichte became the first head of its Faculty of Philosophy. It was via the philosophy developed in his Jena years, however, that Fichte was to have the most influence.

7.1 Reinhold's "proposition of consciousness" and Schulze's critique

After taking up the chair in philosophy at the University at Jena in the Duchy of Weimar in 1787, Reinhold had established Jena as the centre of critical philosophy throughout the early 1790s. At the end of the decade, Jena was to become significant as home to many of the writers and aesthetic critics who were effectively to create the movement of "romanticism", and many of these had been inspired by the Kantian philosophy transmitted to them via Reinhold's lectures.[1] While starting as an expositor of Kant, Reinhold quickly became critical of Kant's own way of *presenting* his philosophy, and wanted to improve on it to be truer to its spirit. Reinhold believed that while Kant had been fundamentally correct in his revolutionary Copernican reshaping of the philosophical project, he had nevertheless neglected to clarify his fundamental principles and concepts. Reinhold consequently set about finding a clear and explicit starting point from which the content of transcendental philosophy could be derived. What was needed, he thought, was some obvious *general feature* of consciousness, which all conscious subjects could acknowledge by simply consulting their own consciousnesses, and this, he believed was to be found in its *representational* character. Reinhold thus formulated his "proposition of consciousness" as follows: "[I]n consciousness representation [Vorstellung] is distinguished through the subject from both object and subject and is referred to both" (FPK: 70). That is, he thought of consciousness as involving three related elements, a "representation", a "subject" and an "object", and that the subject was aware of the separation and relation of the elements. For example, in being conscious of this tomato before me, I am conscious of a certain representation which I refer *to* the tomato itself, grasping the representation (or appearance) as distinct from that *of which* it is a representation (or appearance). Similarly, I am conscious of *myself* as the subject *for whom* this representation of the tomato *is* a representation of the tomato, a subject which is different from the representation itself. This threefold distinction between subject, object and representation constitutes, Reinhold thought, the essential structure of consciousness.

Kant had adopted the term *Vorstellung* from contemporary German writers who had used it to translate the way the term "idea" had been used in English-language philosophy from the seventeenth century. While usually translated back into English as "representation", the term derives from the components *vor*, meaning *before*, and *stellen*, meaning *to place*, and it thus carried the connotations of something being *placed before* the conscious mind. With characteristic emphasis on the importance of the notion of "representation" for Kant, Reinhold seemed to have brought into focus one of the most central notions that Kant himself had used but never elaborated. In fact, in a letter to his student, Marcus Herz, in 1772, two years after the Inaugural Dissertation, but nine years before the appearance of *Critique of Pure Reason*, Kant commented that his philosophy up to that time

> still lacked something essential, something that in my long meta-
> physical studies I, as well as others, had failed to consider and that

which in fact constitutes the key to the whole secret of metaphysics hitherto still hidden from itself. I asked myself this question: What is the ground of the relation of that in us which we call "representation" to the object?

(Corr: 10.130)

Reinhold's development of the "principle of consciousness" might therefore be considered as a belated but explicit answer to the question Kant had asked himself two decades earlier.

Reinhold's account of the structure of consciousness was attacked, however, by the philosopher G. E. Schulze, writing, as noted, under the name Aenesidemus.[2] Schulze, a sceptic influenced by the writings of David Hume, was critical of the idea one could infer from the *Vorstellungen* with which one was acquainted to either some "thing-in-itself" to which the representations referred or the mind itself which was somehow responsible for doing the representing. The legitimacy of the first inference—from the representation to the object—had been famously criticised by Berkeley, and that of the *second*—from the representation to the *mind*—had been criticised by Hume. Aenesidemus's point was, thus, that the Kant–Reinhold view of the mind couldn't withstand this familiar sceptical attack.

Fichte entered this debate by responding to Aenesidemus's attack on Reinhold and Kant, in a review published in 1794.[3] However, Fichte was not simply interested in defending Reinhold, as he was also unhappy with Reinhold's analysis of the mind's basic operations, and Fichte's criticism of Aenesidemus quickly became a criticism of the object of Aenesidemus's attack. What resulted was therefore a modification of the Kant–Reinhold view of the mind.

Fichte's response here was thus complex. Schulze had been critical of Reinhold's idea that one could infer from the representations (*Vorstellungen*) of one's acquaintance to both some "thing-in-itself" and to the mind itself. First, Fichte agreed with Schulze as to the illegitimacy of the former inference, thereby ruling out the intelligibility of any independent "thing-in-itself" doctrine within transcendental idealism. But along with this, he criticised, as involving a type of category mistake,[4] the underlying *conception* of the mind implicit in the *second* of these two inferences. There, the mind is thought of as another type of entity regarded "in itself", and Fichte criticises Schulze's inability to think of the faculty of representation as anything other than a "thing [Ding]"—"Is it" Fichte mocks, "round or square?" (RA: 143). That is, in setting up the picture to which he applies the torch of Humean scepticism, Schulze construed the mind as a "thing-in-itself, *independent* of his *representing* it", but he also thought of it as "a thing *that represents*", but surely this, claimed Fichte, is not the way to capture the nature of *self*-consciousness.[5] To counter Schulze's implicit hypostatising of the mind (a hypostatising, it will be recalled, that is the target of Kant's treatment of the "paralogisms" in the *Critique of Pure Reason*), Fichte goes on to claim that "the faculty of representation exists *for* the faculty of representation and *through* the faculty of representation" (ibid.).[6] That is, the mind is not the sort of thing that can intelligibly be considered "in itself" *independently of* how it is *for itself*, as Schulze seemed to assume. As something whose existence is so dependent on its own self-awareness, the mind, on Fichte's account, had become one of the paradigmatic objects of strong-TI metaphysics.

For Fichte, Schultz's criticisms of Reinhold had brought out problems inherent in Reinhold's idea of the representational character of consciousness. Reinhold had attempted to conceive of a consciousness's *self*-knowledge, using the same notion of representation as applied to the conscious subject's knowledge of *empirical* objects. Reinhold thus considered that, as self-conscious, the mind "stands before" itself in much the way that external objects stand before it. But Fichte wanted to claim that the consciousness of *objects* itself presupposes an even more basic form of awareness characterising the subject's own *self-consciousness*, and that self-consciousness is *not* to be understood on the model of the consciousness of other objects. The self does not know itself in the same way as it knows things *other* than itself. Here Fichte developed Kant's idea that part of what it was for a conscious subject to have beliefs is for it to grasp those beliefs as its own—it must ascribe those beliefs *to* itself. Fichte referred to such self-awareness as "intellectual intuition" and conceived of this as a type of "self-positing" in which an "I" seemed to *bring itself* into existence.

7.2 Fichte's reconceptualising of the mind as self-positing process

With the radical idea of the mind as a kind of *process* of "self-positing", Fichte attempted to combine the two ways of understanding implicit in his critique of Schulze—the idea that what or how the mind is "in itself" is necessarily "*for* itself"; and the idea of its having a form of being other than that of a "thing".[7] If we think of the "positing" of x as something like the *activity* in which we become aware of x, then the mind is, by its very nature, self-positing, and what it is aware of in this awareness is itself *as* that very activity, not some quasi object underlying that activity and *acting*. This anti-hypostatising idea he tried to capture with the neologism of the mind as a *Tathandlung*,[8] something factual in the way an action or performance would be factual rather than the way an object is factual (RA: 141). This explicit de-entification of the mind was a crucial step for Fichte, as standardly the mind had been thought of as a type of "substance", the cognitive processes of which were regarded as involving changes in its "accidental" properties. But Fichte seemed to imply that there could be no separate underlying substance involved. There could be no-*thing*, no substratum, naturally persisting beneath the changes in the mental states to be regarded *as* the bearer of these states.[9] The mind seemed to be holding itself in existence, merely by "its" being aware of itself. This was Fichte's answer to the demand for a conception of the self as *radically independent*, and hence, *autonomous* and *free*, that had been implicit within the German philosophical movement at least since Leibniz. Following Kant, Fichte grasped this self-positing nature as grounded in the self's *moral* life.

We might see Fichte's move here as underlining Kant's own de-entification of the mind in the Paralogisms, and as thereby sharpening the distinction between Kant's idealism and any form of *spiritual realism*, such as that of Berkeley. Kant's *Critique of Pure Reason* is all too easily read as a type of sceptical thesis concerning our capacity to have knowledge of the traditional objects of metaphysical inquiry, "things in themselves", such as the soul and God. Read in this way, the pursuit of metaphysical knowledge of such entities has resulted in reason having been pushed beyond its limits, bringing about the problems Kant charts in the sections on the paralogisms, the antinomies and the transcendental ideal. But as many commentators have pointed out, the thesis that these things are *unknowable* seems to imply their possession of features somehow responsible for their unknowability (at the very least, in knowing them to be unknowable we seem to know *something* about them). In any case, the unknowability thesis (transcendental scepticism) seems to imply a kind of realism: the thesis that there is something that such things in themselves are *really* like in some mind-independent way that is responsible for their cognitive unreachability for finite creatures like us. But Fichte's criticism of the presuppositions of Schulze and Reinhold, together with Fichte's conception of "self-positing", suggests a different picture: it is a mistake to think of (in this case) *minds* in such a realistic way. Minds are not the sorts of entities that have a nature, a way they are "anyway", independently of how they are known, in this case, known by *themselves*. On *this* construal of transcendental idealism, the realm of metaphysics is made up of objects which are in no way the ultimate denizens of a "mind-independent" reality.

This point bears crucially on the general nature of post-Kantian idealism. The post-Kantian idealists are often said to have wanted to *re-establish* metaphysics in light of Kant's *critique* of metaphysics, and this ambition is interpreted as involving a *return* to something like the pre-Kantian conception of metaphysics. But this reading is wrong in a number of ways. First, Kant never abandoned the project of metaphysics *per se*; he just wanted to establish it on a critical, scientific basis. Next, the thesis ignores the extent to which the idealists were *idealists*, rather than *spiritual realists*. Fichte, despite his clarification of the difference between idealism and spiritual realism, is perhaps the easiest to read *as* a spiritual realist. And when viewed as an assertion by a spiritual realist, the idea of the self-positing "I" reads something like an account of the mode of existence of the orthodox Christian God: the *concept* of the "I" has something about it to imply its necessary existence. Here, one starts with the idea of something that *really* exists in a "mind-independent" way, and then one asks after the grounds of its existence, finding that it can have no grounds other than *itself*. On this reading, Fichte's "I" looks like a spiritualist variant of Spinoza's "substance". But alternatively, we might read Fichte as developing that aspect of Kant in which the objects of metaphysics are no longer considered as potential inhabitants of a mind-independent reality, but rather, are affirmed as members of a mind-*dependent* one. It is this radical reconceptualising of the task of metaphysics, in line with the "strong" interpretation of transcendental idealism, that we will see taken up in Hegel's "absolute idealism", and it will emerge out of crucial moves found in Fichte.

7.3 Fichte's project of the *Wissenschaftslehre*

In mid-1794 Fichte published the first two parts of a three-part work he entitled, *Foundations of the Entire Doctrine of Science* (*Grundlage der gesamtem Wissenschaftslehre*), which he completed, with the third part, in 1795. This work, intended to accompany his lectures at Jena, was his first attempt (of *many*) at a systematic presentation of his distinct variety of transcendental idealism, under the title *Wissenschaftslehre*. It was, until relatively recently, the version that was most widely known as representative of this general project, and it was the form of the project most familiar to Fichte's idealist successors. Part I presented the "Fundamental Principles of the Entire *Wisenschafteslehre*"; Part II, the "Foundation of Theoretical Knowledge"; and Part III, the "Foundation of Knowledge of the Practical".

At the outset of Part I, "Fundamental Principles", Fichte describes his task as that of discovering the "primordial, absolutely unconditioned first principle of all human knowledge", a first principle "intended to express that *Act* which does not and cannot appear among the empirical states of consciousness, but rather lies at the basis of all consciousness and alone makes it possible" (Fnds: 93). In this attempt to establish his philosophy on a first, certain principle—an ambition that was to be criticised by the "antifoundationalist" turn among Fichte's "romantic" followers—Fichte appeals to those "laws of common logic" that must hold of the *form* of any possible objective *content* of consciousness, "laws" such as that of any thing's identity to itself (A = A) which is "accepted by everyone and … admitted to be perfectly certain and established" (ibid.: 94).

In Kantian fashion, Fichte treats this feature of any object whatsoever (and so not only *existent* objects, but also, say, possible ones as well), as a matter of *logical form*. We will not be surprised, then, to find that such a law is grounded in the unity of the knowing subject itself. Thus, this idea of a self-identity, which insures a necessary connection between the premise and conclusion of any valid inference about a thing, must be "*in* the self, and posited *by* the self, for it is the self which judges" (Fnds: 95). Fichte moves from the issue of the self-identity of any *object* for consciousness to that of the *subject* of consciousness itself, the "I". Thus in place of A = A, we now have *I* = *I* which, he says, has an entirely different meaning. While for the A of A = A, the question of its *existence* does not arise (a reflection of Kant's denial that existence is a conceptual predicate), Fichte asserts, in an analogue of Descartes' famous *cogito* argument, that from the knowledge of "I am I" can be deduced "I am"! A quasi-Cartesian starting point for the *Wissenschaftslehre* has therefore been found: "The self begins by an absolute positing of its own existence" (ibid.: 99).

In the next two sections (§§2–3) of "Fundamental Principles", Fichte establishes two further principles which, while they cannot be *derived* from that of identity, are nevertheless "reciprocally based upon it" (Fnds: 120). The second principle, which he eventually names the "principle of opposition", concerns the *difference* or *opposition* between the knowing subject and whatever content it is conscious *of*. The logical basis of *this* principle is the proposition, "–A is not equal to A", a logical principle that cannot be simply *derived* from A = A,[10] but which depends upon the *I* = *I*, because the positing of something other than the self depends on the self *doing* that positing, and that self *just is* the process of self-positing.

Fichte grapples with the difficulty that his second principle—the "principle of opposition [Satz des Gegensetzens]", which proceeds from the empirical I's conscious awareness of something *other than* itself, a "not-I [Nicht-Ich]"—is inconsistent with the *absolutely* self-positing I of the first principle. This is because according to the second principle the I is *conditioned* by something opposed to itself, that is, conditioned "as to content", but, according to its very concept, the I is wholly determined by *itself*. It *is* self-positing. A third principle, which Fichte calls the "grounding principle", then, is needed to reconcile the first two. It has the I positing *both* itself *and* the not-I *as* somehow opposed.

The second and third parts of this version of the *Wissenschaftslehre* are now devoted to an attempt to reconcile the apparent contradiction implicit within the three principles articulating the notion of self-positing from which that work had commenced. The relation of the I (now finite because of its opposition to the not-I) and the not-I within his third principle can be understood in either of two ways: first, with the not-I determining the finite I, a direction of determinacy we think of as basic to *knowledge*; next, with the finite I determining the not-I, a direction of determinacy we think of as central to *intentional action*. Parts II and III of the work, therefore, will consider the structures of theoretical and practical reason in turn.

As a whole, the 1794/5 *Wissenschaftslehre* is far from being an easy read, and, moreover, Fichte was soon to repudiate its mode of presentation in later versions, possibly under pressure of some of the feedback he was receiving from his lectures. Nevertheless, he establishes some important results in attempting to sketch how theoretical and practical knowledge might be given foundations from this broadly Kantian point of view. We can easily recognise analogues of the various parts of Kant's transcendental idealism within Fichte's peculiar attempt to derive everything from first principles. Importantly, something like Kant's notion of the non-conceptual content of empirical intuition turns up in the "Foundation of Theoretical Knowledge" in the form of Fichte's account of the "checks [Anstossen]" that the positing I encounters to its positing activity and that are responsible for the apparently *passive* aspects of the content of knowledge.

Fichte's idea of a "check" to the theoretical I's active positing is meant to account for the determination of whatever given sensory content consciousness comes to have, but it is meant to do so without any problematic reference to an external "thing in itself" responsible *for* the check: "The objective to be excluded has no need at all to be present; all that is required—if I may so put it—is the presence of a check on the self, that is, for some reason that lies merely outside the self's activity, the subjective must be extensible no further" (Fnds: 189).[11] For Fichte, the significance of the check lies in its investing of consciousness with determinate content, but in such a way that this content is encountered by the I as a type of obstacle which the I attempts to overcome. Going back further than Kant to Leibniz, we might say that what the I is attempting to overcome in going beyond the check is some conscious content presented in the form of *clear* but *confused* (*indistinct*) ideas. It will be remembered that, according to Leibniz, I have a confused idea of something when I can recognise the thing among others "*without* being able to say what its differences or properties consist in" (DM: §24, emphasis added). The I's *positing* activity, it would seem, attempts to drive knowledge of something beyond a clear but confused idea of it to a clear and *distinct* one.[12] The complete significance of this will become clear in Part III, as there the equivalent of a "check" will be something like what is normally thought of as the sensory presentation of an inclination or desire.

In Part III, Fichte starts to talk of the I's cognitive activity as a consequence of its *drives* (*Trieben*), in a way similar to what we have seen in Schiller's *On the Aesthetic Education of Man*.[13] The apparent convergence between Fichte and Schiller here is significant: Schiller was, after all, a colleague of Fichte's at Jena, and in a footnote added to the Thirteenth Letter of *Aesthetic Education*, in the context of a discussion of the cognitive drives, Schiller refers to Fichte's conception of the "reciprocal relation" of matter and form in *Foundations of the Entire Wissenschaftslehre*, the first two parts of which had only appeared about six months before. "Both principles are, therefore, at once subordinated to each other and co-ordinated with each other, that is to say, they stand in reciprocal relation to one another: without form no matter, and without matter no form" (AE: letter 13, para. 2, note).[14] Curiously, Fichte himself takes up the language of drives in Part III of the *Foundations*, published about another six months after the appearance of the *Aesthetic Education*, and with the idea of a cognitive *drive* we might get a clearer idea of what Fichte had in mind with regard to the earlier description of the self's positing activity and the "checks" that both limit and add empirical content to its knowing.

Throughout the discussion in the "Foundation of Theoretical Knowledge" of the contradiction within the three principles, Fichte had reiterated that this problem cannot be satisfactorily resolved *within* the discussion of theoretical knowledge. Considered in its theoretical capacity as "intelligence in general", the I must be regarded as *dependent* on the object (not-I) known, but this is in clear conflict with the fundamental conception of *self-consciousness*, the idea that "the I, in all its determinations, must be absolutely posited by itself, and must therefore be wholly independent of any possible not-I" (Fnds: 220, trans. modified). The mysterious status of the "check" cannot be explained: the I needs a "check" in order to have actual *content*, but we are not to understand the I as being checked *by* something beyond itself. In Part III, in the context of the I's *practical* reason, he offers a resolution by appealing to his strongly actional conception of the I as, as he puts it, "a *striving* towards determination [ein *Streben* zur Bestimmung]" (ibid.: 231).[15]

In the language of the "drives" and "striving" of Part III, the I's positing is a type of "infinitely and indeterminately outreaching activity of the I" (Fnds: 220) in which it strives to overcome the checks through which it is limited within the apparently non-conceptual givens of "intuitions" or "clear but confused ideas".[16] We might think of this overcoming as involving the further conceptualisation of these apparent sensory givens as when, say, in science we move from talking of a surface as coloured *red* to describing it as differentially reflecting electromagnetic radiation whose wavelength is in the order of 630–700 nanometers. When we think of colour in this way we reflect on the fact that our empirical concept "red" is highly "perspectival" and conditioned by our own natures and circumstances. In the "Copernican" imagery of Kant, we have driven "outwards" from our terrestrial location to a place from where we can reflect back on ourselves and our limitations as perceivers. But our very ability to do this, of course, reflects the fact that we have driven *beyond* those limitations.[17]

In Part III, Fichte develops this idea in the context of a radicalisation of Kant's thesis of the primacy of practical reason. From the practical perspective, all theoretical cognition must be interpreted in the light of the conception of the I as striving: "All reflection is based on the striving, and in the absence of striving there can be no reflection" (Fnds: 258).[18] In the course of such primordial striving, a subject experiences obstacles and restrictions. These are experienced *negatively*, as restrictions to the I's freedom and as what *ought* not to exist.[19] The striving doctrine now promises a resolution of the contradiction between the absolute self and the conditioned self, since the content correlative to the absolute or independent aspect of the I will be presented to the I not as a *fact* but as the content of a *demand*, something having the modality of an "ought to be" rather than an "is". When Fichte later goes on to identify this demand that "everything is to be dependent upon" the I with Kant's *categorical imperative* (Fnds: 230n2), we grasp something of his relation to Kant's idea of the "primacy of practical reason". Kant had meant by this idea that practical, not theoretical, reason could be "pure" and dependent on nothing other than itself. Fichte's claim for the primacy of practical reason was even stronger: "it is not in fact the theoretical faculty which makes possible the practical" he asserts, "but on the contrary the practical which makes possible the theoretical" (ibid.: 123).[20] It is only because we are the kinds of beings capable of being radically self-determining in our moral lives that it makes sense to even talk of us as rational, and as hence capable of knowledge of the world.

Fichte's appeal to *practical* reason as the ultimate context within which the contradictions of "positing" are to be overcome would be the target of a range of criticism after the appearance of the first *Wissenschaftslehre*. We get an early hint of the thrust of these criticisms in Schiller's reference to Fichte in the footnote to the Thirteenth Letter of the *Aesthetic Education*, and against the background of his criticism of *Kant*, we might anticipate the nature of his complaint here. "In the Transcendental method of philosophizing", Schiller states,

> where everything depends on clearing form of content, and obtaining Necessity in its pure state, free of all admixture with the contingent, one easily falls into thinking of material things as nothing but an obstacle. … Such a way of thinking is, it is true, wholly alien to the *spirit* of the Kantian system, but it may very well be found in the *letter* of it.
>
> (AE: letter 13, para. 3, note 2)

In the next decade, Hegel would argue that this was exactly the problem with Fichte's version of transcendental philosophy. Schiller, with his allusion to the "letter" and "spirit" of Kantianism, also seems to be charging Fichte with "thinking of material things as nothing but an obstacle". While working on his *Aesthetic Education* in 1794, Schiller had rejected for publication in *Die Horen* a lecture by Fichte entitled, "Concerning the Difference between the Spirit and the Letter within Philosophy". In it, Fichte essentially argued against the type of *aesthetic* solution to the problems of Kantianism that Schiller had recommended in the *Aesthetic Education* (EPW: 192–216).[21] But it was also in the context of his practical philosophy that Fichte was to develop an idea to be seized upon by others, especially Hegel. This was the concept of "recognition".

7.4 Intersubjective recognition as a condition of self-consciousness

In the 1794–95 *Wissenschaftslehre* Fichte's invocation of the primacy of the *moral subject* in Part III had allowed the idea of the I's external limitation to be replaced by the *normative* idea of its *self*-limitation. It was with this idea that Fichte tried to suggest an answer as to how the *check* "would not set bounds to the activity of the self; but would give it the task of setting bounds to itself" (Fnds: 189), and it was this idea that pointed to his subsequent analysis of the role of recognition—*Anerkennung*—in the *Foundations of Natural Right* (*Grundlage des Naturrechts*) published a year later. With his notion of recognition Fichte would effectively break the grip of the radically isolated and individualistic conception of the mind as "monad" that Leibniz had shared with Descartes, and with which Fichte himself had started his *Wissenschaftslehre*. With it too he reintroduced something of the interactive, mutually influencing conception of monads that Kant had attempted to articulate in his own early attempts to go beyond Leibnizian monadology.

It is in relation to the modern notion of human rights that Fichte introduces his idea of recognition or acknowledgement (*Anerkennung*), and it is in that context that its significance becomes intuitively plausible. We think of others as "having" rights, but it is difficult to conceive of rights as anything like properties belonging to individuals as part of our natural makeup—properties like their height or hair colour, for example. There is thus a tendency to regard the capacity to have rights as somehow dependent upon or derived from other "natural" human properties, like the possession of intelligence, but then it can be asked why *this* should count as a basis for ascribing rights to particular beings. From a certain perspective, this could be seen as simply an anthropocentric prejudice—why *don't* we ascribe such rights to nonhuman animals, for example? But Fichte's theory seemed to offer the general outlines of an answer to these difficult questions by affording rights a normative status not simply consequent upon any non-normative properties possessed by the being to whom the rights are ascribed. To ascribe a right to a person is to attribute to them a "status" by which one regulates one's own behaviour towards them in certain ways. To recognise *your* property, for example, is for me to restrict *my* behaviour in the case of the things *you* own, rather than simply do with them as I like. Thus to have a right is to have a status like that of the "person" to whom one has made a *promise*: such a person can legitimately demand that the *promiser* behave towards them in certain ways—can demand that they *fulfil* the promise made to them—simply in virtue of their having been made the promise. The possession of intelligence and the capacity for rights seem, then, intimately linked from this perspective. Rights and intelligence are features of communal beings who have their interaction shaped by the capacity to hold each other to commitments that they have freely entered into. In the domain of right, the "check" to an action does not come from some merely brute obstacle—it comes from a *demand* addressed to me *as* a rational agent. In recent moral and political philosophy this idea has re-emerged in discussions of the "second-person standpoint" (Darwall 2006).

Fichte starts his own deduction of the concept of right in the *Foundations of Natural Right*, with an initial "theorem" which parallels his claim from the *Wissenschaftslehre* of the primacy of the practical conception of the I: "A finite rational being cannot posit itself without ascribing a free efficacy [freie Wirksamkeit] to itself" (FNR: 18).[22] With the second theorem, however, he introduces his new radical claim of the necessity of the intersubjective existence of a being, capable of ascribing such free efficacy to itself: "The finite rational being cannot ascribe to itself a free efficacy in the sensible world without also ascribing such efficacy to others, and thus without also presupposing the existence of other finite rational beings outside of itself" (ibid.: 29).

Fichte's starts his "proof" with a restatement from the *Wissenschaftslehre* of the contradiction between the absolute independence of the I and its limitation by the object or "not-I". The practical I must think of the object of which it is conscious as both conditioning it and as having no independent efficacy (FNR: 31). The solution to this contradiction then offered is to "think of the subjects' being-determined as its *being-determined to be self-determining*, i.e. as a summons [eine Aufforderung] to the subject, calling upon it to resolve to exercise its efficacy [sich zu einer Wirksamkeit zu entschliessen]" (ibid.). This "summons", which replaces the vague *Anstoss* doctrine of the 1794–95 *Wissenschaftslehre*, must be conceived as coming from *another rational being*.[23] Fichte then goes on, in the "third theorem", to claim that "the finite rational being cannot assume the existence of other finite rational beings outside it without positing itself as standing with those beings in a particular relation, called a relation of right" (ibid.: 39).

With Fichte's theory of rights we actually have the rudiments of a much more general reconceptualising of the distinctly human mode of existence than one merely applying to our status as *legal* beings. From the early-modern period on, the emerging naturalistic conception of the world separated questions of how the world *is* from questions of how it *ought to be*. If the norms to which we held ourselves were *simply reflections of how we are*, then they seemed to lose their distinctively *normative* status. For example, if adherence to norms comes to be understood instrumentally, as a device employed to satisfy given desires, their grip on the agent becomes merely conditional.[24] The only alternative source for the origins of *unconditional* norms seemed to be the will of a transcendent God—an idea found in the early "natural law" tradition, for example. On this view, we hold ourselves to norms and standards because they ultimately come to us as commands from a transcendent will. But Fichte's theory seemed to diffuse any such authority of a transcendent legislator into the community itself. There is no *further* source for the authority of norms than the fact that they are shared by a community of agents who hold themselves and each other to certain behaviours they have each freely committed to.

In this regard, Fichte represents a crucial phase in the ongoing Enlightenment tradition of finding a basis for human normativity in the human realm, rather than in the will of a transcendent God. Moreover, with Fichte's notion of the recognition dependence of right, we can get a sense of how the programme of strong TI might be developed. While the bearers of rights, we might say, are somehow ultimately "natural" beings—members of the species *Homo sapiens*—they only exists *as* bearers of rights in as much as they are so recognised by others, whom they recognise in turn. In this sense, to be a bearer of rights or other normative status is to be more than a natural entity; it is to be "mind dependent" in the sense of a type of "mindedness" necessarily distributed over a community of mutually recognising beings. After Fichte, the development of such a sense of *communally* instantiated mindedness would find support from a variety of sources, not the least of which would be the revival of ancient conceptions of rational mindedness (*Nous*) that would be taken up by Hegel with his notion of *Geist*, or spirit.

A year after the appearance of the *Foundations of Natural Right*, Fichte published a work on moral philosophy, *The System of Morality* (*Das System der Sittenlehre*), but not long after this he became the target of a public accusation of atheism, which ultimately led to his dismissal from Jena.[25] By this time, however, Fichte had put his stamp on this remarkable intellectual community, and his thoughts had been critically appropriated by a variety of other thinkers. Fichte moved to Berlin, where he was eventually appointed to the chair of philosophy at the newly opened University of Berlin, where he taught until his death in 1814.

8

THE JENA ROMANTICISM OF FRIEDRICH SCHLEGEL AND FRIEDRICH SCHELLING

Karl Friedrich von Schlegel (1772–1829) is remembered as a central member of the *Frühromantiker* ("early romantics"), a group of avant-garde poets, literary theorists, and scholars who gathered in Berlin and Jena in the second half of the 1790s. Those at Jena included the poets Novalis (Friedrich von Hardenberg) and Friedrich Hölderlin; and at Berlin, the theologian and linguistic theorist Friedrich Daniel Ernst Schleiermacher and the poet Ludwig Tieck. While nineteenth-century romanticism was to become a conservative and backward-looking movement—a "counter-Enlightenment", privileging tradition and religion over modernity and a sense of "progress"—it was, in its early phases, marked generally by a politically and culturally progressivist outlook and an experimentalist literary and aesthetic practice. Nor was romanticism in its early phases marked by the type of excessive emotionalism and rejection of rationalism with which it is commonly associated. The Frühromantiker had in fact been deeply engaged with the idealist philosophies of Kant, Reinhold and Fichte and developed distinctive points of view, especially aesthetic ones, within the emerging idealist form of philosophy.

Together with his brother, the philologist and literary theorist August Wilhelm, Friedrich Schlegel had edited and contributed to between 1798 and 1800 the main organ of early romantic aesthetics, the *Athenaeum*. Here and elsewhere, often in fragmentary aphorisms, he developed his distinctive philosophical theory of nature of modern "romantic" literature (as he christened it) and valorised the role of "irony" in modern thought. Socially, Friedrich and August Wilhelm and their remarkable partners, Dorothea Veit Mendelssohn, and Caroline Böhmer Schlegel, also formed the hub of a network of interlinking intellectual and personal relationships that bridged Jena and Berlin. Friedrich spent time in Berlin, where he had frequented the famous salon of Henrietta Herz, wife of Kant's former student Marcus Herz. The relationship that he formed there with the then married Caroline was to become the topic of his philosophical novel, *Lucinda* (1799).

From 1790 to 1795, Friedrich W. J. von Schelling (1775–1854) was a student at the seminary at Tübingen, where he had developed close friendships with

Friedrich Hölderlin and Georg Wilhelm Friedrich Hegel. Hölderlin was the first of the three to have made the pilgrimage to Jena, the centre of transcendental philosophy, and in 1797, after a period in Leipzig, Schelling too went to Jena, where (unlike Hölderlin) he came into close contact with the circle around the Schlegels. By the time of Schelling's arrival Hölderlin had left to rejoin Hegel in Frankfurt, but later Hegel himself was to join Schelling in Jena. By then Schelling had been appointed to a chair of philosophy.

At first Schelling had seen himself as simply developing the views of Fichte's idealism by augmenting Fichte's more subjectivistic version of transcendental idealism with a *philosophy of nature* inspired by Plato and Spinoza. After Hegel joined him at Jena in 1801, however, and, possibly at Hegel's prompting, Schelling became more critical of Fichte. For a few years, Hegel and Schelling worked closely together, during which time Schelling developed his "identity philosophy", an attempt to combine transcendental idealism and philosophy of nature.

The intellectual relations between Schelling, Hegel and the various Frühromantiker are complex and controversial. Schelling was more closely associated than Hegel with the Schlegel circle, and Schelling is most commonly thought of as the most philosophical representative of romanticism. Hegel was to become very critical of romanticism, which he particularly identified with the writings of Friedrich Schlegel, but had, nevertheless, been clearly influenced by both Hölderlin and Schelling and even, perhaps, Schlegel himself. Schelling's *personal* relations with the Schlegels were complex, to say the least. Supposedly engaged to Caroline's daughter from an earlier marriage, Auguste, Schelling was in fact having an affair with Caroline, the wife of August Wilhelm Schlegel. Things became murkier when, following Auguste's death from an acute illness, Caroline divorced August Wilhelm and married Schelling. Local gossips were accusing Caroline of having murdered her daughter, and the ensuing scandal drove Schelling and his new wife from Jena in 1803. Around this time Hegel's relationship with Schelling was starting to sour, and soon Hegel was clearly demarcating his philosophy from that of Schelling. In turn, Schelling later became critical of both Hegel and Schelling's own earlier philosophy.

By the first years of the new century, the Frühromantiker circle at Jena started to break up. Fichte had been driven out of Jena in 1799; Novalis had died in 1801; and Hölderlin had succumbed to the psychosis that was to end his intellectual and creative life. Friedrich Schlegel gradually became more socially and politically conservative, in 1808 converting to Catholicism together with Dorothea. Hegel was later to take this as a symptom of the unsustainability of his initial "ironism".

Having relocated to Würzburg, Schelling published, in 1809, a proto-existentialist work, "On Human Freedom", that was to be his last work published before his death in 1854. He continued to write extensively; however, in these writings he became critical of idealism and philosophy more generally and realigned his views more with traditional Christianity. During the years in which Hegel came to be celebrated, after his appointment to Fichte's chair at the University of Berlin in 1820, Schelling remained largely invisible; however, he was appointed to that same chair of philosophy at Berlin after Hegel's death in 1831, specifically to counter what was seen as Hegel's dangerous influence. Here we will be concerned only with the idealism of his early period.

8.1 Friedrich Schlegel: transcendental poetry and the unpresentable absolute

Until recently, the Frühromantiker have typically been thought of as poets, novelists or literary/cultural critics, but not philosophers. This has started to change, however, and the distinctly philosophical content of romanticism is becoming increasingly recognised, and its complex links with the more central lines of idealism have been mapped.[1] This applies especially to the complex figure of Karl Friedrich von Schlegel.

While the influence of Fichte on the Jena romantics has been long recognised, Jena romanticism has been typically seen as a type of applied Fichteanism in the realm of aesthetics and literary studies (Haym 1870: 260). Recent research has revealed a much deeper engagement by the romantics with the emerging post-Kantian form of idealism, however. Far from simply enthusiastically and uncritically assimilating and applying Fichte's ideas, Schlegel, Hölderlin, Novalis and others were active in criticising Fichte's thought. Importantly, in the writings of the romantics, the transcendental idealism of Kant and Fichte was linked to Plato, seen though *Neoplatonic* spectacles,[2] and Plato was admired especially for the role he gave to *myth* within his philosophy. For the romantics the ineradicable role of myth and allegory was consequent upon the limitations of conceptual thought for the presentation of "the absolute".[3] But the resources of myth had been lost in the modern world, and in *Dialogue on Poetry* (1800), Schlegel called for a "new mythology" founded on art (DP: 81–88).

In 1795, Schiller, in *On Naive and Sentimental Poetry*, and Schlegel, in *On the Study of Greek Poetry*, had put forward similar theses about the distinct forms of sensibility characterising ancient and modern poetry. Schiller had called the spirit expressed in modern poetry, with its inner, subjective character, *sentimental*, Schlegel called it *romantic*. In *Dialogue on Poetry*, Schlegel notes that "[t]he modern poet must create all things from within himself" (DP: 81) in much the same way as done in Fichte's idealist way of philosophising. "[U]p until to now, however, each poet [does this] separately and each work from its very beginning, like a new creation out of nothing" (ibid.). Modern poetry thus "lacks a focal point" in contrast to the situation in antiquity where a common mythology allowed "[a]ll poems … [to] join one to the other, till from ever increasing mass and members the whole is formed. Everything interpenetrates everything else, and everywhere there is one and the same spirit, only expressed differently" (ibid.).

We might say that, for Schlegel, ancient mythology was the direct poetic expression of Plato's unifying "world soul". It was the "hieroglyphic expression of surrounding nature in this transfigured form of imagination and love" (DP: 85), "a work of art created by nature" (ibid.: 86). In it we see "the first flower of youthful imagination, directly joining and imitating what was most immediate and vital in the sensuous world" (ibid.: 81–82). The new mythology, however, will incorporate the reflective subjectivity of the modern sensibility. Thus in contrast to the ancient, it "must be forged from the deepest depths of the spirit; it must be the most artful of all works of art, for it must encompass others; a new bed and vessel for the ancient, eternal fountainhead of poetry, and even the infinite poem concealing the seeds of all other poems" (ibid.: 81–82).

In fact, the new poetry—"transcendental poetry"—would in this way be like transcendental philosophy. And:

> just as we wouldn't think much of an uncritical transcendental philosophy that doesn't represent the producer along with the product and contain at the same time within the system of trans-cendental thoughts a description of transcendental thinking: so too this sort of poetry should unite the transcendental raw materials and preliminaries of a theory of poetic creativity—often met with in modern poets—with the artistic reflection and beautiful self-mirroring that is present in Pindar, in the lyric fragments of the Greeks, in the classical elegy, and, among the moderns, in Goethe.
>
> (AF: fragment 238)

Thus, "this poetry should describe itself, and always be simultaneously poetry and the poetry of poetry" (ibid.).

Schlegel has subsequently been known most as a literary theorist, and even with early romanticism's philosophical credentials restored, he is per-haps still unlikely to be considered a philosopher in any traditionally recognisable sense.[4] This is linked to his rejection of systematic, con-ceptually articulated thought for the type displayed in fragmentary and ironic form in wit and aphorisms,[5] the style he regarded as characterising the romantic. This form can seem to represent a type of anti-philosophy rather than philosophy proper; however, as Hegel clearly recognised, the anti-philosopher is importantly different to the non-philosopher, and while decidedly unsympathetic to Schlegel, Hegel saw a definite philosophical significance in his writings, albeit a negative one.[6] For Hegel, Schlegel's irony expressed a type of narcissistic self-deification in which laws and conceptual norms had lost any purchase on behaviour and thought, becoming the mere playthings of thought. Moreover, this, he thought, represented a self-annihilating extreme form—a type of living *reductio ad absurdum*—of Fichte's "subjective" brand of idealism.[7]

However, Hegel's unflattering characterisation of Schlegel seems to miss a dimension to the philosophy that underlay this aesthetic practice, and the picture of the nihilistic ironic subjectivist sits uneasily with other aspects of Schlegel's outlook, especially his attraction to Platonism and the "objective" nature of classical culture.[8] A more sympathetic reading and appreciation of Schlegel is possible, in which he appears more a philosopher who, having taken a type of "linguistic turn", was seriously engaged with the aesthetic and communicative conditions for the emergence in a reader of a type of *self-reflective* understanding of the limitations of language and thought.

It was Schlegel's companion from Berlin, F. D. E. Schleiermacher, who is usually identified as occupying the key place within the history of "hermeneutics", as a general science of meaning and interpretation, as it developed towards the end of the eighteenth century (Gadamer 1992: 173–97), but Schlegel too played a significant role in the revolutionary decades in the development of this form of thought.[9] Influenced by the linguistic and historicist ideas of Kant's former student, J. G. Herder, Schlegel was interested in the possibilities and limits of human communication and in the role of forms of communication within the constitution of the human *community*. The highly reflective nature of distinctively modern, as opposed to classical, poetry involved a distinct type of relation between writer and reader which he describes as one of quasi-religious community. "The synthetic writer", he notes,

> constructs and creates a reader as he should be; he doesn't imagine him calm and dead, but alive and critical. He allows whatever he has created to take shape gradually before the reader's eyes, or else he tempts him to discover it himself. He doesn't try to make any particular impression on him, but enters with him into the sacred relationship of deepest symphilosophy or sympoetry.
>
> (CF: fragment 112)[10]

The *displacement from* an immediate absorption within those contextualising things and events within the environing world that Schlegel saw as characteristically expressed in modern literature is clearly another expression of Kant's "Copernican" turn. The modern work of art is one in which the spectator or reader is positioned in a way so as to be *no longer* totally absorbed in the represented world. Rather than take what is presented as a reality pure and simple, the receiver simultaneously feels her own "view" as one that is perspectivally conditioned, a particular aspect of a greater whole. But this nevertheless seems to allude to a type of unconditioned "view from nowhere" *from which* this perspectivity could be grasped. And yet such an allusion to an all-encompassing aperspectival view could be no more *than* allusion: effectively following Kant, Schlegel thinks of the world as *omnitudo realitatis* as *never* able to be known; it is only ever capable of being expressed allegorically. It is this insight that is expressed ironically. "Irony", as Manfred Frank puts it, "is that which refers 'allegorically' to the infinite, exposing its provisionality and incompleteness" (Frank 2004: 181). But as in Kant, the *desire* to attain to the whole cannot be overcome, and, moreover, this unachievable goal functions to drive us forward, as Rüdiger Bubner puts it, in a "continuous effort to see through the one-sided partialities and finite limitations of our current perspectives" (Bubner 2003: 208).

One of Schlegel's favourite metaphors for the experience of this type of simultaneous perspectival and aperspectival take on the world comes from Fichte: the subject is "suspended" or "oscillates" between two contradictory cognitive relations to the world, one of which presents the world *from* a finite perspective, the other of which alludes to the greater whole within which the first view is grasped *as* limited and perspectival. This is what is conveyed in irony, as irony itself "is the form of paradox" (CF: fragment 48). Thus besides his use of myth, another aspect of Schlegel's attraction to Plato was the *literary form* of dialogue itself that was the context of Socrates' famous irony. The type of playful dialogical context of ancient Athens was the one in which philosophical truth could emerge, one in which speech could sufficiently disengage with the substance of discourse to allow it to reflect upon itself and thereby discover and overcome its own internal limitations.

> Socratic irony ... originates in the union of *savoir vivre* and scientific spirit, in the conjunction of a perfectly instinctive and a perfectly conscious philosophy. It contains and arouses a feeling of indissoluble antagonism between the absolute and the relative, between the impossibility and the necessity of complete communication.
>
> (CF: fragment 108)

And it is this "indissoluble antagonism between the absolute and the relative" that is what is given expression in romantic poesy, and in particular in one of its distinctive modern forms, the novel. Thus novels, he notes "are the Socratic dialogues of our time" (CF: fragment 26). It is important that the *impossibility* of complete communication has to be itself made explicit in the communication by the adoption of an allegorical, ironical or fragmentary form in which the complete but impossible one is paradoxically invoked to demonstrate the *incompleteness* of what is actually said. That the fragment is "like a miniature work of art" and "complete in itself, like a porcupine" (AF: fragment 206), suggests something absolute that is complete in itself, but by explicitly *being* a fragment it brings attention to its incompleteness, and by analogy, to the suggested incompleteness of the "absolute" itself.[11]

There are clear parallels between Schlegel's espousal of irony and that promoted later by Friedrich Nietzsche and, in recent times, by Richard Rorty and other postmodernist readers of Nietzsche.[12] It is not surprising, then, that Schlegel attracted criticisms similar to the types directed at Rorty and other contemporary postmodernists. Criticisms here are typically made along the lines first expressed by Hegel—that of the impossibility of maintaining a commitment *to* the values to which one is meant to be attached, albeit, *ironically*. Effectively, these criticisms amount to the accusation of "nihilism", but it is important to stress that Schlegel's intention had been to give a *response* to the phenomenon of nihilism, an issue that had been put on the agenda by Jacobi in his criticisms of contemporary Spinozism.

8.2 Schlegel and the critique of foundationalism

Friedrich Jacobi had used the term *nihilismus* to characterise the problems attendant upon an Enlightenment move from faith to conceptually articulated world view, and he did so by invoking the ancient idea of the regress of reasons. For example, if I am asked for the justification of some belief, and I appeal to some further supporting belief, I can, in turn, be asked for the justification of *that* further belief. The only way to prevent an infinite regress of this kind, which threatens the rationality of *all* belief, thought Jacobi, is to appeal to some type of *immediate* certainty. Only something like *self-justifying* immediate knowledge, he argued, could stop this regress—a knowledge of something that was "causa sui", the cause of itself, and so subject to no *further* condition of its existence. Here, there were only two alternatives possible: Spinozism or faith.

Spinoza, he believed, had been the thinker who had been most consistent and systematic in his demand for rational explanations, and congruent with this, his thought had terminated in a conception of the totality of the extended material world as the ultimate existence that was, as it were, the cause of itself. For Jacobi, Spinoza was an atheist who exemplified the nihilistic, atheistic consequences of any form of thought committed to rationalism. Within this monistic material world there could be no God and no basis for a distinction between good and bad, for, as Spinoza himself had suggested, all that good could mean was the augmentation of the power of those "finite modes" of it that we think of as individual bodies. The only other way out of the infinite regress of rationalism would be to acknowledge the limits of reason and make a "leap of faith" to the existence of *something* other than this meaningless whole, something whose existence must be presumed if one was to prevent the spiral into atheism and nihilism.

Schlegel agreed with Jacobi's diagnosis of the infinite regress, but disagreed with his assessment of Spinoza and, at least in the period under discussion here, rejected the solution of the *salto mortale*, or "mortal leap", into faith in God. Here Schlegel has been portrayed as an early critic of

122

philosophical *foundationalism* and its attendant "myth of the given" (Beiser 2003: 123–26). While accepting the power of Fichte's development of Kant's critical philosophy, Schlegel points to the problems of the "foundationalist" dimensions of Fichte's approach, dismissing the idea of "intellectual intuition" as mere "mysticism", and he responds to the sceptical dilemmas of the post-foundational perspective on philosophy in subtle and suggestive ways. Thus, rejecting the idea of an absolute starting point for philosophy, Schlegel appeals to the alternative of a philosophising that begins "like the epic poem, in the middle",[13] and suggests replacing the idea of a grounding of knowledge in a *single* first principle, as in Fichte's *Wissenschaftslehre*, with that of a *plurality* of principles. "What if ... an externally unconditioned yet at the same time conditioning and conditioned *Wechselerweis* were the foundation of philosophy?"[14]

This move is sometimes described as the expression of a *coherence* theory of truth, but I suggest that Schlegel's thought here amounts to something quite different, indeed more radical and philosophically interesting. The coherence theory of truth seems a natural development of Kantianism:[15] it is what is suggested when the "fact world" that is correlated with Kant's transcendental unity of apperception is denied any metaphysically real status that would be required to think of a judgment as true in virtue of its "correspondence" with independent reality. But Kant's formal idealism *does* deny the fact world just this status: it is the world of "appearance". There then seems little for "truth" to mean other than *what* it is that unifies the totality of judgments into those of *one world*.

Schlegel's formulae suggest, however, that we cannot start from the assumption of anything like the unity of Kant's transcendental unity of apperception or its associated fact world. The plurality of principles that make up the *Wechselerweis* is not the unity of a group of principles which mutually support each other because of their logical coherence. Nor is there any remnant of the unity of an "I"—absolute or empirical—that could be the "I" for whom these principles stand as principles. Hegel interprets Schlegel as the extreme consequence of Fichte's subjective idealism which achieves a type of *reductio ad absurdum* of its starting point. But this relies on a disavowal of Fichte's infinite I leaving the empirical I unrestrained, and yet this "I", as Schlegel claimed in 1804, is in no sense a unity, but is itself *self-contradictory*. "The authentic contradicting-ness in our I is that we feel at one and the same time both finite and infinite."[16] It is this self-contradictory nature of the I that correlates with the content of Schlegel's *Wechselerweis*. In one place, Fichte's first principle of "the I posits itself absolutely" is replaced with two principles: "'The I posits itself' and 'The I should posit itself' are not two propositions deduced from a higher one; one is as high as the other; further they are two first principles, not one. *Wechselgrundsatz*."[17] These alternatives between *is* and *ought* are not two mutually supporting principles, and while not contradictory in the formal sense, they are certainly contradictory in spirit. The normative nature of the second formula presupposes that the "I's" self-positing is something that might not otherwise happen and so undermines the descriptive status of the former.

But the contradictory nature of Fichte's assumed content of intellectual intuition should not come as a surprise to a *Kantian*. This is exactly what Kant had claimed would happen once one attempts to formulate any such "metaphysical" truth. And Schlegel's response to this discovery has a certain Kantian feel to it as well. By contrast to thinking of these objects as capable of being presented in conceptual thought, another, aesthetic and *symbolic* way of presenting them must be found. Moreover, it must so present them as to bring out this antinomial, or contradictory, structure. This would be the Kantian justification of the promotion of irony.

Schlegel's idea of some kind of *reciprocal* determination between *principles* was an extension of the notion of "reciprocal determination", not new to the idealist tradition. In the *Critique of Pure Reason* Kant conceives the category of community (*Gemeinschaft*) as that of a "reciprocity between agent and patient [Wechselwirkung zwischen dem Handelnden und Leidenden]" (CPuR: A80/B106) and the idea of the relation "*reciprocally*, of one person to the condition of others" (CPrR: 5.66) appears as the third category of relation in the analogous table of categories in the *Critique of Practical Reason*. Fichte too had used the idea of reciprocal determination in his "third principle" in which the I posits both the I as finite and the not-I to which it is opposed, here the "Wechselbestimmung" capturing the bidirectionality of the relation of the (finite) I to the non-I. Appealing to Fichte's concept of reciprocal action, Schiller *too* had invoked the idea of a "Wechselwirkung" operating between the otherwise antagonistic sensuous and formal *drives*. With this, both principles "are, therefore, at once subordinated to each other and co-ordinated with each other … without form no matter, and without matter no form" (AE: letter 13, para. 2, note 1). Virtually all these ideas of reciprocity would be employed by Hegel in his theory of spirit, but Schlegel's idea of the unity of mutually opposed *principles* would be of particular use to Hegel.

Questioning the self-sufficiency of the very *concept* of the absolute I in this way then gives a quite different connotation to Schlegel's otherwise Jacobian scepticism about the ability of the finite I to ever conceptually know the absolute. To think of oneself as cut off from a type of cognitive grasp of the whole that would be available to God still presupposes that the unachievable goal is meaningful. Here, then, Schlegel moves somewhat as we will see in Schelling. The Fichtean absolute, infinite I, against which the finite I can be understood only as *limited* (by the non-I which is itself a product of the absolute I's positing) once again looks like an instantiation of the voluntaristic God found in orthodox Christian theology which is beyond the reach of human knowledge. Hegel was to try to capture the problem with this concept of the infinite by saying that an infinite understood as *opposed* to something finite would thereby, by the type of principle of reciprocal determination noted above, *be discounted as* properly infinite. As Manfred Frank has noted of Schlegel, "With Hegel and Schelling ... he shares the insight that the concept of finitude is dialectically bound to that of infinity and cannot be isolated from it" (Frank 2004: 178–79). But while Schlegel seems to break free from the opposition of foundationalism and scepticism represented by Fichte and Jacobi in ways that suggest parallels with Hegel (ways that Hegel perhaps was not fully appreciative of), Schlegel nevertheless still seems to remain within the overall framework of a Kant-inspired metaphysical scepticism marking him off from Hegel.

Schlegel's replacement of Fichte's linear, foundationalist idea of deduction from a first principle with the one of a mutually determining set of principles was a further step away from the foundationalist philosophy of Fichte, but Schlegel's scepticism constituted a retreat from Fichte to Kant—or from strong to weak TI. In contrast, Schelling was to go in a more sustained sense *beyond* Fichte.

8.3 Schelling and Plato's world soul

It is common to consider as the first expression of the distinctly "German idealist" phase of post-Kantian idealism, a two-page document of controversial authorship composed sometime in 1796 or early 1797.[18] It appears to have been a product of the enthusiastic interactions of three remarkable students who had been at the Tübingen seminary through the early 1790s, Schelling, Hegel and Hölderlin. The document—given the name, "The Oldest Systematic Programme of German Idealism"—like Schlegel's *Dialogue on Poetry*, calls for nothing short of the creation of a "new mythology", a new type of *poetic* philosophising which will "give wings to our physics, which progresses laboriously with experiments" (OSP: 3). All the parts of this new philosophy, which will encompass both nature and the moral world of interacting free spirits, will be unified by "the idea of *beauty*, taking the word in a higher Platonic sense" (ibid.: 4). The document looks forward to the developments in the thought of all three contributors, and it clearly looks back to Schiller's diagnosis of the problems of Kantian formalism in *Aesthetic Education* and the solution he offered there of the "aesthetic state". However, it also looks back to a document written by Schelling before the appearance of Schiller's letters, a work that seems to be the historical template for the mythologically presented philosophy of nature—the physics with wings—called for in the "Oldest Systematic Programme". This was a commentary by the nineteen-year-old Schelling on Plato's *Timaeus*.[19]

This work, only recently discovered, has added weight to the thesis of the importance of Platonism and Neoplatonism for the development of the post-Kantian idealism of Schelling and Hegel. It is clear that the young seminarians had become enthusiastic about the Spinozist pantheism that had become the talking point of German intellectual circles, as a result of Jacobi's igniting of the "pantheist dispute" in 1785 with his *Briefe*. But Jacobi had not only introduced the German reading public to Spinoza but also to Giordano Bruno, and thereby, indirectly to Nicholas of Cusa. In fact, popular forms of Christianity in the German states had long had a deep-running Neoplatonic pantheistic-tending stream which had found expression in heterodox thinkers like Meister Eckhart (1260–1328) and Jacob Böhme (1575–1624), who had often been associated with the heresies of "free thinkers" as well as with populist social movements. This, as we have seen in the case of Schiller, had especially been the case in the German region in which the three seminarians were born and educated, the Duchy of Württemberg. Moreover, at the time, this movement seemed to be undergoing a revival. In the 1780s Böhme had been taken up by the Catholic philosopher Franz von Baader,[20] and in the 1790s Plotinus himself was being read under the urgings of Novalis, who had stressed the proximity of Plotinus' views to those of Kant and Fichte (Beierwaltes 2004: 87–88).

What Schelling had attempted in his *Timaeus* commentary was a *Kantianised* reading of the elaborate cosmology of Timaeus' long speech, in this late Platonic text become canonical for Neoplatonism.[21] Thus, Plato's account of the fashioning of the world by the *demiurge* (crafts worker) and the formation of a *world soul* was read by Schelling as an analogical or mythological way of expressing the Kantian idea of the *constitution* of the world by reason. But in this way, besides *Kantianising* Plato, Schelling was reciprocally *Platonising* Kant's transcendental philosophy, as the notion of the world soul clearly broke down any abstract opposition of human and divine intellects in a way foreshadowed by §§76 and 77 of the *Critique of Judgment*. Rüdiger Bubner has summed up the result this way:

> Nature is thought in relation to man, conceived as a totality that is projected out of man himself and his own immanent potentiality. Nature is thus more than the world of phenomenal appearances that are to be grasped as standing collectively under the order of laws prescribed by the understanding. For nature now presents itself to knowledge as an already organised interconnection of parts, as if it represented the externalization of some inner reality, or as if the human spirit had posited nature over against itself as an after-image or reflections of its own being.
>
> (Bubner 2003: 21)

Schelling, Hegel and Hölderlin had clearly all been antagonistic to the type of politically conservative orthodox Christian appropriation of Kantian philosophy that they found among their teachers at Tübingen,[22] and were attracted to alternatives. In place of Kant's already idiosyncratic Christian-Neoplatonic ("Augustinian") interpretation of Plato, Schelling was thus substituting his own equally idiosyncratic *pagan* Neoplatonistic reading, a move in general accord with the Spinozist ideas the three seminarians were also to find attractive, as well as the "aesthetic paganism" introduced into German culture by Winckelmann. Of the three, it was the precocious Schelling who was first to make an impression on intellectual culture, and to be appointed to a chair in philosophy, at the University in Jena in 1798. In the decade extending from his youthful *Timaeus* commentary until 1804, the year he left Jena, Schelling developed an influential version of post-Kantian idealism that came to be known as "identity philosophy", in which he linked Fichte's version of transcendental idealism to a *philosophy of nature* inspired by Plato and Spinoza. In works like *Ideas for a Philosophy of Nature* (1797), *On the World Soul* (1798) and *First Outline for a System of the Philosophy of Nature* (1799) Schelling developed ideas he first sketched in his *Timaeus* commentary, and it was in his philosophy of nature where he made explicit his concerns about Kant's Copernican revolution.

8.4 Schelling's philosophy of nature

In *Ideas for a Philosophy of Nature*, Schelling poses what he describes as the fundamental philosophical question: "How a world outside us, how a Nature and with it experience is possible" (IPN: 10). Such a question, asking after the *possibility* of the external world and "with it experience", rather than with Kant, asking after the *conditions* of the experience of the world, could look anti-Kantian indeed, but Schelling's question may not be as far from Kant's as it at first appears. As recent scholarship on Kant has shown, even in the *Critique of Pure Reason* Kant's transcendental deduction of the "formal" conditions of experience seemed to creep over into its "material" conditions.[23] That is, against the grain of his "transcendental *idealism*" at places Kant seemed to be arguing that the conditions being explored pertained to how the world *must itself be*. This indeed seemed to be part of the development of Kant's transcendental idealism after the *Critique of Judgment* and up to the *Opus Postumum*, where Kant in fact had attempted to "deduce" the reality of an order of connectedness among forces constituting the universe that he identified with the ancient concept of the *aether*.

Asking after the conditions of experience Schelling says that it is only after the knowing subject itself has "disentangled itself from the fetters of nature and her guardianship" that nature *could be there* as something knowable *for* the knower. "Disentangling" oneself from the fetters of nature clearly has something to do with the move of Copernican reflection, but the very idea that the knowing subject must become "disentangled" from the world presupposes an earlier state in which mind and world are somehow "entangled".

As soon as man sets himself in opposition to the external world … the first step of philosophy has been taken. With that separation, reflection first begins, he separates from now on what Nature had always united, separates the object from the intuition, the concept from the image, finally (in that he becomes his own *object*) himself from himself.

(IPN: 10)

Reflection presupposes the act of breaking with the original unity of nature, and the philosophy of nature will be directed to understanding this original unity.

Again it is useful to take our bearings from Kant's Copernican turn here. As we have seen, the Copernican turn had been the condition for the coming into focus of what I have termed a "fact world"—a world of *logically unifiable* "facts". To use the standard terminology that Fichte, Schelling and others adopt in describing the separation of knower and known is to talk of the separation of "subject" and "object", but it must be kept in mind what is meant by these heavily theory-laden terms. For Kant, the "subject" was the formally conceived "transcendental unity of perception" or the "I think" that accompanied all representation. For Fichte it was the self-positing "I" that posited itself as opposed to a non-I that in turn limited the positing "I". The "object" existing for such a subject, I have suggested, for Kant was ideally the object *qua* component of a knowable or judgeable "fact" that could be unified with other facts in the project of coming to know the world *as a unified whole*. For Fichte, it was an object first known in sensory intuition that was subsequently cognitively "worked up" to the status of component of a unified world. What had been well left behind in these developments was the more commonplace idea of the "I", such as found in Descartes, in which it was conceived as naming a distinct mental substance.

It is clear that Schelling substituted for Fichte's "absolute I"—from which the posited finite subject and object emerged as opposed—the idea of a *primordial nature*, in which, as in Spinoza's substance or Cudworth's world soul, both subject- and object-like aspects somehow coexist. While attracted to the Spinozism against which Jacobi had been issuing his warnings, Schelling was intent on showing that it was *not* at all nihilistic in the way that Jacobi claimed, but rather was compatible with the human freedom at the centre of, but imperfectly realised in, Kant's philosophy. Spinoza could thus be reconciled with the idealist philosophy of Kant and Fichte, but such a reconciliation had to work against the grain of that reading of Spinoza shared by many of his admirers as well as his critics, that identified Spinozism with a type of materialism. Thus the version of Spinozism that became incorporated into German idealism, with the thought of figures like Schelling, had specific inflections. The somewhat "mechanical" conception of Spinozism as inherited from the seventeenth century was replaced by a more "organic" version, more compatible with the talk of organic forces, emerging with Blumenbach, Kielmeyer and Schiller, and more like Cudworth's Neoplatonist "plastic power".

Schelling had quickly become an enthusiastic follower of Fichte, but was dissatisfied with what was gradually perceived as the excessive intellectualism of his conception of the "I" in which material nature was presented as something posited by the absolute I, as a type of obstacle against which the reciprocally posited *finite* I was destined to strive.[24] Platonists had always identified conceptual knowledge with freedom conceived as detachment from the environing things attracting bodily desire, a detachment symbolised by Plato's image of the soul's *wings* or Eckhart's idea that "in the intellect, I am as close to a point located a thousand miles beyond the sea as I am to the place where I am presently standing" (SW: 114). But this very same detachment from the particularity of the place and time of one's environmental location could also be experienced as *alienation*, and it was against this that Schelling wanted to reassert the ineliminability of the "I" at home in the materiality of nature—hence his attraction to the pantheism of Spinoza. This same line of thought was pursued by Hölderlin, who also posited an original *Sein* (being) preceding the separation of "subject" and "object" of cognition but not as equivalent to Fichte's "absolute I", which had been understood as entirely subject, untainted by spatiotemporal location.[25] In a way somewhat like Schelling's thinking that "reflection" separated the mind from an original participation in the material world, Hölderlin spoke of the original "division" of subject and object as the consequence of a "judgment".[26]

To the Tübingen colleagues, this gave a certain ambiguity to Kant's reflective Copernican turn. From one point of view, cognitive reflection upon the things of one's environment, converting them into components of the "facts" of a fact world from which one was equidistant, could be understood as freedom; from another, a recipe for homelessness. It was the localistic need to "belong" to some specific time and place that was to become dominant in the nationalistic forms of "romanticism" to be seen as opposed to the cosmopolitan universalism and intellectualism of the earlier "Enlightenment" from the seventeenth and eighteenth centuries.[27] But truer to the Leibnizian reconciliationist impulse, the early romantics of the "Jena decade" did not see this particularism as simply *opposed* to Enlightenment universalism but in need of reconciliation with it, and this was to characterise the thought of Schelling as well, at least in this early period. And far from being a piece of romantic "emotivism", Schelling's concern with the negative effects of reflection engage with a deep philosophical problem, one that had already been signalled by Kant in his concerns about the "subjective" conditions of the application of the moral law.

As the philosopher Thomas Nagel has pointed out, while reflection may purport to lead to a kind of "view from nowhere" onto the world, one can *act* in the world, only from *somewhere in particular* (Nagel 1986). Schelling's call for a fundamentally *active* conception of the human essence that must in some sense represent a *return to the world*, or more precisely, a return to some particular *environs* within it, represents the attempt to maintain a unity between theoretical and practical reason. Rather than think of passive contemplation of the whole as an *end* of our existence, as had Plato, Schelling considers such reflection as itself just a *stage* on the way to becoming genuinely human and so genuinely free. From this point of view, being permanently located in the "reflected" point of view would be a kind of "spiritual sickness". When humans "break out of" nature, as it were, they upset an "original equilibrium of forces and consciousness", and although this is the precondition of their freedom and rationality, the point of such reflection must be to *re-establish* something like the original equilibrium "through freedom" as "only in equilibrium of forces is there health". Philosophy, therefore, must assign to reflective consciousness "only *negative* value" (IPN: 11).

It is here where Schelling's distinctly ambiguous relation to Fichte emerges, its antagonistic aspect not having become obvious until pointed out by Hegel, in 1801 in his *Difference between the System of Fichte and Schelling*. On the one hand, in Fichtean spirit Schelling asserts the following:

> So far as I am *free* … I am not a *thing* at all, not an *object*. I live in a world entirely my own; I am a being that exists, not for other beings, but *for itself*. There can be only deed and act in me; from me effects can only *proceed*: there can be no passivity in me, for there is passivity only where there is effect and counter-effect, and this is only in the interconnection of things, above which I have raised myself.
>
> (IPN: 13)

Moreover, he uses this to criticise any attempt to understand the mind *mechanically*. Suppose I were a "mere piece of mechanism", he says, how could I then ask such questions, since

> what is caught up in mere mechanism cannot step out of the mechanism and ask: How has all this become possible? *Here*, in the midst of the series of phenomena, absolute necessity has assigned to it its place; if it leaves this place, it is no longer this thing. … *That* I am capable of posing this question is proof enough that I am, as such, independent of external things; for how otherwise could I have asked how these things themselves are possible *for me*, in my consciousness? One would therefore have to think that anyone who so much as raises this question is by that very fact refusing to explain his ideas as effects of external things.
>
> (IPN: 14)

From the reflective position, one can appreciate how Descartes could have thought of the mind as a *non-material* and so (for him) *non-extended* substance. But that the mind cannot be thought of as a mechanism, does not, for Schelling, rule out one thinking of its continuity with *nature* conventionally thought of as "external" to the mind. The nature *from which* the mind had disentangled itself in adopting the "reflective" point of view should not *itself* be thought of as "mechanical". The type of mechanical natural philosophy to which many German thinkers had been opposed at least since the time of Leibniz's opposition to Newton was inadequate to the mind's original nature.[28] Rather, it was what *appeared* as nature *to* such a mind, *after* it emerged and looked back, as it were, from its transcendental perspective.[29]

Schelling's early experiments with reconciling Spinozism and Platonism with the transcendental philosophy of Fichte and Kant found an at least *relatively* stable resolution in the so-called "identity philosophy" of the early years of the new century. This was also a period of intense collaboration between Schelling and Hegel, and the identity philosophy left its mark on Hegel's own distinctive outlook.

8.5 Art and mythology

After departing from Jena, and especially after the rift with Hegel a few years later, Schelling's philosophy was to move increasingly away from the conceptuality of philosophical discourse to the symbolic and analogical expression of art and religion. The strongly Neoplatonic features of Schelling's early attempt to synthesis Kant and Spinoza are displayed in his development of Kant's idea that art and religion could be understood in terms of the symbolic expression of ideas. Thus in his *Philosophy of Art* (1802–3) Schelling notes that "[p]articular things, to the extent they are absolute in that particularity, and thus to the extent they as particulars are simultaneously universes, are called ideas. Every idea is = universe in the form of the particular" (PA: §27), and that "God" is to be understood as "the unity of all forms". As with Leibniz and others influenced by the Neoplatonic tradition, for Schelling the beautiful self-sufficient perfection of the universe as a whole manifested itself in those particular things conceived as "absolute in that particularity". This was the underlying idea driving his linked theories of aesthetics and religion: "*The basic law of all portrayals of the gods*", he wrote, "*is the law of beauty*, for beauty is the absolute intuited in reality" (PA: §33).

Like Kant, Schelling interprets religious mythology as a figurative representation of something *discursively* represented in "ideas". The "same syntheses of the universal and particular that viewed in themselves are ideas, that is, images of the divine, are, if viewed on the plane of the real, the gods" (PA: §28). Effectively repeating Kant's critique of the transcendental illusion, Schelling criticises the idea that the reality of the gods can be understood on the model of the reality of the objects of the world of experience and understanding. In support, he appeals to the religious orientation of the Greeks:

> Anyone who is still able to ask how such highly cultivated spirits as the Greeks were able to believe in the reality or actuality of the gods ... proves only that he himself has not yet arrived at that stage of cultivation at which precisely the *ideal* is the real and is much more real than the so-called real itself. The Greeks did not at all take the gods to be real in the sense, for example, that common understanding believes in the reality of physical objects.
>
> (Ibid.: §29)

Schelling's point seems to be, rather, that the reality of the Greek gods was expressed in what they enabled those who revered them to *do* and the way such gods enabled them to *live*.

Rather than being the objects of "mere understanding" or "reason", the gods would be properly objects of the faculty of the imagination or "fantasy". This, as we have seen, does not make them "unreal"; rather, imagination is just that faculty which presents the synthesis of the absolute with the limitation of particularity in the form of an *image*.[30] Thus we have to think of art and the imagination as something like a representational medium in which these "real" things—real because of their efficaciousness—have their reality, just as the world of science exists *in* the representational medium that we call the understanding.

> The creations of art must have the same reality as, indeed an even higher reality than, those of nature. The figures of the gods that endure so necessarily and so eternally must have a higher reality than those of human beings or of plants, yet must simultaneously possess the characteristics both of individuals and of types, including the immortality of the latter.
>
> (PA: §38)

And neither should we think of the imagination as a faculty for the production of merely or primarily inner or subjective imagistic representations; it is external media such as poetry, painting, sculpture that give reality to the gods. An essential conceptual link between religion and art is thus forged by Schelling: mythology is the "necessary condition and first content" of art (ibid.); and art, that form of presentation (*Darstellung*) of the absolute itself for finite subjects, by means of particular beautiful things, is the medium of mythology. Thus, the gods "can have no independent, truly objective existence except in the complete development of their own world

and of a poetic totality that we call mythology". Only within this mythological world "are abiding and definite forms possible through which alone
the eternal concepts can be expressed" (ibid.). In contrast, the theoretical
representations of the scientific understanding, in virtue of their objectification of the known, cannot, as Kant had pointed out, encompass the
absolute itself—that is, the absolute as having a unity, beyond being the
synthetic sum of all knowable objects. Moreover, as we have seen, because
it is from the reflective point of view, and hence premised upon *separation*,
the world of scientific understanding cannot include the active knower *in*
the known. In contrast, this is just what art is able to achieve, "without
suspension of the absolute".

In short, with Schelling it is wrong to think of the gods of religions as
simply erroneous or failed attempts to represent the world in the explanatory mode of the understanding. They exist in the products of the imagination and play a regulative role in the beings who imagine them. We have
to think of art and the imagination as something like a representational
medium in which these "real" things exist, just as the world of science
exists *in* the representational medium of the understanding:

> The creations of art must have the same reality as, indeed an even
> higher reality than, those of nature. The figures of the gods that
> endure so necessarily and so eternally must have a higher reality
> than those of human beings or of plants, yet must simultaneously
> possess the characteristics both of individuals and of types, including
> the immortality of the latter.
>
> (PA: §38)

One gets a similar idea of the role of art in making gods present in the
world in the more recent philosophy of Hans-Georg Gadamer, who also
justifies the "exemplary significance" of religious art, in his discussion of
the ontology of picturing (Gadamer 1992: 134–44). We should not think of
the picturing as being paradigmatically of independently existing things, on
the model, say, of a mere copy, as in a passport photo. Rather there is a
more primordial type of picturing within which the object has its "being"
added to, as it were, by the very event of its being pictured; the thing
experiences an *"increase in being"* (ibid.: 140). For Gadamer too, mythology
provides the fundamental exemplar. "Herodotus' notorious statement that
Homer and Hesiod created the Greek gods", remarks Gadamer, "means
that they introduced the theological system of a family of gods into the
varied religious tradition of the Greeks, and thus created distinct forms. By
articulating the gods' relations to one another it set up a systematic whole"
(ibid.: 143). That is, the poetry of Homer and Hesiod, by unifying and sys-
tematising that represented in fragmentary form within local cults, "added
to" the being of those "gods" by giving them a more determinate form than

they had hitherto received, thus enhancing their effectiveness. The plastic arts took this process a step further by giving a fixed enduring form to what otherwise would only have existed at the less determinate level of verbal meaning; nevertheless, Gadamer denies that this thesis amounts to the Feuerbachian reversal of the "imago dei thesis" (ibid.). It is not that humans create the gods in their own image because the humans only gain an "imaginably" determinate nature in a culture where the gods are already presented to supply normative models to guide and shape characteristic patterns of social life itself. We will see this idea developed by both Hegel and Nietzsche in their own distinctive ways.

9

HEGEL'S IDEALIST METAPHYSICS
OF SPIRIT

Georg Wilhelm Friedrich Hegel (1770–1831) was born and schooled in
Stuttgart and, as we have seen, attended the seminary ("Stift") in nearby
Tübingen where he formed friendships with Schelling and Hölderlin. When
he joined Schelling at the University of Jena in 1801, the glory days of the
first wave of post-Kantian idealism were coming to an end. Fichte had been
banished, and the early romantic circle was fragmenting. The local view of
Hegel seems to have been that he was little more than a spokesperson for
his friend Schelling's excursions into idealism and nature philosophy, an
assessment that Hegel apparently struggled against for a large part of his
career and which is still extant in some circles today.

At Jena, up until the closure of the university in 1807, when Napoleon's
troops invaded and occupied the town, Hegel experimented with various
ways of conceiving the structure of his idealistic system. He was completing
his first great work, the *Phenomenology of Spirit*, during the occupation of the
town that brought the first part of his career to a standstill. Deprived of a
university position for the next decade, Hegel worked as the editor of a
newspaper and as the headmaster of a high school, but nevertheless published his three-volume *Science of Logic*. In 1816 he was appointed to an
academic post at the University of Heidelberg, during which time he published the first edition of his *Encyclopaedia of the Philosophical Sciences*, and
in 1818 he was appointed to the chair of philosophy that Fichte had occupied
at the University of Berlin.

During Hegel's twelve years in Berlin his influence and fame grew. His
Elements of the Philosophy of Right appeared in 1820, as a handbook to
accompany his lectures. Also from his Berlin period we have records of his
course of lectures on philosophy of religion, philosophy of history, aesthetics, and the history of philosophy. Hegel died in 1831 during a cholera
epidemic, although perhaps not of cholera, as has traditionally been
assumed. After his death, Hegel's followers split over the interpretation of
his attitude to religion, the "left Hegelians" taking Hegel's philosophy as
fundamentally a form of humanism, their "right" opponents seeing it as a
philosophical defence of Christian theism.

9.1 The puzzle of Hegel's attitude to religion and metaphysics

In a lecture from his series on philosophy of religion at the University of Berlin in 1827, Hegel claimed that "the content of philosophy, its need and interest, is wholly in common with that of religion. The object of religion, like that of philosophy, is the eternal truth, God and nothing but God and the explication of God" (LPR: 78).[1] From this avowal, it would seem evident that the "right Hegelians" were correct and that Hegel had turned his back on Kant's "Copernican revolution" to embrace a pre-critical, "theo-centric" metaphysics. However, to a number of influential recent interpreters, Hegel was *the* philosophical modernist, a *post*-Kantian in a developmental, as well as temporal, sense—the philosopher who preserved and developed those aspects of Kant's thought that were directed against the metaphysics of the early-modern period and its essential links to religious belief.[2] How could such a picture be reconciled with statements from Hegel like the one above? To clear the way for understanding Hegel's philosophy we will have to understand something about his attitude to religion and how this bears on his relation to Kant and the project of transcendental idealism.

Kant had undermined traditional proofs for the existence of God and treated "the idea of God" as a product of the rational capacity in which humans shared. But interpreted *weakly*, transcendental idealism seemed *agnostic*: there was at least a *place* for God among the unknowable "things in themselves". Nevertheless, Kant's apparent marginalisation of God from philosophical inquiry is usually seen as in keeping with the modernism of his approach, and in contrast, Hegel is commonly taken as regressing to something like the earlier outlook of the seventeenth century. When Kant's approach is examined in light of strong TI, however, things can seem different. If metaphysics is not about what exists "in itself", but what reason produces out of its own activity, and if the *idea* of God *is* produced necessarily as a regulative idea by reason itself, then it is far from clear that the question of God has been so "marginalised". Rather, the philosophical question posed about God has been transformed.

For Kant, the *regulative* role played by the idea of God in cognitive life was most thematic in the idea's contribution to the *moral* life and character of the individual. And despite Kant's attempt to separate philosophy from the content of religious belief, his "idea" of God had a distinctly Christian, specifically *Augustinian*, shape. In contrast, Schelling's account of the Greek gods that had their proper existence in the imaginary realm of "art", and had thereby structured the inner and outer lives of the members of a community, could be seen as resulting from Schelling's having extended Kant's notion of "God" as an action-guiding "symbolic" expression beyond Kant's otherwise orthodox Christian assumptions. Hegel's own early "theological writings" had shown this same criticism of orthodox Christianity and attraction to the "aesthetic paganism" of Schelling and Hölderlin,[3] but by the time of Hegel's "mature period" in Berlin, his attitude to Christianity had changed. He now seemed to think of Christianity, and particularly of its Protestant form, as an especially *apt* mode of religious representation for the modern world. The question of *which* religion suited contemporary life was, however, separate from that of his philosophical understanding of the nature of religion itself and the status of its objects. Kant had produced an entirely new—"idealistic"—way of thinking about the objects of religion, and there is no reason to believe that Hegel had reverted back to "spiritual realism".

Thus, while Hegel in Berlin outwardly lived the life of a Lutheran, this image seemed out of step with what he taught *about* religion in the lecture hall.[4] Indeed, the unorthodox nature of Hegel's attitude to religion attracted attention from the time of his arrival at Berlin in 1818. Only a few years after his appointment, he had started to attract accusations of "pantheism" and, a little later, "atheism" from more orthodox thinkers. Even to his closest associates, Hegel's mature attitudes to religious belief were far from clear, and when the smouldering issue of the implication of his philosophy for religion erupted after his death, both "left Hegelians" like Feuerbach, who saw Hegel's God as no more than an anthropological projection of our own "species being", and their "right" opponents, for whom Hegel's philosophy was nothing less than a full-blooded form of theism, would claim to represent his actual views.

The actual version of Christianity that Hegel did embrace in his Berlin years was, as Cyril O'Regan has argued, a distinctly unorthodox one (O'Regan 1994). As a Württembergian like Schelling and Hölderlin, he had clearly absorbed the influence of the peculiarly "Swabian" form of Protestantism, a form of religious culture that may have made them receptive towards the revival of Spinoza in the 1780s and the philosophies of Plotinus and Proclus in the 1790s. As Manfred Baum has pointed out, Schelling and Hegel read Plato in light of the middle- and Neoplatonist interpretations (Baum 2000: 207), and the Neoplatonic characteristics of Hegel's thought came to be widely acknowledged during the nineteenth century: Feuerbach, for example, describing Hegel as "the German Proclus" (PPF: 47).

The Neoplatonism that marked Swabian Protestantism went back to thirteenth- and fourteenth-century thinkers of the "German Dominican" school such as Albert the Great, Meister Eckhart and John Tauler, and tropes from the discourse of this school such as the "negation of negation" and the "unity of opposites" are redolent in Hegel's writings. Strenuously opposed to the nominalist and voluntarist picture of God as radically removed from human experience and knowledge, Eckhart had pictured God as *within*: "no mystic in the history of Christianity", writes Bernard McGinn "was more daring in the way in which he explored how real union with God must go beyond the uniting of two substances that remained ontologically distinct in order to reach total indistinction" (McGinn 2005: 182). The doctrine of the Trinity and the Incarnation were, for Eckhart, understood in terms of the process of the divination of *mankind*, a doctrine that for more orthodox Christians came dangerously close to a pantheistic heresy, and the *roots* of this heresy might be traced to the ambiguous conception of the "soul" (*psyche*) that such Platonistic forms of Christianity had inherited from the Greeks.

Plato thought of the soul as immortal, but Aristotle was, at best, equivocal. Identifying the soul as the *form* of the body, and distinguishing plant, animal and rational souls, Aristotle had seemed to suggest (in DA: bk 2, 413b) that while the *activity* of the intellect (*Nous*) was separable from the body, the soul itself was no such separable (or hence immortal) thing.[5] Such a separation of the concepts of super-individual *Nous* and individual *psyche* is said to have been incorporated into later Neoplatonic thought. Plotinus, for example, from the logical doctrine that the universe is, at the same time, both one *and* many, conceived of this relation in terms of the three "hypostases" of *the One, Nous and Soul*. The plurality of souls, all egressing from "the One" by being individuated by bodies, was now thought of as encompassed by *Nous* as by "some huge living organism" (Enn: Ennead IV, treatise 8, ch. 3) and as *regressing* back to the one by making it the object of contemplation.

Plato's disembodied and Aristotle's embodied conceptions of the soul pulled Neoplatonism in different directions. Following Plato, Plotinus had still conceived of individual souls as *essentially* manifestations of *Nous*, but as temporarily "imprisoned" in the worldly bodies from whence they received their non-rational features.[6] But in both Plotinus and Proclus adherence to the form–matter distinction seemed to count against any conception of the soul as a *nonmaterial substance*. From Hegel's point of view, however, the Christian doctrine of the Incarnation transformed the Neoplatonic elements that had gone into the Christian thought of the Trinity,[7] strengthening the *necessity* of the process in which divine *Nous* came to be *embodied* in mortal beings, symbolised by Jesus. This increased the more "Aristotelian" characteristics of the soul over the "Platonic" ones,[8] and pushed the conception of God in a pantheistic direction.[9] Furthermore, the third "person" of the Trinity (the "Holy Spirit") evoked once more the *communal* conception of the mind already present in Plotinus.[10] On top of this and generally following Kant's "symbolic" analysis, all these doctrines were then conceived as expressing in a type of pictorial language of historical narrative, *eternal* truths that Hegel thought properly captured *conceptually* in philosophy.

9.2 Hegel's critique of Kant's idea of God

The God implicitly representing the cognitive and practical norms of Kant's transcendental idealism tends, as we have seen, towards an orthodox Christian one, in particular one reflecting the more voluntaristic characteristics of St Augustine's God. Christian voluntarists had always stressed God's transcendence of the human viewpoint, and this is reflected in that weakly transcendental idealist side of Kant's philosophy that posits noumena or things-in-themselves as objects transcending human epistemic capacities. In his early essay, "Faith and Knowledge", from 1802, we find Hegel explicitly critical of this combination of theological voluntarism and weak TI in Kant. At the outset of the essay he notes that recently the "opposition of faith and knowledge" had "been transferred into the field of philosophy itself" (FK: 55). Hegel goes on to imply that Kant's unknowable thing-in-itself was the result of an incorporation into philosophy of the God of faith, unknowable to reason. "Reason", he claims,

> having in this way become mere intellect, acknowledges its own nothingness by placing that which is better than it in a *faith outside and above* itself, as a *beyond*. This is what has happened in the *philosophies of Kant, Jacobi, and Fichte*. Philosophy has made itself the handmaid of a faith once more.
>
> (Ibid.: 56)

This criticism seems more in the spirit of Fichte's or Schelling's criticism of "the letter" of Kant's critical philosophy, rather than a reversion to *preKantian* metaphysics. Thus, a few lines earlier Hegel had claimed that "Reason had already gone to seed in and for itself when it envisaged religion merely as something positive *and not idealistically*" (FK: 55, emphasis added). Presumably, this is a trap to which Kant had fallen prey. In his treatment of religion Kant had merely *assumed* the voluntarists' picture of God, a picture then reflected philosophically in the transcendence and unknowability of the thing in itself. Furthermore, the clear suggestion seems to be that in this respect Kant was being *unfaithful* to his own idealism—the strong TI at the heart of Kant's transcendental turn.

These brief comments at the outset of Hegel's philosophical career, I believe, present in a highly condensed way an attitude to Kant's critical philosophy that was to persist throughout Hegel's subsequent writings. From his early "theological" writings, Hegel was critical of the "positivity" of orthodox Christianity and criticised such religions by appealing to natural *völkisch* ones, such as those of the ancient Greeks, where acceptance of the gods somehow fitted naturally with everyday experience and was not in need of the artificial enforcement of an externally imposed dogma. Of course, any such type of ahistorical advocacy of the norms of ancient society could not withstand the growing awareness of the distinctively "modern" reality emerging from the aesthetic writings of Schiller and Friedrich Schlegel. Hegel came to believe that *something* about the Christian God of modernity would reflect a distinctly contemporary experience, just as the longing of romantic poesy reflected that experience. But in this Hegel did not simply become reconciled to a transcendent Christian God, as had, for example, Schlegel. Rather, this enlightened criticism of "positivity" remained. And since the transcendental scepticism at the heart of Kant's weak TI was itself a reflection of this same positivity, Hegel was critical of that dimension of Kant's philosophy. But what was left when one eliminated the unknowable thing-in-itself from Kant's philosophy was still meant to be taken in the spirit of critical philosophy. We might say that the version of idealism that Hegel purports to find beneath the letter of Kant's official account of transcendental idealism is that more optimistic approach to metaphysics reflected in the Preface to the first edition of the *Critique of Pure Reason*, where it is said of metaphysics that it:

> is the only one of all the sciences that may promise that little but unified effort … will complete it. … Nothing here can escape us, because what reason brings forth entirely out of itself cannot be hidden, but is brought to light by reason itself as soon as reason's common principle has been discovered.
>
> (CPuR: Axx)

But Kant had developed this idea in such a way that something *was* hidden—the thing in itself, the philosophical equivalent of the voluntarists' radically transcendent God.

9.3 The project of a "phenomenology of spirit"

It is often overlooked that Kant had regarded his *Critique of Pure Reason* not as a way of bypassing metaphysics but as a propaedeutic to a new, scientific, rather than dogmatic, metaphysics. Hegel too had early in his career conceived of such a propaedeutic: he called it a "phenomenology of spirit".

The term "phenomenology" had in fact been coined by a correspondent of Kant, the German scientist–mathematician J. H. Lambert (1728–77), and in a letter to Lambert sent by Kant to accompany a copy of his Inaugural Dissertation, Kant had described metaphysics as needing a "necessary propaedeutic" to determine the "validity and limits" of the use therein of the "principle of sensibility" (Corr: 10.98). It is fairly clear that the project of such a propaedeutic was what was realised eleven years later in the *Critique of Pure Reason*, but by that time Kant had apparently dropped the use of the term "phenomenology", at least for that purpose. Its use by Hegel a quarter of a century later had clear continuities and discontinuities with Kant's, despite the vast disparity between their philosophical styles. Hegel's "phenomenology" is still a "propaedeutic" to metaphysics, his *idealist* metaphysics—or more specifically, to his *system* of philosophy, comprising *logic*, *philosophy of nature*, and *philosophy of spirit*, as set out in his *Encyclopaedia of the Philosophical Sciences*.

Hegel's *Phenomenology* is a propaedeutic in the sense of a work intended to bring the readers to where they could undertake properly *logical* thought, amounting to something like a systematic deduction of the "thought determinations" in a way reminiscent of Kant's deduction of the "categories" in the *Critique of Pure Reason*.[11] Hegel refers to this goal of the *Phenomenology*, perhaps misleadingly, as "absolute knowing [absolutes Wissen]", a phrase which appears to suggest to the reader the achievement of a type of comprehensive "God's-eye view" onto the whole of existence— the Copernican point from which the world as a totality, an *omnitudo realitatis*, might be grasped.[12] In many ways, however, such an understanding is predicated upon a conception of "knowing" which Hegel was determined to undermine, in the very process of reaching "absolute knowing"—the conception that knowing is fundamentally a relation between an independently understandable knowing subject and some known object. To think of absolute knowing in this way is to think of knowledge of the whole on the model of determinate knowledge of a constituent of the whole—the idea criticised by Plotinus and other Neoplatonists.

Hegel himself tells us something about his own conception of the method to be employed there in the Introduction to the *Phenomenology*. Modern philosophy, he notes, alluding to Descartes, starts with *doubt*, but in such doubt it is usually presupposed "that the Absolute stands on one side and cognition on the other, independent and separated from it" (Phen: §74), with the puzzle being how cognition could then bridge the gap and make contact with the object. That is, such doubt presupposes what Schelling described as the "reflective" starting point, in which the mind stands over against the world as "subject" to "object". Scepticism that this could be achieved is that of weak TI. One of Hegel's standard moves will be to point out that any world standing over *against* cognition, because it doesn't *include cognition itself*, could never be thereby thought of as the *whole* world, in Hegel's terms, as "absolute" or "infinite".[13] Therefore the reflective model of knowledge could not be adequate for philosophy *qua* knowledge of the Absolute. But Hegel equally resists Schelling's recourse to some original intellectual intuition, some kind of *prelapsarian* knowledge of which the mind is capable *prior* to its separation from the rest of nature. To circumvent this problem, Hegel then considers a new path by regarding the *knowing itself* as a part of the Absolute, and does this by considering *forms of knowing* (as opposed to the putative objects of knowledge) as themselves constituting "appearances" or "phenomena" to be reflected upon.

The switch from discussing "knowing" to talk of (the plural) *forms* of knowing reflects changes in thinking about knowledge that had followed in the wake of Kant. Kant himself had concluded the *Critique of Pure Reason* with a three-page chapter entitled "The History of Pure Reason", which "will present in a cursory outline only the difference of the ideas which occasioned the chief revolutions" in metaphysics (CPuR: A853/B881). Later, in Part II, "Foundation of Theoretical Knowledge", of his 1794 *Foundations*, Fichte described the *Wissenschaftslehre* as a "pragmatic history of the human mind" (Fnds: 198–99), it being the underlying processual character of the mind as a never-satisfied "striving" that allowed it to have a history.[14] Following Fichte, in Schelling's *System of Transcendental Idealism* of 1800, this programmatic statement concerning philosophy as a history of the mind finds itself expanded out into the idea of a "history of self-consciousness" in epochs (STI: 2). These "historicist" and "contextualist" dimensions to knowledge are developed in Hegel, and the discipline of "phenomenology" will thus examine the series of possible forms consciousness can adopt *in* its claims to know the world. Phenomenology will observe

> the path of the natural consciousness which presses forward to true knowledge; or as the way of the Soul which journeys through the series of its own configurations as though they were the stations appointed for it by its own nature, so that it may purify itself for the life of the Spirit, and achieve finally, through a completed experience of itself, the awareness of what it really is in itself.
>
> (Phen: §77)

The turn to forms of knowing as worldly appearances does not imply that Hegel has adopted some merely *empirically* historicist approach to knowledge, and in no sense does he chart simply *different* forms of knowledge that might be conceived "relativistically". Rather, the "series of configurations" through which knowledge passes are to be revealed as internally related, such that each new form of cognition will be seen to (in some sense) grow out of and, retrospectively, resolve problems affecting the preceding one. That each individual form of cognition is guaranteed to *have* such problems is a consequence of the feature of reason that Kant had noted in his *critique* of the claims of "pure reason". For Kant, reason had a natural tendency to overstep its own boundaries, an idea that Hegel repeats with the notion that "consciousness … is something that goes beyond limits". Since, following Fichte, Hegel takes the limits confining reason as imposed by reason *itself*, it is of the very nature of reason to be *self-transcending*. "[S]ince these limits are its own, [consciousness] is something that goes beyond itself" (Phen: §80).[15]

In Kant, the propensity of cognition to go beyond its proper limits entangles it in contradiction, as revealed by the "antinomies" of pure reason, and Kant had taken this as a warning to prevent reason from so transcending its limits in this way. Hegel, with his idea of a *series* of knowledge forms, sees this entanglement in contradiction *positively*. It is contradiction that leads reason to attain a more encompassing standpoint from which the perspectivity of the earlier opposed viewpoints can be appreciated, and their contradictions resolved.

As has often been pointed out, Hegel's procedure in the *Phenomenology* seems to presuppose a "phenomenological we", the reflectively positioned *readers* who are meant simply to follow the self-correcting "natural consciousness" as it passes through the series of individual forms of knowing via which it educates itself "to the standpoint of Science" (Phen: §78)—that is, the "absolute knowing" from which logical thought is possible. At this final point, having passed through the totality of possible shapes, natural consciousness will grasp that it is relativised to *none* of them but can somehow participate in them *all*. However, at the terminus of the process, the original gap between the "phenomenological we" and the natural consciousness is itself overcome, as the reader, who has occupied the position of the phenomenological we, attains this knowledge as well. When the natural consciousness is presented as looking back and surveying the path along which it has come, in a type of *recollection*, the *reader* of the *Phenomenology* is presumably meant to realise that the "pragmatic history of the mind" that has unfolded before it is, in fact, the history of *its own mind*. The reader has brought to the reading of this text an ensemble of cognitive capacities that, rather than being simply "given", have been acquired as an inheritance from the cultural history which has just been outlined. This, then, is Hegel's answer to Schelling's problem of reflection. In the absolute knowing reached by the collective mind in its self-correcting progress, reflective consciousness is reunited with that first-order consciousness that belongs within the world, but there is supposedly no reliance on any primitive "intellectual intuition". The circle has been closed: the reader's knowing of itself is at the same time a knowing of something within the world, an evolving "spirit" distributed over a plurality of knowers, that has "itself" thereby achieved "self-consciousness".

When the work has reached the point of absolute knowing, the reader of the *Phenomenology* will now be in the position to make *explicit* the "logic" that has been *implicit* in the series of forms of consciousness throughout. This is, indeed, the task Hegel would undertake in the *Science of Logic*, a few years after the *Phenomenology*. No substantial engagement with Hegel's phenomenological investigations is possible here, but a short survey of the initial shapes of consciousness and self-consciousness, and of the transitions between them, might both convey something of Hegel's method and give a foretaste of what might be expected of his *logical* investigations.

9.4 Self-negating shapes of consciousness

In the first three chapters of the *Phenomenology* Hegel charts the progress of a single consciousness through a series of what we might think of as separate *epistemic–ontological attitudes* (that is, attitudes that define both the fundamental nature of what is known, and the fundamental nature of the knowledge by which it is known) that he labels, "Sense-certainty", "Perception", and "the Understanding".[16] Each of these attitudes is a version of a generally realistic orientation within which that which is known within experience is taken to be some independent "in-itself [das Ansich]"—something that is there "anyway" with the nature that it has independently of the knower. But these three separate "shapes" of consciousness are differentiated by the respective assumptions involved regarding the fundamental characteristics *of* that independent "in-itself".

The advocate of the first of these shapes thinks of that which is immediately and receptively apprehended as "the richest kind of knowledge", and "the truest knowledge" (Phen: §91) and as issuing in a type of knowledge which exceeds conceptual comprehension. That is, what are presented in *Sense-certainty* are regarded as the ultimately *simple* components of being, and like the contents of Kantian intuitions, these simple objects are meant to be things given immediately in experience, and are meant to be given as the singular referents of a type of mental pointing—each presented as a "pure 'This'", the "singular thing [das Einzelne]" (ibid.). Hegel attempts to show the incoherence of the idea of anything's being "given" in the sense of being immediately present to a consciousness while still being "determinate" or cognitively relevant. Even concepts like "this", "here" and "now" do not pick out their referents in an immediate and direct way, since each application of the concept will implicitly involve a contrast. For example, for "this" to pick out a determinate reference it will need to be distinguished from a contrasting "that"; what counts as "now" will depend on what is taken to count as "then"—and so on. Without such contrast there would be nothing to tell us whether "now" stretches over a second, a day or a year; or "here", the room, the city or the country that I'm presently in. In short, this looks like Hegel's way of making the sort of criticism against a Newtonian "transcendental realism" of space and time to which Leibniz and Kant had been, in their ways, opposed.[17]

This insight—that contrasting relations (or "negations") between concepts are essential to establishing the way concepts apply to the world—is crucial for Hegel, who names this phenomenon "determinate negation".[18] In "Perception" we see the principle applied at the level of empirical concepts such as colour concepts, where we might think that an important consideration in determining what span of the colour spectrum is picked out by the concept "red" is tied up with the question as to the point at which a neighbouring colour word like "orange" would apply. That is, we might think that whether or not "red" can be said of just this colour depends on whether or not "orange" or some other contrasting colour term is appropriate and thereby *excludes* its being red.[19]

However, Hegel's point about determinate negation goes beyond the relatively straightforward one about the role of contrasts in conceptual determination, as not only do words like "this", "here" and "now" have contraries to mediate their application to the world, but also, Hegel suggests, these concepts *turn into their contraries* in the course of being applied to the world, and hence generate insoluble contradictions that invalidate Sense-certainty as an attitude. What he seems to mean is this. Being relativised to the perspective of the particular subject applying the terms and to the context of their application means that the content of such judgments will not be stable. Thus, if I say "now is day" and that judgment is *true*, in twelve hours time it will be false, because by *then* "now" will be *night* (Phen: §95).

As Hegel also seems to think of this dynamic character as applying equally to *spatial* oppositions, what he appears to have in mind here is that such spatial and temporal determinations should be thought of as functioning within the experience of *mobile* agents in the spatiotemporal world, agents for whom "here" can become "there", just as "now" inevitably becomes "then". I take it that Hegel is saying of a mobile perceiver whose *referential* powers were limited to the use of such egocentric indexicals as "this", "here", "now", and whose *predicative* powers were limited to saying something *of* these "entities" (along the lines of the "protokoll" sentences proposed by some logical positivists–"here red", "now hot", etc.), would not be able to make meaningful claims at all. The world of such a being would be utterly chaotic:

> The *Here pointed out*, to which I hold fast ... in fact, is *not* this Here, but a Before and Behind, an Above and Below, a Right and Left. The Above is itself similarly this manifold otherness of above, below, etc. The Here, which was supposed to have been pointed out, vanishes in other Heres, but these likewise vanish. What is pointed out, held fast, and abides is a *negative* This, which *is* negative only when the Heres are taken as they should be, but, in being so taken, they supersede themselves; what abides is a simple complex [einfache Komplexion] of many Heres.
>
> (Phen: §108)

The collapse of Sense-certainty as a cognitive attitude will result in its being replaced by a new shape of consciousness, "Perception", the object of which is "the thing with many properties". Effectively, the purportedly immediate *bare this*s of Sense-certainty will be replaced by objects conceived as underlying *primary substrate* within which *properties* inhere. In the first instance, says Hegel, the properties will be taken as simply inhering in the substrate in a way that makes them indifferent to each other, but if all such properties were in fact "indifferent" to each other in this way, they could not be determinate, "for they are only determinate in so far as they differentiate themselves from one another, and *relate* themselves *to others* as to

145

their opposites" (Phen: §114). Here too, the principle of "determinate negation" applies: in Hegel's example, "[w]hite is white only in opposition to black, and so on" (Phen: §120). That is, the concepts "white" and "black" are not *indifferent* to each other, because an object's being white *precludes* its being black. But other empirical concepts *are* "indifferent". For example, an object's being white does not preclude its being *square*, say. The object of "Perception" then, cannot just be a bundle of properties inhering indifferently in a simple substrate; rather the substrate must have some internal structure which reflects the different relations within which properties can stand to each other. This reconceptualising of the object will ultimately force a transition to "the Understanding", in which the perceivable object as mere substrate is replaced by something else—perhaps something like the "substantial forms" which in Aristotle's *Metaphysics* came to replace his earlier, simpler conception of individual substances in the *Categories*, and which could be appealed to in the nomological explanations of science.

Besides the fundamental role played by the idea of "negation" in Hegel's account, these early chapters bring out something of the importance that the notion of "recollection" will play for Hegel. We see from the account of Sense-certainty that a properly cognitive being presumably could not simply exist in some constant and enduring *now* in the way that, for example, a musician might strive to be "in the moment". What was once *now* must be capable of becoming *then*: it has to be retained or recalled, as it were, *as* something no longer immediately present. Indeed, appealing to the morphology of the German words, Hegel will attempt to establish a link between what *has been* (that which is "gewesen", past) and its *essence* (its "Wesen"), with which he attempts to give sense to the role Plato had given to "recollection" in philosophical knowledge.[20] It is with just such a recollection that the *Phenomenology* as a whole will itself conclude. By recalling the complete history of all the particular shapes that it has gone through, and by grasping that what "abides" is "the negative", that is, the propensity of any particular shape of spirit to transform *in some necessitated way* into a different shape, we are thought to achieve the objective of "absolute knowing".

9.5 Self-consciousness and the recognitive theory of spirit

The transition from chapter 3 to chapter 4 of the *Phenomenology*, "The Truth of Self-Certainty", also marks a more general transition from contemplating shapes of "consciousness" to considering those of "*self*-consciousness", and it is in the course of chapter 4 that we find what is perhaps the most well-known part of the *Phenomenology*, the account of the "struggle of recognition" and the ensuing "master–slave dialectic", where Hegel examines the necessity of intersubjective conditions for the existence of any individual "self-consciousness". As in Kant, Hegel thinks that the capacity for one to be "conscious" of some object other than oneself requires the reflective awareness of oneself as the one *for whom* the object *is* an object. In a further step, however, and expanding on an idea found in Fichte, Hegel makes the meeting of this requirement rely one's recognition (or acknowledgment— Anerkennung) of *another, different subject*, who in turn reciprocally recognises one's self. Such embodied patterns of mutual recognition thereby constitute the "objective spirit", as a condition of individual self-consciousnesses as such.

The first shape of self-consciousness is its analogue of "Sense-certainty", which, rather than taking some immediately given *object* as the most certain existence, takes *itself* to be the most certain and fundamental. This is the shape of *Self*-certainty. Because it itself is taken as the basic reality, it takes what *had been* taken to be an independent "in-itself" to be something entirely *of its own* determining. This subject feels assured that its own internal states are the "truth" of its external objects. That is, this is basically a *willing* subject who thinks of external objects in terms of what *it* intends for them. Hegel hence refers to it as "desire in general". Clearly this form of self-consciousness is modelled on Fichte's idea of the absolutely self-positing subject, and Hegel accordingly refers to this form of self-consciousness with the Fichtean formula for the absolute ego, "I = I". We might speculate that if this form of self-consciousness imagined a deity to represent its norms, it would choose something like Newton's all-powerful world-creating God.

But this purely desiring self-consciousness assigning no independence to its objects beyond what it intends for them, like the shapes of *consciousness*, has a contradiction at its core. This has to do with the fact that, as a form of willing or desiring, it leads to the *annihilation* of its objects that mediates it, and this, paradoxically, reveals how in fact it is *dependent* upon such objects. For example, if Self-certainty desires some unique state of affairs to obtain, and brings it into existence, then that state of affairs can no longer *be* something desired—one cannot *desire* what one already *has*. As this form of self-consciousness had grasped itself just *as* a generalised desire, the achievement of its desire thereby brings about its own annihilation. Paradoxically, then, it *is* dependent upon something beyond its control. It is dependent on the reinstitution of some desire once satisfied. The very concept of the will found within the voluntaristic extreme of the Christian tradition is, it would seem, incoherent.

Just as with consciousness, in self-consciousness contradictions like this will plague each individual shape, and new shapes will replace the old in such ways as to solve those contradictions. Also, each successive shape of self-consciousness will be coordinated with a differently conceived object of consciousness of which it regards itself as "the truth". The only object, it will turn out, that will properly "satisfy" self-consciousness will be, not an ordinary object, but *another I*, another *self-conscious subject*. Hegel sums this up:

> A self-consciousness exists *for a self-consciousness*. Only so is it in fact self-consciousness; for only in this way does the unity of itself in its otherness become explicit for it. ... A self-consciousness, in being an object, is just as much "I" as "object".
>
> (Phen: §177)

This *unity of a self in its otherness*, an otherness which must be *another self*, describes the relation that Hegel conceptualises with the Fichtean notion "recognition" or "acknowledgement" (*Anerkennung*): "Self-consciousness exists in and for itself when, and by the fact that, it so exists for another; that is, it exists only in being acknowledged" (ibid.: §178). Hegel adds,

> With this, we already have before us the concept of *spirit*. What still lies ahead for consciousness is the experience of what spirit is – this absolute substance which is the unity of the different independent self-consciousnesses which, in their opposition, enjoy perfect freedom and independence: "I" that is "We" and "We" that is "I".
>
> (Ibid.: §177)

That is, what Hegel means by "spirit" is not some strange immaterial *entity* like either Newton's or Berkeley's God. It just *is* this configuration of mutually recognising individual subjects whose existence *as* subjects depends upon this joint act of recognition. Moreover, the world of such interacting "spiritual" beings is in some way emergent from, and presupposes, a world of interacting *living* beings, a realm of organic nature in which individuals have the type of "entangled" existence that Schelling had posited in his *philosophy of nature*. In ways not entirely unlike those found in modern "functionalist" accounts of the mind, Hegel is struggling to find a way to describe a non-dualistic conception of the mind's embodiment in the organism, or in Aristotelian terms, of the relation of the "rational soul" to the "plant" and "animal" souls.

Thus, Hegel's discussion of the realm of spirit emerges against the background of a largely Schellingian account of the interactions between living beings driven by natural desires. In Schelling's Neoplatonist-inspired account, the realm of life itself could be conceived "henologically", as a unity or universal, *from which* organisms were precipitated as particular living things during their individuated existence, and *back into which* they would be resorbed on their death. As he had put it in 1797, "Individual products have been posited in Nature, but Nature implies a *universal* organism.—Nature's struggle against everything individual" (FOS: 6).[21] Hegel too conceives of "life" in such terms:

> Thus the simple substance of Life is the splitting-up of itself into shapes and at the same time the dissolution of these existent

differences; and the dissolution of the splitting-up is just as much a splitting up and a forming of members.

(Phen: §171)

But it would be misleading to see too much continuity between Schelling's life-philosophical solution to the mind–body problem and Hegel's. Schelling's life-philosophical approach was in fact taking him away from Fichte's development of Kantian strong TI, while it was Hegel's project to reconcile the opposing idealist and life-philosophical perspectives represented by Fichte and Schelling, respectively, within Hegel's *absolutely* idealist development of strong TI. While in some contexts he might be seen as advocating a quasi-naturalistic account of the mind as emergent from nature, in others he would still be advocating a view of "nature" as a posit, as it were, of spirit. In Hegel's own "Philosophy of Nature", for example, he would treat nature itself as "the Idea in the form of otherness" (PN: §247). While the idea of spirit as embodied within patterns of intersubjective recognition between finite human beings is indeed at the heart of Hegel's solution to the thorny issue of self-consciousness, spirit itself will have to be understood at its various levels—the levels of "subjective", "objective" and "absolute" spirit—that emerge in the *Phenomenology*.

With this introduction of the notion of recognitively structured "spirit" in chapter 4, the *Phenomenology* starts to change course, the earlier tracking of "shapes of consciousness" effectively becoming replaced by the tracking of distinct patterns of "mutual recognition" between subjects, shapes of "spirit" itself, that had been signalled with the idea of the primitive form of community between master and slave. Thus, while the first four chapters were concerned with shapes of consciousness and self-consciousness—"subjective spirit"—we now start to track historical patterns of *objective* spirit, and after that, those core areas of human practice noted as the forms of "absolute spirit": art, religion and philosophy.

Subjective spirit is spirit embodied in individual finite beings, and the study of subjective spirit, which is found in the first section of Hegel's systematic *Philosophy of Spirit*, is roughly equivalent to what we think of as "philosophy of mind". Thus in the theory of subjective spirit, Hegel will be seeking to understand such factors as the conditions that allow a being to be conscious and to have directed, conceptually shaped thoughts about the world. One of the most fruitful aspects of Hegel's approach to "mindedness" is the way that he links the conditions of such individual intentional existence to social life. A little like the picture found in the twentieth century in the thought of Wittgenstein and others, Hegel's stresses that it is only in virtue of an individual's belonging to a realm of normative social practices that include the expressive powers of language that individuals can possess such intentionality. The study of the conditions of subjective spirit then takes us to *objective* spirit—spirit as it is "objectified" in those forms of supra-individual culturally encoded normative (or rule-following) practices that any individual "subjective spirit" internalises. When Hegel studies "objective spirit", as he does in the *Philosophy of Right* (which corresponds to the second part of the *Philosophy of Spirit*) he engages with overtly normative phenomena, such as systems of explicitly worked out laws to which members of a community subject themselves, as well as more generally culturally specific "sociologically" normative practices to which individual hold themselves in their social life.

Hegel's recognitive conception of spirit is most commonly dealt with in the context of objective spirit (e.g., as in R. Williams 1997), but it is also at the heart of his theory of *absolute* spirit. Thus in the *Phenomenology*, the presence of God in the world is dealt with in terms of a pattern of recognition between self-conscious subjects: God is manifest in the world as the voice of the reconciling "Yea" in the intersubjective practices of confession and forgiveness—the *Yea*, in which, Hegel says, "the two 'I's let go their antithetical *existence*". God, we must remember, is for Hegel, an *idea* related to Fichte's "absolute I" and Kant's "ideal of reason". Hegel goes on: this reconciling *Yea* is

> the *existence* of the 'I' which has expanded into a duality, and therein remains identical with itself, and, in its complete externalization and opposite, possesses the certainty of itself: it is God manifested in the midst of those who know themselves in the form of pure knowledge.
>
> (Phen: §671)

But "God", as we have seen, is equally the content of philosophy as of religion, and this imagistically represented God will soon be replaced by the purely conceptual content of philosophy. The divine in each of us, represented imagistically in God's having sent his "son" into the world for the redemption of its inhabitants, is the same as the capacity for pure, conceptual thought.

9.6 Phenomenology, logic and metaphysics

It is needless to say that Hegel's project of a phenomenology of spirit as meant to take the reader to the "logical" stance from which philosophical thought can be carried out is a massively ambitious one. Even among sympathetic Hegel scholars, the questions of both its nature and success are extremely controversial.[22] For one thing, it is clear that Hegel means something quite different by the term "logic" than is meant in the "formal" logic dominant in contemporary philosophy, but exactly what it is committed to beyond that is far from clear. As involving a progressive unfolding of "thought determinations", Hegel's logic can seem akin to the "category theory", where Aristotle attempted to describe the most basic determinations of "being". Moreover, such an "ontological" reading of the logic is reinforced by the fact that "logic" forms the first part of Hegel's tripartite philosophical "system", as articulated in the *Enyclopaedia of the Philosophical Sciences*, and leads into the more substantial philosophies of *nature* and *spirit*. This seems to suggest that the general features of existence limned in the logic are then filled out as one focuses more on specific *types* of existence.[23]

It is understandable then that Hegel's logic is often identified as a type of "ontology", akin to that of, say, Aristotle or Spinoza. The distinctness of Hegel's ontology, then, is sometimes said to reside in the role given to the *Phenomenology of Spirit* as a type of critical prolegomena to the doing of a traditionally conceived metaphysics (Stern 2002), or as an "epistemological argument" for type of ontology contained in the following "Logic" (Horstmann 2006).[24] But for those who stress the continuity between Hegel's philosophy and Kant's critical project (Pippin 1989), this type of ultimate identification of Hegel's logical thought with a traditionally conceived "ontology" falsely attributes to Hegel an entirely *pre-Kantian* conception of metaphysics—one that has forgone the characteristic "modernism" of Kant's critical project. For them, Hegel's "Logic" is more akin to Kant's "transcendental logic", a logic with a *content* (and so more than "formal logic") but which cannot be thought in any way *realistically*, as if presenting aspects of the way the world is "anyway". It is the structure generated out of "reason" itself—the reason that can be seen evolving in history.

This issue of the nature of Hegel's "metaphysics" is perhaps the deepest one separating those scholars involved in the revival of Hegelian thought in the last decades of the twentieth century, but some clarification of this issue might be achieved by appealing to Henrich's distinction between a *unity*-focused Platonist "henology" and a *being*-focused Aristotelian "ontology" (Henrich 2003: 86). After all, Hegel himself does make considerable use of, at least, the nomenclature of those Neoplatonist philosophers who challenged the idea that anything could be predicated of "the One", including the concept, "being". Thus in the *Lectures on the History of Philosophy* Hegel refers to the "great sagacity" expressed in Proclus' treatment of the One and its "negations." "Multiplicity is not taken empirically and then merely abrogated; the negative, as dividing, producing, and active, not merely contains what is privative, but also affirmative determinations" (LHP: vol. 2, 438). Indeed, Hegel's constant use of the notion of the Neoplatonists' treatment of "negation" would seem to be relevant both to the narrowly "logical" dimension to the *Science of Logic* and to the more "ontological" issues broached there as well.[25] The theme established early in the *Phenomenology* that what "abides" is something "negative" is indeed at the heart of much of Hegel's supposedly "logico-ontological" thought.

In a well-known passage in the Preface to his *Phenomenology of Spirit*, Hegel broaches the relation of his thought to that of Spinoza, who, with his concept of "substance", we can think of as a clear "ontologist".[26] While Spinoza had conceived "the absolute" as "substance",[27] it must, Hegel claims, be equally understood as "subject" (Phen: §17). On first reading it might be thought that, with this idea, Hegel is advocating a picture in which a divine personality or self-consciousness is somehow *added to* Spinoza's substance, resulting in a picture which is both closer to orthodox Christian theology and one with which Hegel has simply *completed* the three errors Kant points to in the genesis of the concept of God, adding "personalisation" to Spinoza's realisation and hypostatisation of "ideas". But it is clear from what is said in the immediately following passages that "subjectivity" has other connotations for Hegel than the traditional personality attributed to God. "Subjectivity" is for Hegel associated with a type of processual form of existence he describes as "pure, *simple negativity*" (Phen: §18), and it is in this spirit that, elsewhere, he links this "negativity" to Aristotle's characterisation of God (*Theos*) as an activity of thought thinking itself, "*noesis noeseos noesis*" (PM: §577). With this conception, Hegel clearly takes an otherwise unrepresentative element of Aristotle's metaphysics that he sees developed later among the Neoplatonists:[28] it is a conception of God, dissociated from Aristotle's own notion of substance.

With his fundamental notion of "substance" (*ousia*), Aristotle had tried to capture the enduring nature of a thing that persisted through its changes, and had thought of those changes as replacements of accidental qualities by their *opposites*. Thus at one time, the same tomato might be on the vine and green, and at another on the table and red. And Aristotle had thought of the relations between properties like "green" and "red" as *negations*: for the tomato to be red *negated* its being green. But Hegel thought that Aristotle had another, deeper, use of a type of "negativity", and says that Aristotle makes conspicuous "the moment of negativity, not as change, nor yet as nullity, but as difference or determination" (LHP: vol. 2, 140). This is the negativity displayed in *noesis noeseos* and in the ways in which Plotinus and Proclus later characterised the "self-emptying" of the absolute *into* the spatio-temporal realm. The cosmos considered in its unity had to be more than just the sum of its particular constituents; but it was *not* to be thought of in the way that Spinoza later did, that is, in terms of a thought determination appropriate *to* any individual constituent—that of *substance*.

For Spinoza, "if something is absolutely infinite, whatever expresses essence *and involves no negation* pertains to its essence" (E: pt 1, def. 6, expl., emphasis added). His famous dictum that "all determination is negation" thus holds for the making determinate of what can be said of a substance by reference to its properties, and these "negations" presuppose an ultimate substance (God) which is a uniformly "positive" ground.[29] But the type of negation that Hegel finds inherent in Aristotle's concept of God, one that is made explicit in the Neoplatonists' conception of the necessity of the emanation of "the One" into "the many", cannot be conceived of as the negation of some ontologically more primitive ground that is without negation. It is in this sense that Hegel appeals to an idea of negation that is not to be conceived as one of a ground free of negation, but which is rather the "negation of negation".[30]

Hegel thus sees in Aristotle's "speculative" concept of God the resources to criticise the ultimacy of Aristotle's own concept of substance and ontologies based upon it. But in turn, he sees Aristotle's problematic notion of substance as relying on an assumption taken over from Plato: for Aristotle, a substance is "abstractly identical with itself" in the way that for Plato an *idea* was statically self-identical (LHP: vol. 2, 138–40). That is, Hegel uses Aristotle to make the same sort of criticism of Plato that is found in Plotinus and Proclus. To think the unity of the world we cannot rely on Aristotle's notion of individual substance and we must give up Plato's "self-identical" conception of "idea" on which it was based. But is this not related to what Kant had said in the *Critique of Pure Reason* where he denied that one could have a "constitutive" knowledge of Platonic unities modelled on the knowledge we could to have of the *parts* of those unities?

Nevertheless, in appealing to the Proclean critique of Plato in the criticism of Spinoza's treatment of "the One" as a substance, Hegel is approaching these issues in a quite different way to Kant. This is clear from their respective responses to Kant's finding that pursuing thought concerning the One results in contradictions. For Kant, this is a signal that reason has overstepped its legitimate limits. In the spirit of weak TI, and following Aristotle's law of non-contradiction, Kant believed that the inevitable appearance of contradictions when one attempts to reason about the ultimate unities of the individual soul, the cosmos as a whole, and God means that one *cannot* reason about these things. For Hegel, however, it reveals something about their "natures" as metaphysical entities of strong TI and as instantiating, in different ways, the idea of the One. It reveals that *contradiction* belongs to its very "natures". And again, he follows a Neoplatonist precedent, that of Nicholas of Cusa: within "the One" we have to think of opposites as *coinciding* (OLI: bk 1, ch. 4).[31]

We are now in a better position to appreciate the complexity of the issue of Hegel's relation to Kant. It is of course true that *contra Kant's critical position*, Hegel advocates the return to a type of "speculative" metaphysical thought that has its basis in reason—"Vernunft". Unsatisfied with Kant's recontextualising of metaphysics uniquely within the realm of *practical reason*, Hegel wanted to unify reason in its theoretical and practical uses. He was not then satisfied with the injunction of weak TI to *resist* the pursuit of speculative metaphysics. But Hegel's dissatisfaction with Kant here is, nevertheless, deeply Kantian, in that it develops Kant's *strong* TI. In response to the antinomies and other contradictions generated by attempts to think about the organic unities, was not Kant himself holding thought to the standards appropriate not to those domains but rather to statically self-identical *things*, the individual *substances* thought by the understanding? And does not that signify a reduction of reason to the understanding, two "faculties" which Kant insisted on separating?

Hegel's death in 1831 is often taken as marking the death of the continental idealist tradition as well. Hegel's own "school" of philosophy had effectively broken up within a decade after his death, and as Hegel had presented his own philosophy as the culmination of the idealist tradition, it is tempting to read the collapse of Hegelianism as effectively equivalent to that of the tradition itself. But perhaps we should not so easily accept this diagnosis. Confident assertions that idealism as a philosophy is "dead" are often made on the basis of crude misunderstandings, particularly of identifying idealism with Berkeley's spiritual realism, and it seems clear that ideas developed within the idealist tradition have gone on to have lives elsewhere. For example, even within the tradition of analytic philosophy that developed in explicit opposition to the "British idealism" of the late nineteenth century, ideas that look to belong to Kant's or Hegel's versions of idealism have once again made an appearance.[32] Moreover, given the generalised ignorance or misunderstanding of idealism for the past hundred years, it is not surprising that forms of philosophy regarded as different from or even antithetical to idealism might, on closer examination, be equally read as close approximations to it. In the final chapter I will look at the philosophies of Arthur Schopenhauer and Friedrich Nietzsche as exemplifying just this ambivalence.

10

SCHOPENHAUER, NIETZSCHE AND THE AMBIGUOUS END OF THE IDEALIST TRADITION

The son of a wealthy merchant in Danzig, Arthur Schopenhauer (1788–1860) studied medicine and then philosophy, first at the University of Göttingen, where he studied under Kant's critic G. E. Schulze ("Aenesidemus"), and then at the University of Berlin, where Schopenhauer encountered Fichte. From 1814 to 1818 he composed his main work, *The World as Will and Representation*, and after an aborted philosophical career in Berlin in 1820, and enabled by his inheritance, he pursued philosophy as a private scholar.

Schopenhauer described himself as deeply influenced by both Plato and Kant, as well as by ideas from Eastern religions, and his philosophy had features similar to those of the early romantics as well as elements of the thought of Fichte, Schelling and Hegel. Despite these influences, Schopenhauer was particularly hostile to the views of the post-Kantians, and he opposed to their *rationalism* a particularly *pessimistic* view of the world as godless and meaningless. Schopenhauer had remained largely unread and unknown until the 1850s when he started to receive attention. He became increasingly well known after his death in 1860, and, especially towards the end of the century, had come to influence a wide audience, especially literary and other artists, such as Wagner, Tolstoy and Proust.

Among Schopenhauer's earliest enthusiastic supporters was Friedrich Nietzsche (1844–1900) who, in 1872, at the age of twenty-eight, published his first major work *The Birth of Tragedy out of the Spirit of Music*. This work bore the stamp of the ideas of the composer Richard Wagner, with whom Nietzsche had become associated, partly through their mutual interest in Schopenhauer's philosophy. Somewhat like Schelling and other "early romantics" of the 1790s, Wagner had sought to effect a transformation in modern European culture by *aesthetic* means and saw his music dramas as playing a role in modern culture analogous to that of tragedy in the ancient-Greek world.

Nietzsche's book was thus infused with ideas about Greek mythology characteristic of the earlier romantics, but now refracted through Schopenhauer's "pessimistic" ideas about the irrationality of "the will". Rather than representing the early Greeks as paragons of a rational, freedom-loving form of paganism keyed into a love of beauty, Nietzsche stressed the essential role played by the dark, irrational aspect of Greek culture. He did this by arguing that the triumph of Greek culture was not the philosophical culture that flourished with Socrates and Plato, but the earlier art form of tragedy that had developed at the time of Pericles. Moreover, he argued that the art form of tragedy itself grew out of the practices of a religious cult associated with the god Dionysus. Nietzsche's work caused a storm among philologists and classical scholars, as it went against the existing rationalistic view of the Greeks that had been fostered by earlier idealist philosophers.

In his later work, especially after the end of his friendship with Wagner, Nietzsche became increasingly opposed to philosophy and romanticism. His late work, known for its "perspectivist" epistemology and apparently "irrationalist" conception of truth, is commonly thought of as initiating a decisive break with the idealist tradition, although some interpreters see Nietzsche's later views as actually coming closer to those of Hegel.

10.1 Schopenhauer's metaphysics of the will

Schopenhauer opens the first chapter of *The World as Will and Representation* with what looks like a classically *Kantian* claim: the world, he says, "is my representation", and this is

> a truth valid with reference to every living and knowing being, although man alone can bring it into reflective abstract consciousness ... [E]verything that exists for knowledge, and hence the whole of this world, is only object in relation to the subject, perception of the perceiver, in a word, representation.
>
> (WWR: vol. 1, §1)

But then, however, he *criticises* Kant for *neglecting* this principle. What Kant had neglected, it turns out, was that he had thought of representations we know in experience ("appearances") as *not* equivalent to "the world". Rather, Kant, he thinks, had identified "the world" with the unknowable realm of noumena or things in themselves with which he had *contrasted* representations. It would seem, then, that Schopenhauer's attempts to purge weak TI of its central problems run along lines that, despite his vocal opposition to them, have much in common with the approaches of the post-Kantian idealists, Fichte, Schelling and Hegel.

According to Schopenhauer, Berkeley had "rendered an immortal service to philosophy" with his idea that what we immediately perceive and naïvely accept as the world is really our own representations, but "the remainder of his doctrines cannot endure". What Schopenhauer alludes to here is Berkeley's spiritualistic recourse to the *mind of God* to explain the contents of the human mind, the inference that Hume had criticised in Berkeley.[1] Schopenhauer, as an atheist, was clearly not going to adopt *that* doctrine from Berkeley. Nevertheless, something *akin* to Berkeley's God as the ultimate reality beyond one's individual mind was going to play a role in Schopenhauer's variation of Kant, and this was to be what he called "the will".

Were it a matter of having to make an *inference* from our representations to something beyond them, then Schopenhauer might have been a type of global sceptic like his teacher at Göttingen, the Humean Schulze. However, Schopenhauer thought that we could know something other than our own representations, and that we did not have to *infer* its existence, we could know it *directly*. What we can know in this way he calls "the will", and we know it directly in the form in which it operates in ourselves; there we *feel* its operations. That is, we can directly "perceive" the will as it is operative in ourselves from the first-person point of view, and we do so when aware of our feelings and emotions (WWR: vol. 1, §21). Schopenhauer thus corrects the dualism he attributes to Kant by replacing Kant's distinction between sensible and intelligible worlds—the world of our representations and what exists in-itself—by a distinction between two ways of regarding the same metaphysical reality. The one world can first be regarded *as* representation, and next *as* will, a distinction that can equivalently be thought of as that between two stances one can adopt to the world, the stances of theoretical and practical reason, respectively.[2] And it is the latter that has epistemological priority: the world grasped as *will* is the underlying truth of representation.

As with Schiller and Schelling before him, Schopenhauer's epistemological thought has a naturalistic dimension, clearly related to his medical training; he came to think of human psychological phenomena as grounded in the dynamics of bodily processes and drives. What we directly encounter in ourselves as some internal drive—the psychological will—is actually an *instance* of something much more general that can be recognised in the world at large. But in his conception of the role of such organically based volitional processes in the natural world, he, in Platonist fashion, inverts the relation between the organic and non-organic, compared with traditionally "materialistic" or "naturalistic" accounts, as found, say, in Hobbes. While in such "naturalistic" interpretations willing is commonly "reduced" to simpler mechanisms of nature, Schopenhauer has a view more like that found in Leibniz's pananimism, or in Schelling's nature philosophy, treating the organic as primary. Instead of understanding willed actions as ultimately made up of the operations of "natural" forces, he understands natural forces—the force of gravity, for example—as ultimately manifesting a type of universal "willing" found paradigmatically in the organic world.

Ultimately, then, Schopenhauer's vision is not unlike Leibniz's original attempt to ground modern mechanically naturalistic accounts of the world on a metaphysical picture of it. But while for Leibniz the underlying reality was that of a totality of monads harmoniously linked by the intentions of a rational and beneficent God, in Schopenhauer, the metaphysical core is the ultimate expression of that theological voluntarist picture that Leibniz had opposed. Leibniz's rational God has now been replaced by the processes of a will shorn of any recognisably rational characteristics.

10.2 The task of transcending the will: morality and art

Despite being opposed to the rationalist metaphysics of Kant and the post-Kantians, as Schopenhauer perceived it, he nevertheless conceived of morality in ways *somewhat like* those of Kant. As mere instruments of the will's incessant and irrational striving, we could hardly avoid being the sorts of individuals who ruthlessly pursue their own desires and trample over others in the process. However, we can *also* grasp that as beings in the world of individuated things, each of us, *as the specifically embodied individual that he or she is*, is really just a "representation", and if we can do *this*, then we can *see through* the type of egocentric perspective that depends on our sense of our individuated selves as separate from others. From there, a type of empathetic feeling *with* others is possible: we learn to see that we are all sufferers together—we are co-sufferers in the world of will where, ultimately, everyone is a loser.

Somewhat like Plato and Kant, then, and much like a traditional religious ascetic, Schopenhauer wants to encourage a morality based on a *disidentifying* with the body that individuates each of us, and especially with that body's urges and desires – the urges and desires associated with those parts of the body that "correspond completely to the chief demands and desires by which the will manifest itself; they must be the visible expression of these desires. Teeth, gullet, and intestinal canal are objectified hunger; the genitals are objectified sexual impulse" (WWR: vol. 1, §20). The individual body is thus regarded as a type of trap from which one seeks to escape, and it is in reflecting on the fact that as individuated we are *only* as represented that we can transcend the egocentric will-determined perspective from which we *do* will.

As we have seen, Kant indirectly linked aesthetics and morality in virtue of the fact that, as he thought, our attraction to beauty was fundamentally *disinterested*, and Schopenhauer, drawing on Kant's approach to aesthetics, does the same. Schopenhauer thus separates the role of pleasure or feeling in aesthetic life from those resulting from the gratification of our desires, seen as manifesting something constitutive of our existence – the "will". Aesthetic contemplation must then be *will-less*. Also as in Kant, aesthetic pleasure cannot be connected with the *matter* being experienced; it must be connected with its *form*, with the most obvious result being a distinction between the beautiful and the *reizende*, the stimulating or charming. Where the pleasure taken in our experience of objects is related to the pleasure we would get from their satisfying our desires, the experience cannot be an aesthetic one.[3]

In book 3 of *The World as Will and Representation*, Schopenhauer characterises the aesthetic mode of contemplation according to *two aspects*—the nature of *subjectivity* involved and the nature of the *object* of such a mode of experience. In aesthetic contemplation, the subject has, subjectively, achieved the status of a "will-less subject of knowledge"; objectively, come to know the object of its experience "as Idea". Two forms of subjectivity can be distinguished by whether or not "the will" is involved. In our most basic form of consciousness we grasp the objects of the world on the basis of the *way those objects are relevant for our interests and desires* – that is, on grounds of their relevance to our experience of *will*. But in aesthetic experience, in contrast, we break out of this "endless stream of willing" and have our attention no longer directed to "the motives of willing" but to things, considered "free from their relation to the will. Thus it considers things without interest, without subjectivity, purely objectively" (WWR: vol. 1, §38). This is how the Dutch still-life painters, for example, considered the everyday and insignificant objects of their paintings, and these paintings conveyed this form of subjectivity as well (ibid.).

While the disinterested contemplation of beauty allows us to achieve this objective state, this is always only attained fleetingly. Beauty "almost always succeeds in snatching us, although only for a few moments, from subjectivity, from the thraldom of the will, and transferring us into the state of pure knowledge" (WWR: vol. 1, §38). For Schopenhauer, the experience of artistic and natural beauty replaces religion in a world where it no longer has any role to play. The quasi-religious significance of aesthetic experience for Schopenhauer is obvious where he talks about "the blessedness of will-less perception" (ibid.) and characterises aesthetic experience as taking us "into another world", a world outside of time and space – it is an experience within which we *in some sense*, step out of our individual bodily existence. But this can be understood in Kantian terms. The objective view here, is one which has, by detaching itself from the *particularity* of the will, become a *universal* view. In it "we are only that one eye of the world which looks out from all knowing creatures, but which in man alone can be wholly free from serving the will" (WWR: vol. 1, §38).

Given the doctrine of the ontological priority of the will, aesthetic contemplation is not just an aid to morality for Schopenhauer, but conveys metaphysical insight. In the aesthetic experience I can disengage my perception of the world from the determining effects of the will, and what is now perceived are the Platonic forms or "ideas" themselves. In line with the Platonist revival at the end of the eighteenth century, Schopenhauer's conception of the ideas was a heavily *Neoplatonist* one, involving no "separation" of the ideas into a transcendental realm. What the ideas are, in fact, are the various grades of the will's *own* objectification. They are, as it were, conceived as distinct levels of the emanation of "the One", now conceived as *the will*.

Schopenhauer now uses this idea to give an account of the various arts. In the Neoplatonist schema, matter is the lowest grade of the emanation of the One, and, correspondingly, for Schopenhauer, the lowest grade of the will's objectification is the force of gravity, and the art that manifests the force of gravity is architecture (WWR: vol. 1, §43). Thus the aesthetic pleasure taken in the appreciation of a building, say, has to do with the ways the opposing forces of rigidity and gravity (as two degrees of the objectivity of the will) are resolved in the eyes of the viewer. In the dynamic interplay of weight and support in the building, we become aware of the qualities of weightiness, massiveness, rigidity and so on. These are no longer empty concepts for us, as they might be if we were approaching the building simply from an engineering perspective, but they appear to our senses in the disinterested pleasure taken in the architectural form.

Schopenhauer now works through the various arts in terms of the ways they manifest the will in its various degrees of objectification. Eventually we come to arts which represent the will in the highest forms of manifestation in expressions of the human will. As Aristotle had claimed, theatre can be thought of as a mimesis of human action, but there is an even higher form of art which manifests the will in a way even beyond that represented in dramatic form. This is *music*, the direct copy of the will itself (WWR: vol. 1, §51). This was in keeping with the general valorisation of music over other art forms in the romantic period, its commonly having been seen as the "purest" or "highest" manifestation of the human creative instinct. But it would be in the work of one composer–dramatist in particular, Richard Wagner, that Schopenhauer's vision of the relation of music to the metaphysical core of the world as will would be most fully realised. And it would be, in turn, in the context of a reflection on the work of Wagner that Nietzsche would reinterpret Schopenhauer's ideas in Nietzsche's great early work, *The Birth of Tragedy out of the Spirit of Music*. Before examining that development, however, more needs to be said on the relationship of Schopenhauer's ideas to those extant within the classical period of post-Kantian idealism.

10.3 Schopenhauer and Fichte's transcendental idealism

After Göttingen, Schopenhauer for a time pursued philosophy at the University of Berlin, where one of his teachers was Fichte. While loudly proclaiming opposition to the views of any of the post-Kantian idealists, Schopenhauer's development of Kant's ideas shows many similarities to the idealism of Fichte. Just as Schopenhauer was to ground cognition in something *deeper*, in "the will", so too had Fichte grounded thinking in a conception of the subject's *striving* which was itself to be understood as a particular instantiation of an impersonal will, the "absolute I". But if Fichte's absolute will was a modern depersonalised analogue of the simultaneously rational and beneficent God of Christian Platonism, Schopenhauer's was that of the arbitrary, almost psychotically arational but all-powerful God glimpsed in the theology of some medieval voluntarists. And like the fate of those conceptions in the passage to early modernity, Schopenhauer's would itself be fit for translation into an increasingly secular and naturalistic world view in the second half of the nineteenth century. Naturalistic analogues of it would spring up in the later decades of the nineteenth as well as the early twentieth century, such as Freud's influential idea of the arational unconscious "primary process" at the heart of all purportedly rational cognitive actions. This quasi-naturalistic context would be that within which Nietzsche would engage with the idealist tradition in his own highly ambiguous way.

It is tempting to view Schopenhauer's conception of the will as a consequence of that very aspect of the thinking of Kant that had been diagnosed and criticised by his Jena critics. In Jena, Fichte had been the most faithful supporter of the revolutionary cause during the time when events in Paris were taking an increasingly bloody turn. In contrast, the increasing violence of the Revolution in the early 1790s had given other otherwise sympathetic observers such as Schiller a reason to step back and reflect on the causes of such a turn. For Schiller, of course, this was a central task of his *Aesthetic Education* where he diagnosed these political events as resulting from an imbalance between the formal and the sensuous drives, an imbalance which he attempted to counter by appealing to the mediating role of the aesthetic in life. A propensity for this imbalance demonstrated itself in Kant's own thought, and Schiller believed the same imbalance was present in the thought of his Jena colleague, Fichte. Hegel, a quarter of a century later, in his *Philosophy of Right*, was to repeat Schiller's diagnosis of, if not his solution to, the worrisome political consequences of the Fichtean will. Thus he saw expressed in the events of the revolutionary Terror of 1792–94 a particularly one-sided configuration of the will that he called the *negative* will. While Schiller had described this aspect of the will as one that strove to clear itself of all "content" that was "contingent", a will devoted to "obtaining Necessity in its pure state" (AE: letter 13, para. 3, note 2), Hegel represented it as the "absolute possibility of abstracting from every determination in which I find myself or which I have posited in myself, the flight from every content as a limitation" (EPR: §5, remark). While Schiller had warned of a conception of the will with which "one easily falls into thinking of material things as nothing but an obstacle", Hegel described the political consequences of unleashing such an unrestrained negative will with its resulting fanaticism of destruction, demolishing the whole existing social order, eliminating all individuals regarded as suspect by a given order, and annihilating any organization which attempts to rise up anew. Only in destroying something does this negative will have a feeling of its own existence.

(EPR: §5, remark)

For Schopenhauer, events like these simply testified to the underlying metaphysical nature of the will, a truth that could be seen in the world at large and in the impulses of one's own subjective consciousness. It was the vision of the "world as will" that was to grip the last and most ambiguous exponent of Continental idealism, Friedrich Nietzsche. Nietzsche's relation to the idealist tradition is ambiguous in the sense that over a century after his death, it is still not clear whether his philosophy marked its ultimate annihilation or gave it hope of renewal.

10.4 The early Nietzsche: Schopenhauer, Wagner and *The Birth of Tragedy*

Nietzsche's great early work, *The Birth of Tragedy out of the Spirit of Music*, emerged from a complex play of cultural and philosophical influences from the first half of the century, largely transmitted via his association with Richard Wagner, the musician and self-proclaimed philosopher, with whom Nietzsche shared an interest in the philosophy of Schopenhauer. Many elements from both earlier romanticism and Schillerian classicism, as well as from the Kantian core common to both, are identifiable in the fundamental ideas of this complex text. They appear, however, as if in a distorting mirror provided not only by Schopenhauer's philosophy but by developments within the philological sciences in which Nietzsche had trained.

After its early Jena-based post-Kantian phase, German romanticism had turned increasingly against the modern world, with its liberal forms of social life, and had looked nostalgically towards the Middle Ages as a period of organic solidarity. Many romantic philosophers became increasingly socially and politically conservative, turning to religion, and especially, like Friedrich Schlegel, to Catholicism.[4] However, in the 1830s and 1840s a new generation of romantic thinkers started to emerge who were critical of the conservative Christian turn and who tended to align themselves with the earlier more pantheist and pagan forms of romanticism from the 1790s. Among these was the composer Richard Wagner, who appealed to a new form of mythology to play the sort of revolutionary role called for in works like "The Oldest System Programme". In his case, the vehicle was to be his own music drama built around the Nordic "Nibelungen" myths, interest in which had been promoted by August Wilhelm Schlegel in the early part of the century, and which had fed nationalist sentiment during the wars against the French (Williamson 2004: 86–87).[5] Actively engaged in politics, Wagner became involved in the insurrection at Dresden in 1849, where he came to be influenced by Ludwig Feuerbach, a leading member of the "left Hegelian" school who, after Hegel's death, advocated an anthropologised version of Hegel's philosophy, with the idea of God taken to be simply a projection of the human essence.[6]

Wagner's left-Hegelian humanism was reflected in the libretto to his *Ring* cycle, started not long after the revolutionary events at Dresden (B. Magee 2001: 56), but his disparate synthesis of early romantic and idealist ideas with socialist politics came to take a turn in 1854, when he read Schopenhauer's *The World as Will and Representation* (ibid.: 133–34). Wagner now came to interpret myth in less political terms and more as a dreamlike, mystical state of representation, and gradually he turned away from his Feuerbachian humanism to promote the idea of a Schopenhauerian pessimistic revelation in Christianity which he saw as somehow derived from Indian rather than Jewish sources. This increasingly conservative and Christian colouring of his thought came to be realised in later operas such as *Parsifal*.[7] However, at the time of his first acquaintance with Wagner in 1869, Nietzsche could regard *The Ring* cycle on which Wagner laboured in a strongly *pagan* light, and as the modern analogue of ancient tragedy.

In *The Birth of Tragedy*, Nietzsche's portrayal of the achievements of ancient drama strongly recalls Schiller's analysis of artworks in *On the Aesthetic Education of Man*.[8] Echoing Schiller's idea of the aesthetic reconciliation of the antithetical formal and sensuous drives, Nietzsche proposed the existence of two antithetical drives in the Greek world, represented by the deities of Apollo and Dionysus, the deities that Wagner had recognised in his essay *Art and Revolution* in 1849 as at the heart of Greek tragedy (AWF: 32–33). But in the details of the drives involved, Nietzsche appealed to an underlying Schopenhauerian metaphysics of the will in a way that gave his account a very different feel to the earlier Hellenism of idealists like Schiller and Hölderlin. This was reinforced by the work of the earlier romantic philologist Friedrich Creuzer, upon which Nietzsche drew (Williamson 2004: 239–40).

Creuzer, who had combined the new approach to philology forged at Göttingen by Heyne and his school with the romantic approach to myth from Schelling and Friedrich Schlegel, had published his *Symbolism and Mythology of the Ancient Peoples* from 1810, while occupying the chair of philology at Heidelberg.[9] While regarding the gods as imagistic presentations giving "ideas" concrete, sensuous form, he gave the notion of a symbol a very irrationalist twist, with the claim that its meaning could never be defined conceptually, but only known through *feeling*.[10] In his philological researches, he claimed to have traced the Greek god Dionysus back through Egyptian to Indian mythology (Williamson 2004: 133). Dionysus, he claimed, was a symbol of the disintegration of living unities within the natural cycles of life and death, and hence of a restoration of the unity of nature, itself. This principle of de-individuation opposed the unifying and integrating processes symbolised in the Greek pantheon by Apollo. The *Neoplatonic* feel of this process was far from coincidental. In it nature as a unity was dispersed into a plurality of living individuals which, in turn, in their disintegration returned to the primordial unity. Creuzer was, with his 1805 translation of *Enneads* III, 8, "On Nature and on Contemplation and the One", the first to translate Plotinus into German (Vielliard-Baron 1988: 213–20). This Plotinian text interpreting the processes of nature according to the idea of *Nous,* or intelligence, was central for the development of idealist philosophies of nature (ibid.: 215–16).

According to Creuzer, the story of the sufferings of Dionysus formed part of Greek initiation mysteries used to achieve states of mystical unity with the world (Williamson 2004: 133). The comparison of the suffering and redeeming Dionysus with the stories of the Christian redeeming God, Jesus, became obvious, and the later teachings of Christianity were interpreted as resulting from a transformation of these more ancient myths. In short, Creuzer had reconstructed a type of religion in which the benefits that Hegel had come to see in the Christian idea of the incarnation of God might be delivered by a different means in the figure of Dionysus, and this alternative type of religion gave expression to a very different form of existence than the Christian one—certainly very different from Christianity in its Augustinian form. That is, the Dionysian rituals were closer to the overtly sexualised and violent celebrations of the life cycle from which they had derived, but these impulses came to be repressed in later Christian and European culture. All these ideas came together in *The Birth of Tragedy* mixed in with a Schopenhauerian metaphysics of "the will", but while Schopenhauer had found the idea of "the world as will" abhorrent, Nietzsche found in the Dionysian impulse something affirmative and attractive, at least as presented through the medium of art.[11]

At one level *The Birth of Tragedy* works as a type of analogue of Schiller's assessment of the conditions of cultural health: a culture is most healthy when the Apollonian/formal drive and the Dionysian/sensuous drive reciprocally limit each other in virtue of being combined in that culture's highest aesthetic products. The state of health declines when the Apollonian/formal drive gains the upper hand. But from Nietzsche's perspective earlier Hellenophiles, such as Schiller and Hölderlin, had naïvely accepted the "rational" and "harmonious" appearance of Greek life at face value, and had been too accepting of Socratic *rationalism*. Against this trend, Nietzsche saw his task as one of unearthing what lay at the basis of this appearance, his method being "to level the artistic structure of the *Apollonian culture*, as it were, stone by stone, till the foundations on which it rests become visible" (BT: §3). To be found in ancient folk wisdom was, he claimed, a pessimistic view of the world very different from the "Greek cheerfulness" of the Homeric stories of the Olympian world: underneath their apparent cheerfulness and life-affirming outlook the Greeks "knew and felt the terror and horror of existence"—that is, the terror that accompanied a grasp of the world as the irrational, Schopenhauerian *will*.[12] It was only by being integrated with Apollonian representation in art that this terror and horror of existence could be transformed into the *optimistic* and *affirmative* view of life naïvely ascribed to the Greeks. But after the high point of the age of tragedy, Greek life suffered the inverse fate, as Apollonian culture triumphed over its Dionysian rival with the rise of philosophy and Socratic rationality. The inheritance of this upheaval, with its various transformations—Christianity and the later rationalist culture of enlightenment—was the actual cause of the malady diagnosed by Jacobi as "nihilism".

With Nietzsche, then, Schiller's concerns about the formalistic rationalism of Kant and Fichte of the formal repressing the sensuous drive became generalised and deepened, and directed at the whole philosophical tradition consequent upon the "Socratism" that had developed in the ancient polis *against* the tradition of tragedy. In this sense, Nietzsche took the side of earlier romantic idealists like Schelling and Schlegel in the affirmation of an aesthetic-mythological culture against a philosophical and reflective one, but in a way that deepened its anti-rationalist dimensions.

It is clear that elements of Nietzsche's philosophy changed over the two decades following *The Birth of Tragedy*. First, he became increasingly critical of the Schopenhauerian dimensions of his early work, but also increasingly antagonistic to Wagner and his aesthetic-philosophical perspective, intent on distinguishing genuinely "Dionysian" art from the sickly "romanticism" to which he now condemned Wagner.[13] The nature of his later outlook and the ways it differed from the earlier one are highly controversial, like the interpretation and assessment of Nietzsche's views generally are. One philosophical dimension of his stance, however, because of the continuity of its theme with earlier idealism, might allow us to assess something of Nietzsche's relation to the earlier tradition: this theme encompasses his so-called "perspectivist" diagnosis and response to the problem of modern nihilism, in the project that he called "genealogy", and his most puzzling doctrine of "the eternal recurrence".

10.5 The later Nietzsche: life after the deaths of tragedy and God

In *The Birth of Tragedy* Nietzsche attributed the decline of tragedy (and Greek culture in general) to the effects of the tragedian whom Aristotle had thought of as the art's greatest exponent—Euripides (BT: §§11–12). With Euripides the tragedy becomes comprehensible in secular, psychologically realistic terms, and the character on stage was now intuitively grasped by the audience as one of them rather than as a personification (Dionysus) of the Schopenhauerian will. With this Euripides introduced "aesthetic Socratism" into tragedy, the rationalist requirement that "to be beautiful everything must be intelligible" (ibid.: §12). This negative approach to the aspirations of any post-Socratic philosophy would be a strong characteristic of all of Nietzsche's subsequent demythologising thought.

In an essay written shortly after *The Birth of Tragedy* entitled "On the Usages and Disadvantages of History for Life" (1874), Nietzsche attacked the rationalism of contemporary *historical* culture in similar terms. At its heart is a critique of the ideal of *reflective, aperspectival* knowledge of the world, the position that, as Schelling had argued, is built on an unbridgeable separation between knower and world, and that thereby paralyses action. The essay starts with an image of the animal-like absorption into the present moment of the child at play, but the child will be cast out of this paradise when it learns the meaning of "it was". This is a phrase that reminds the human being "what his existence fundamentally is – an imperfect tense that can never become a perfect one" and that "being is only an uninterrupted has-been, a thing that lives by negating, consuming and contradicting itself" (UDH: 61).

Nietzsche presents his contemporary historical culture not as an acknowledgment of this Dionysian temporality of historical existence but as its *denial*. The objectivity that the modern historian seeks, "that aesthetic phenomenon of detachment from personal interest" (UDH: 91), is conceived as a type of view from nowhere or no-when that aspires to the blessedness of the child's atemporal play.[14] But this yearning for this detachment from embeddedness in the world just is what Nietzsche in his later works would diagnose as a symptom of weakness and decadence or, in Jacobi's terms, nihilism—a state seen in Plato and Schopenhauer, and characterising particular religions like Buddhism and Christianity.

The child's punctate presence in the moment and the idea of a comprehensive aperspectival view of history from the viewpoint of eternity are pictured as the opposing lost and unattainable ends, respectively, of a continuum on which individuals are located. Individuals live *within* the flow of time, but, having learnt the "it was", we can no longer live within this flow in the mode of other animals, as we have retained our lived past via the representations of memory. But how much of the past *can* or *should be* retained? A person with too much memory, and an incapacity to forget, would surely be paralysed by this overload, so there must be a way of *drawing a border or horizon* around what is retained. But such horizons themselves can be narrower or wider, and so human life forms will differ according to whether the borders of historical sense are narrow, like those of the parochial "dweller in the Alps", or wide like those of the liberal whose historical sense is "more just and instructed" (UDH: 63). The latter represents an Enlightenment goal, but while the alpine dweller may live in "superlative health and vigour" the enlightened liberal may be one who "sickens and collapses because the lines of his horizon are always restlessly changing, because he can no longer extricate himself from the delicate net of his judiciousness and truth for a simple act of will and desire" (ibid.). An exemplary instance of the link between the narrowness of a horizon and the capacity for action is provided by someone passionate whose horizon will be intensely focused on the object of that passion:

> It is the condition in which one is the least capable of being just; narrow-minded, ungrateful to the past, blind to dangers, deaf to warnings, one is a little vortex of life in a dead sea of darkness and oblivion: and yet this condition – unhistorical, anti-historical through and through – is the womb not only of the unjust but of every just deed too; and no painter will paint his picture, no general achieve his victory, no people attain its freedom without having first desired and striven for it in an unhistorical condition such as that described.
>
> (Ibid.: 64)

Nietzsche's reflections were occasioned by what he perceived as the hypertrophy of a type of historical culture in Germany that had turned history into a "science". Quoting Goethe, "I hate everything that merely instructs me without augmenting or directly invigorating my activity" (UDH: 59), Nietzsche's criticism of contemporary historical learning is thus an analogue in the case of *historical* knowledge of Schelling's earlier criticisms of the objective, reflective point of view which simply *opposes* the knower to the known. Like Schelling, Nietzsche recognises the problems this creates for an agent for whom history is meant to serve life and who has to act *in the now*. The problem being diagnosed, then, is the now familiar one of the nihilistic consequences of a "Copernican" reflective consciousness, but specific to the medium of time.

Nietzsche's idea of knowing from *within* an historically changing horizon recalls Kant's idea of the finite conditions of experience and knowledge, but now deprived of any objectivity that could be derived from their universality, and it prefigures his later "perspectivist" approach to epistemology, expressed in pithy claims along the lines that "facts is precisely what there is not, only interpretations".[15] Briefly, the idea is that rather than knowledge ever being a matter of a correspondence to the world "as it is in itself", all human forms of apprehending the world are made from some particular perspective ultimately rooted in some values or interests. "The apparent world, i.e., a world viewed according to values; ordered, selected according to values, i.e., in this case according to the viewpoint of utility in regard to the preservation and enhancement of the power of a certain species of animal" (WP: §567 [March–June 1888]). The diagnosis of the degree to

167

which such power, or "will to power", is being enhanced or diminished with any such perspective will be the task of the method of "genealogy", a technique seen at work in the essay, *On the Genealogy of Morals*. But one might even see *this* idea as having had a type of historical precedent in the idealist tradition, in view of Fichte's famously declaring in the first introduction to the *Wissenschaftslehre* of 1797, that "[w]hat sort of philosophy one chooses (between idealism and realism) depends … on what sort of man one is. … A person indolent by nature or dulled and distorted by mental servitude, learned luxury, and vanity will never raise himself to the level of idealism" (FISK: 16).

Even in the early history essay, however, Nietzsche was aware of the traps of any naïve perspectivism which simply rejected *any* conception of the transcendence of one's finite horizon as meaningless, as he there alludes to the idea of a "most powerful and tremendous nature" which:

> would be characterized by the fact that it would know no boundary at all at which the historical sense began to overwhelm it; it would draw to itself and incorporate into itself all the past, its own and that most foreign to it, and as it were transform it into blood.
>
> (UDH: 63)

For a self-conscious perspectivism, this "most powerful and tremendous nature" looks like a Kantian "ideal", and we might expect to find it represented symbolically in the form of a "god" or God. Indeed, *something along* these lines seems to unfold in Nietzsche's later period, with his conception of the "Übermensch".

After his break with Wagner, Nietzsche had become increasingly hostile to the romantic and idealistic elements of *The Birth of Tragedy*, and turned to a type of naturalistic orientation that is usually said to mark the work of his "middle period", an orientation that had more in common with English and French materialism than German idealism.[16] Thus in works like *Daybreak* and *The Gay Science*, he adopts a decisively psychological and somewhat evolutionary approach to human phenomena, proclaiming such a scientific psychology as the means for ridding society of religious myth.[17] These works then seem to signal a radical and somewhat "materialist" departure from the idealist tradition, akin, say, to the departure that might be traced from Hegel, through Feuerbach, to Marx and Engels. The rationalistic side of idealism, culminating in Hegel, is now seen as *another version* of a God-centred view of the world which is not even to be argued with but exposed or unmasked as part of an illusory realm of *Vorstellungen* or, as in the Marxist tradition, "ideology", masking a quite different underlying order—that of the "will to power", an idea with clear connections to Schopenhauer's "will". But *philosophy* cannot do this, as it is itself expressive of a declining form of life:

These wisest men of all ages—they should first be scrutinized closely. Were they all perhaps shaky on their legs? late? tottery? decadents? ... This irreverent thought that the great sages are *types of decline* first occurred to me precisely in a case where it is most strongly opposed by both scholarly and unscholarly prejudice: I recognized Socrates and Plato to be symptoms of degeneration, tools of the Greek dissolution, pseudo-Greek, anti-Greek (*Birth of Tragedy*, 1872).

(TI: 473–74)

Congruent with the "naturalistic" turn of the middle period, it is tempting to think that genealogy can be no *philosophy*, but must rather be something like *science*, and that Nietzsche's break with idealism is final.

And yet, he still signals a difference in approach between *his* genealogy and what might be thought of as one carried out in a modern naturalistic spirit, the approach of the "English" genealogists.[18] Moreover, despite the anti-romantic, anti-idealist tone of the middle period, his most well-known later work, *Thus Spoke Zarathustra*, has many of the marks of the type of early-romantic thought which was central to the emergence of post-Kantian idealism. Thus it takes the form of an *artwork*—a fiction about Zarathustra's attempt to create a new religion, the central teaching of which is presented in the form of *myth*. Moreover, the myth addresses one of the key topics of the idealist tradition since its Leibnizian inception, our representation of time and the question of the possibility of time's transcendence: the myth of the "eternal recurrence". And while it is often discussed as if Nietzsche is here interested in a *cosmological thesis*, an interpretation that would be at home with a naturalistic construal of his later thought, it is equally open to one that puts it more squarely within the idealist camp.[19]

In a section entitled "On the Vision and the Riddle", we are shown Nietzsche's fictionalised creation, the character of Zarathustra, making his way up a mountain, impeded by the "spirit of gravity", a creature half dwarf–half mole sitting on his shoulders and whispering discouraging comments in his ear. The "gravity" that the spirit represents is one that tugs equally on Zarathustra's mind as on his body, and the dwarf's comments pertain to Zarathustra's ultimately earth-bound nature that affects him even in his capacity as a thinker. Zarathustra is a "stone of wisdom" who hurls himself high, presumably attempting to achieve a Platonic view from "nowhere" and "no-when", a perspective from which he can grasp *what* is *as it is* "in itself", but gravity—signifying the embeddedness of the mind in the material world—will ensure that this attempt will ultimately fail. Zarathustra finally tries to rid himself of this burden by challenging it with his "most abysmal thought"—the thought of the eternal recurrence.

Zarathustra and his dwarf have reached a gateway labelled "Moment". Pointing it out, Zarathustra says,

Behold this gateway, dwarf! ... It has two aspects. Two paths come together here: no one has ever reached their end.

This long lane behind us: it goes on for an eternity. And that long lane ahead of us – that is another eternity.

They contradict one another [widersprechen sich], these paths; they abut on one another: and it is here at this gateway that they come together. ...

But if one were to follow them further and ever further and further: do you think, dwarf, that these paths would be in eternal contradiction?

(TSZ: 178)

At its most obvious level, the question is about the "shape" of time: either time is linear and the paths are eternally opposed, or it is circular, and they somehow eventually meet. As mentioned earlier, some have taken this as a quasi-scientific cosmological thesis in line with Nietzsche's "naturalistic" middle-period persona, but as Alexander Nehamas has pointed out, it is hard to see how construed as such this thought could have the psychological effects on the thinker that this "abysmal thought" is supposed to have (Nehamas 1985: ch. 5). Clearly the "circular" conception of time is connected with the outlook of ancient religions with their Dionysian celebrations of the cycles of life–death–rebirth, and as such contrasts with Christianity's view of cosmological time as stretching linearly between creation and the "last things", but it would be overly hasty to regard this as involving the choice between some kind of "atavistic" pagan outlook and the modern Christian one.[20] But if it is neither of these, then what?

In a later part of the narrative, Zarathustra's animal companions recite to him *what they take to be* Zarathustra's doctrine:

Everything goes, everything returns; the wheel of existence rolls for ever. Everything dies, everything blossoms anew; the year of existence runs on for ever.

Everything breaks, everything is joined anew; the same house of existence builds itself for ever. Everything departs, everything meets again; the ring of existence is true to itself for ever.

Existence begins in every instant; the ball There rolls around every Here. The centre is everywhere. The path of eternity is crooked.

(TSZ: 234)

What is portrayed here, according to Nehamas, is "nothing more than the Dionysian view of nature" and, as he points out, it is significant that it is expressed *not* by Zarathustra himself, but by *animals*, whom he accuses of "turning his thought into 'a hurdy-gurdy song'" (Nehamas 1985: 147).[21] But we should also take note of the words "the centre is everywhere [die Mitte ist überall]", the oft-repeated phrase within the tradition of Christian Neoplatonism, found in Meister Eckhart as applied to God, and extended to a theory of space by Nicholas of Cusa, where it was also meant to capture the perspectival nature of knowledge to be exploited later by Leibniz and the idealists following in his wake. Nietzsche was clearly familiar with Eckhart; for example, he quotes Eckhart's infamous "I ask God to rid me of God" in *The Gay Science* (GS: §292). It would be highly improbable that Nietzsche wasn't familiar with the metaphor of the sphere whose centre is everywhere.[22]

Nehamas links this "Dionysian" view of nature to Leibniz and Kant (Nehamas 1985: 75), and notes that Nietzsche himself had associated the view in his early work with Schopenhauer. Indeed, as we have seen, the idea of the "interconnectedness" or "knottedness together" of all things that Leibniz seems to have taken from Bisterfeld's idea of "immeation" goes back to the Neoplatonists, and the idea became popular in the "naturephilosophical" dimensions of the idealism of Hegel and the early Schelling, where it was seen in distinctly *Kantian* terms.[23] It could be said that the difference of the Neoplatonist from the "Dionysian" versions of this image was similar to that alluded to by Plotinus himself in "Nature and Contemplation and the One",[24] where he distinguishes *his* account of "the earth and of the trees and the vegetation in general" from that of the Stoics. While they claimed this nature "to be devoid of reason and even of conscious representation" Plotinus insists that such productive nature can either "harbour" or "produce by means of" contemplation (*theoria*) (Enn: Ennead III, treatise 8, ch. 1). There is a parallel between the productivity of nature and that of handicraft:

> in the case of workers in such arts there must be something locked up within themselves, an efficacy not going out from them and yet guiding their hands in all their creation; and this observation should have indicated a similar phenomenon in Nature; it should be clear that this indwelling efficacy, which makes without hands, must exist in Nature, no less than in the craftsman.
> (Ibid.: Ennead III, treatise 8, ch. 2)

Or, as he also puts it "every life is some form of thought, but of a dwindling clearness like the degrees of life itself" (ibid.: Ennead III, treatise 8, ch. 8).[25] It was this apparently "idealist" aspect of Plotinus that led post-Kantians in the 1790s to read him as a type of "proto-post-Kantian"!

Is it not possible to read Nietzsche's discussion of the "Dionysian" conception of time put forward in the myth of the eternal recurrence in this light, rather than as either an atavistic celebration of Dionysianism itself, or as some quasi-naturalistic cosmological thesis? Having reached the gateway

"Moment", Zarathustra, as we have seen, poses the question to the dwarf of the relation of the two paths, that leading to the future and that leading from the past: if one were to follow them ever further and further, would they be in "eternal contradiction"? The dwarf replies "disdainfully" in the affirmative: "Everything straight lies ... All truth is crooked; time itself is a circle", to which Zarathustra responds "angrily", telling him, the spirit of gravity, not to treat this "too lightly" (TSZ: 178).

The contemptuous tone of dwarf's reply to Zarathustra is consistent with the dwarf's earlier discouraging comments. Zarathustra is a "stone of wisdom" that throws himself high, "but every stone that is thrown – must fall!" (TSZ: 177) This *sceptical* knowledge is expressed by the "spirit of gravity", we might say, *in the spirit of gravity*. That is, it is a thought that is meant to *impede* Zarathustra and weigh him down—to prevent his thought from escaping the earth's gravitational pull. Here the doctrine clearly expresses an enervatingly negative "will to power" and is meant to undermine Zarathustra's striving. The message is that if time *is* circular and *there is* no extra-temporal place from which to know the world *sub specie aeternitatis*, then the very telos of the wisdom that Zarathustra seeks cannot be even coherently conceived. But for *this* answer Zarathustra has only scorn, and *he* then goes on to expressing his abysmal thought thus:

> Behold this moment! ... From this gateway, Moment, a long eternal lane runs *back*: an eternity lies behind us.
>
> Must not all things that *can* run have already run along this lane? Must not all things that *can* happen have already happened, been done, run past?
>
> And if all things have been there before: what do you think of this moment, dwarf? Must not this gateway, too, have been here – before?
>
> And are not all things bound fast together in such a way that this moment draws after it all future things? *Therefore* – draws itself too?
>
> For all things that *can* run *must* also run once again forward along this long lane.
>
> And this slow spider that creeps along in the moonlight, and this moonlight itself, and I and you at this gateway, whispering together, whispering of eternal things – must we not all have been here before?
>
> – and must we not return and run down that other lane out before us, down that long, terrible lane – must we not return eternally?
>
> (TSZ: 178–79)

In terms of their *content*, the idea of the circularity of time, the versions of the thought given by Zarathustra, his animal companions and the dwarf all seem much the same—they all *affirm it*. But Zarathustra is seeking a life-

enhancing form of representation of the "circularity" thesis. The significant difference must have to do more with the way the doctrine is expressed, and there *is* a difference here. The dwarf's contemptuous expression, as well as the joyful one of the companions, is about a universal—"time"—while Zarathustra's is about something singular, *this* moment; and this contrast is further emphasised by the string of indexical terms in the final few sentences of Zarathustra's account: the demonstratives, "this slow spider", "this moonlight itself" and the first- and second-person pronouns "I", "we", "you". That is, the dwarf and the animals presumed to utter the thought *as* a type of eternal thought, and to utter it from the "transcendental" or "reflective" position, despite the fact that the content of the thought *undermines this position*. In contrast, Zarathustra explicitly speaks from *his* present, the moment of his "now", affirming that *it* will eternally recur. The thought must be expressed in explicit relation to the "I" that thinks it, some analogue of Kant's transcendental unity of apperception, but one that does not annul its identity with the actual individual thinking it.

We should recall the relation posited by Kant between the transcendental I and the idea of God, and surely some analogue of this relation is what Nietzsche is appealing to here. Moreover, his attempts to bridge the universality of the transcendental I and the singularity of any individual I surely recall the attempts of the post-Kantian idealists to mediate this relation. Kant's "I" is universal inasmuch as the thought that it accompanies is *free* of indexicality; Zarathustra's, in contrast, is meant to draw attention to the role of the "I" as the *centre* of all indexical terms, such as "here" and "now". It is meant to affirm the perspectival nature of any thought uttered, and affirm it, as it were, *as* a perspectival claim. Read in this way, the endeavour of Zarathustra–Nietzsche looks like one more attempt after Kant to reconcile the separation of the finite and conditioned human perspective and the reflective God's-eye view of the Copernican turn.

For the later Nietzsche, the conception of the Übermensch is the one of a being who can live on the basis of such an understanding of time, and Nietzsche is explicit about the fact that such a being would have "divine" powers. For example, to live with such a conception of time would imply that one could "will the past", as the circularity of time annuls the distinction between the fixity of the past and the affectability of the future. To live according to the norms of such a god would be to aspire to live free of resentment against one's conditionedness by the past, to be free of what Nietzsche refers to as "revenge against the past". Whatever cards you were dealt, you would have it that it had not been otherwise; you would affirm it as just what you *would have* willed, had you been the dealer. And seen in *this light*, Zarathustra's teaching appears as akin to that of Leibniz's *Theodicy*. Leibniz had meant his philosophy to affirm that the world as created by the Christian God is the best of all possible worlds. Zarathustra's theodicy of the eternal return is meant as a thought which, in the mind of an individual thinker, would affirm that his or her life was, for them, the best of all possible lives.

POSTSCRIPT: IDEALISM AFTER THE END OF (ITS) HISTORY

In most accounts of the history of modern philosophy, idealism is portrayed as having expired at the end of the nineteenth century, a victim of an increasing secularisation of high culture and the unrelenting valorisation of the empirical sciences as models of rationally acquired knowledge. In professionalised philosophy in the Anglophone world, for example, this eclipse of idealism would seem to have been finally secured by the triumph of the "analytic philosophy" of Russell and Moore over the "British idealism" that briefly bloomed in the last decades of the nineteenth century. In a very different context, and in a very different way, idealism is taken as having been replaced by another approach claiming the legitimacy of science, the historical materialism of Marx and Engels. And yet as with the case of Nietzsche's assault on idealism we might ask whether these various critics had the right beast in their sights when they pulled the trigger.

Consider Marx's claim, for example, to have stood Hegel's idealistic account of history on its head, inverting it into its materialistic opposite. "My dialectic method", Marx had claimed in 1873,

> is not only different from the Hegelian, but is its direct opposite [or contrary, "Gegenteil"]. To Hegel, the life-process of the human brain, i.e., the process of thinking, which, under the name of "the Idea", he even transforms into an independent subject, is the demiurgos of the real world, and the real world is only the external, phenomenal form of "the Idea". With me, on the contrary, the ideal is nothing else than the material world reflected by the human mind, and translated into forms of thought ... With him it is standing on its head. It must be turned right side up again.[1]

In short, for Marx the "mystical" perspective of Hegel had to be replaced by a secular, scientific one. But again, does not this materialist criticism, by construing idealism as its opposite, conflate it with an "immaterialism" or "spiritual realism"? Understood as an expression of strong TI, however, Hegel's approach to history should not be interpreted in terms of any causal efficacy of mental items or ideas. Rather, it amounts more to the claim that any characteristic "form" or pattern discernible in history is not to be considered "realistically" but rather *idealistically*. This of course bears on the significance of just that feature of Hegel's approach to history that has been a constant object of criticism in the twentieth century—its teleology. But might not even the "teleology" of Hegel's distinctly philosophical version of history appear in a different light when its idealist infrastructure is correctly understood?

Ontological versus benign teleology

In the case of the analytic philosophy to emerge after the collapse of British idealism, it could be plausibly argued that *naturalism* was the form of philosophical self-conception to become dominant eventually. Nevertheless, even there "naturalism" has never been without its critics,[2] and many such critics have appealed to conceptions of philosophy which have something in common with what I have called strong TI. Moreover, within these disputes can be seen the return of philosophical conceptions which, with their stress on irreducibly normative considerations and the theme of the intersubjective grounding of reason have given contemporary forms to an idealism of a distinctly Hegelian hue.[3] Within conceptions of this kind considerations of teleology have been reintroduced, as can be seen in a controversy between two leading twentieth-century analytic philosophers, Hilary Putnam and Bernard Williams.

Hilary Putnam is known for his broadly Kantian criticisms of the role of the notion of a "God's-eye view" within the approach he criticised as "metaphysical realism". Putnam's targets here have included Bernard Williams's conception of an "absolute conception of the world" towards which, Williams had claimed, scientific knowledge converges (Putnam 1992: ch. 5). Williams's idea had originally been invoked in order to contrastively characterise the type of truth and justification of which ethical claims are capable.[4] Evaluative judgments, he had it, could be thought to be *true* and capable of a degree of argumentative justification in the way other "perspectival" judgments could be so considered. Nevertheless, he claimed, they could not be considered to be "objectively" true, where this equated to the idea of independence from *all* perspective. They were thus denied the type of convergence on the "absolute viewpoint" that was presupposed in the natural sciences, and so could not be conceived as being about the way the world is "anyway"!

Williams's own distinction might be seen as effectively amounting to a combination of an "idealist" approach to evaluative judgments (they could be true from a certain shareable point of view) and a "realist" approach to natural science, which aims at accounting for how the world is "anyway", independently of all points of view. But how is one to understand *philosophy itself* on such a view? Putnam interpreted Williams as regarding the absolute conception as the goal of *philosophical* inquiry, but, in response, Williams has denied that this was ever his intention (B. Williams 2000). According to Williams, the claims of philosophy are themselves to be understood as ineradicably perspectival ones for the same reasons as those invoked by Putnam: philosophy must account for *normative phenomena* within the world such as the nature of semantic relations. Philosophy thus belongs to the realm of discourse more like that of our evaluative judgments than like that of our natural scientific ones.[5] Moreover, this is not simply a problem about physics *per se: no* science conceived in the natural explanatory mode, it would seem, could be adequate. While evolutionary explanations might, for example, seem better candidates in accounting for our linguistic practices, natural selection does not explain human cultural practices *per se,* "but rather the universal human characteristic of having cultural practices, and human beings' capacity to do so". Regardless of the identity of the science in question, if the normativity of semantic relations prevents them from being part of the "absolute conception of the world", this only brings out the fact that achieving such a view

> would not be particularly serviceable to us for many of our purposes, such as making sense of our intellectual and other activities. For those purposes—in particular, in seeking to understand ourselves—we need concepts and explanations which are rooted in our more local practices, our culture, and our history.
>
> (Ibid.: 484)

For Williams, then, philosophy should *not* aspire to an account of the way the world is "anyway" or, we might say, the way it is "in itself". Rather, it attempts to describe relations that hold within the world from the perspective of our normative practices, and this we might describe as in line with strong TI. But we might regard his claim that our philosophical concepts and explanations are necessarily "rooted in our more local practices, our culture, and our history" as manifesting the particularly *Hegelian* side of his thought. Like Hegel, then, Williams invokes the necessarily *historical* dimension of philosophical reflection: such a philosophical "memory", internal to the practice of philosophy itself, must address the relation between our present normative orientations and commitments (such as a commitment to science or certain liberal political values, for example) and the earlier configurations from which they arose and which they replaced. Here historical reflection cannot aspire to the type of "objectivity" that is the goal even of the empirical *Geisteswissenschaften,* as this is the type of historical narration that would lead to relativistic nihilism. Rather, such histories need to be recounted from the normative commitments *of the present point of view* from which our present commitments will be regarded as more rational than those they replaced: it will in some sense, therefore,

177

be Whiggish or, as Williams says, "vindicatory", lest "the history of our outlook ... interfere with our commitment to it, and in particular with a philosophical attempt to work within it and develop its arguments" (B. Williams 2000: 489). Williams notes that the type of "wide-screen versions" of stories about the "unfolding of reason" or the "fuller realization of freedom and autonomy" as told by Hegel and Marx are not at all popular within contemporary philosophy, but "we *must* attend to it, if we are to know what reflective attitude to take to our own conceptions" (ibid.: 488).[6]

From such a Whiggish perspective, philosophical history can only be understood as leading up to the present, as what is being *accounted for* is just the ensemble of fallible and rationally correctable criteria which inform those judgments that we presently conceive of as rational, the very criteria that allow us to conceive of ourselves as rational judges. This, as I have suggested, is close to the conception of "absolute knowing" found at the conclusion of Hegel's *Phenomenology of Spirit*, a conception that *cannot* be equated with notions like the aperspectival "God's-eye" or "absolute" point of view discussed within contemporary analytic philosophy. The unity of absolute knowing must be one that is grasped "henologically" rather than "ontologically", or "idealistically" rather than "realistically". In Hegel's terms, the "infinity" found here must be one that *includes* rather than excludes the finitude of temporal perspective—the view from "now", an idea repeated in Nietzsche–Zarathustra's notion of the eternal recurrence.[7] Of course Hegel's teleological story of modernity as the fulfilment of a form of rational humanity that starts with the Greeks is not Nietzsche's conception of history from the Greeks to the present, as they each identify with different sets of values within this tradition. But what I take them to have in common is an idealistic understanding of the form of their respective histories that can be traced back to Leibniz's and Kant's critiques of any metaphysically realist conception of time itself. Crucially, in these narratives whatever necessity is to be found cannot be regarded as there "anyway", as perhaps it is in some Marxist conceptions of the "iron laws of history". It is, rather, a necessity that holds only for some knowing subject in as much as he or she affirms some evaluatively "thick" self-conception that links that individual in history to others with whom he or she identifies as of the same community. Hegel's innovation here was to take such an idea of self-constitution through recognition of one's historical community as applying not simply to the "givens" of nationhood or religion but to a trans-historical evolving community of *free and rational* beings.

Williams's clarification of his views about the relations between the aspirations of science and philosophy may remind us that the idealist project, when viewed through the interpretative lens of strong rather than weak TI, does not regard philosophy as relying on the possibility or otherwise of some super-scientific access to the world as it is "anyway". Like Williams, idealism, with its commitment to some form of "empirical realism", is content to leave the task of finding out what exists in the world anyway to the empirical sciences. The naturalists who, today, equate philosophical knowledge with that of the empirical sciences tend to do so on the assumption that a philosophy that rejects that reduction could only do so on the basis of having some extra- or super-scientific pretension. From the perspective of strong TI, however, such naturalism in philosophy looks like no more than the expression of a desire to rid our culture *of* philosophy. And while it might be the case that historical forces in play in modern life *will in fact* endanger the future of philosophy, the idea of philosophers *arguing for* the correctness of such a happening seems a strange prospect.

In the reading of the idealist tradition I have sketched here, idealism arose as a way of doing philosophy that could coexist without competition with science, and it could do so by means of a metaphilosophical reinterpretation of what philosophy *qua* "metaphysics" had always been. Perhaps idealism, properly understood, could still provide hope for a coherent and plausible modern philosophy, and a third alternative to the scientistic naturalism and the opposing, revived orthodox theism of the early twenty-first century.

NOTES

Introduction

1 And here I count my own earlier book on Hegel (Redding 1996) as manifesting such a reluctance to confront the question of the sense in which Hegel was an idealist.
2 Kant paraphrases critical idealism here as "the principle of the ideality of space and time" (ibid.), but the point could equally be made with respect to the *conceptual* form of objects.

Chapter 1: The seventeenth-century background to the emergence of continental idealism

1 Quoted in Max Jammer 1954: 56.
2 The "infinite-sphere" metaphor is said to first appear in a work called the *Book of Twenty Four Philosophers*. On the history of the metaphor see Karsten Harries (1975, 2001), Dietrich Mahnke (1937), and Elizabeth Brient (2002: pt 3).
3 In particular, in the 1584 work *La Cena de le Ceneri* (*The Ash Wednesday Supper*) (Bruno 1995).
4 In fact, it was the thesis of the spatial *plenum* that provided Aristotle with his definition of a thing's place as the limit surface of the surrounding body.
5 Plato, *Republic*, book 10.
6 In their biographies of Newton, both Christianson (1984) and Westfall (1980) emphasise More's general influence on Newton's understanding of the role of God in the world. The importance of More's influence has also been supported in the more general accounts of Koyré (1957: 159–68), Jammer (1954: 40–47, 108–12), and Grant (1981: 244–45, 252–54). Not all have been convinced, however. See, for example, Hall (1990).
7 See, for example, Jammer (1954: 41). On the idea that for Proclus space itself is an immovable, indivisible, and *immaterial* body, see Siorvanes (1996: 133).
8 Christianson describes Newton by 1663–65 as having become "steeped in the Platonism of Henry More and its compelling emphasis on the Book of Nature" (Christianson 1984: 248).
9 McGuire (1995) argues that although Newton was influenced in his conception of space in many ways by More, Newton's way of thinking about space still differs from that of More, given the influence of Gassendi's mechanistic account.
10 For an account of the systematic links between Newton's theological, metaphysical and scientific beliefs, see Force (1990).
11 On the spread of Böhme's ideas among the radical Protestant sects during the time of the English Civil War, see Hutin (1960: ch. 3).

12 For a helpful account of Augustine's account of creation see Knuuttila (2001).

13 This is argued, for example, in Burnyeat 1982.

14 Theologically, Newton held to the anti-Trinitarian doctrine of Arianism.

15 Of course, it is not unusual for each side of such intellectual wars to characterise its opponent in terms that that opponent would reject. But it is particularly clear in the case of the emergence of Continental idealism, for here, in particular, the model for understanding the idealists has, in fact, come from the *anglophone* side of the divide.

16 Paul Franks links Kant's attitude to Swedenborg's spirits and to Newton's conception of space in this suggestive way: "As the Newtonian God is supposed to be omnipresent in space without being a space-filling body, so the pre-critical, Kantian mind is supposed to be omnipresent in the human body without being the body that fills that space. But just as Newton has no way to explain the special, noncorporeal way in which God is supposed to inhabit space, so Kant has no way to explain the special, noncorporeal way in which the mind is supposed to inhabit space" (Franks 2005: 32).

17 See, for example, the account given in McGinn (2005).

18 Michael Allen Gillespie has stressed the dark side of the nominalist tradition and its link to nihilism: "[R]ather than establish man as lord of nature and his own destiny, it leaves him afloat in a universe utterly dependent upon a capricious divine will. Nominalism points not toward the dawn of a new enlightenment but toward the dark form of an omnipotent and incomprehensible God" (Gillespie 1995: 23). As we will see, the attraction to Plato and Aristotle of figures within the Continental idealist tradition, such as Leibniz and Hegel, was part of a response to what they perceived as the nihilistic consequences of nominalism.

19 In a certain sense, Berkeley's later objections to Newton's concept of absolute space include the same point. Space cannot be seen as something "eternal, uncreated, infinite, indivisible, immutable" but *other than God* (PHK: §117) presumably because such an independent existence would in some sense *constrain* God. However, to make God spatial was to come too close to identifying God, in a pantheistic way, with the extended world.

20 "[H]e is a good and just master; his power is absolute, but his wisdom permits not that he exercise that power in an arbitrary and despotic way, which would be tyrannous indeed" (Th: 60).

21 As the world is a "whole assemblage of contingent things" its cause must be an intelligent will, as the actual world is one of many possible ones, and so must have been *chosen*. And as this intelligent cause must be infinite in all ways, and so "absolutely perfect in *power*, in *wisdom* and in *goodness*", it "cannot but have chosen the best" (Th: 127–28).

22 Leibniz seems to have shared the same antipathy to the combination of voluntarism and nominalism that had been exhibited by the Cambridge Platonists John Smith and Ralph Cudworth. On Cudworth's anti-voluntarism, see Darwall (1995: ch. 5) and Gill (2006: ch. 4). In contrast More had a very voluntaristic view of God, one he shared with Newton.

23 For such a defence of Berkeley see, for example, Luce (1945). On this reading, perceptible objects are to be conceived as something like collections of Russellian sense-data, with the requisite distinction between the act of perception itself and what it is that is perceived.

24 The same combination of "Platonist theory of spirits" with "what most people consider to be extreme Nominalism" is commented upon by Richie (1967: 50). Stoneham (2002: 220) refers to nominalism as Berkeley's "working assumption" and notes that Berkeley intended to be a "full blooded nominalist". Berkeley

himself had aligned his philosophical position with the Pythagoreans and the Platonists in *Siris* (WGB: vol. 5, 263, 266).

25 Locke thinks that it requires "some pains and skill to form the *general idea* of a *triangle*" (EHU: bk 4, ch. 7, para. 9), but Berkeley thinks it impossible, inviting his readers simply to observe whether they could form the idea of a triangle which is "*neither obliques, nor rectangle, equilateral, equicrural, nor scalenon, but all and none of these at once*" (PHK: 13). On the assumption that "idea" here means something like "image", the attempt is clearly futile. Ayers (2005: 47) stresses the "heavily nominalist, imagist account of universal knowledge" in Berkeley's "Introduction", noting that he is "laying claim to a more rigorous nominalism and imagism than his celebrated predecessor", John Locke.

26 Berkeley seems later to have tempered this earlier strong identification of spirit and will with one in which "understanding" plays an equal role; however this issue remains unresolved in his philosophy.

27 See, for example, Luce (1945: 25) and Roberts (2007: 4).

Chapter 2: The monadological world of Gottfried Wilhelm Leibniz

1 Thus Mercer (2004: 118) describes Leibniz as combining a metaphysics "thoroughly rooted in Aristotelian thought", with a Platonist *epistemology*. Sources for the strand of Christian Neoplatonism in Leibniz's thought include the Cambridge Platonists, and in particular Cudworth, Anne Conway and Franciscus Mercurius van Helmont, from whom he may have taken the term "monad" (Wilson 1989: 161; Merchant 1979) and the Platonist Trinitarian theologians teaching at the Calvinist academy at Herborn, J. H. Alsted and J. H. Bisterfeld, the "Herborn Encyclopaedists" (Loemker 1961, 1972: 143–45 and 190–93; Hotson 1994).

2 If monads act, but are not acted *upon*, this of course rules out the possibility of their *interaction*, as interacting involves *both* acting and being acted upon. This was to be important for the relation of Kant, and the post-Kantians, to Leibniz.

3 Modern scholars trace Leibniz's conception of "harmony" to Bisterfeld's notion of "immeation". See, for example, Rutherford (1995: 36–40). The Trinitarian dimension of the notion of harmony is treated in Antognazza (1999).

4 And this is seen as a difference of perfection. Circular motion can go on infinitely, whereas linear motion has finite starting and end points.

5 This is the theme of his *Theodicy*.

6 On the way in which Leibniz's idealism differs from Berkeley's "phenomenalist" idealism, see, for example, Garber (2005) and Shim (2005), and for the opposing view, Adams (1994: ch. 9). In an influential article, Garber (1985) argued that in the 1680s and 90s Leibniz had held that the ultimate components of the world were corporeal substances which necessarily combined matter and form, although the idea of the distinctness of Leibniz's middle period from later monadological conception was criticised by Adams (1994: ch. 11). Pointing to Leibniz's Christian Platonist inheritance, Smith (2004) has identified Adams's error of reading even the later Leibniz as a type of Berkeleian immaterialist: "On the 'Platonic-Aristotelian' picture, it is neither the case that there is nothing but spirit, nor that there is independently existing matter. Rather, all actual matter serves as the body of some soul or soul-like form. Just as for Aristotle prime matter has only conceptual reality but is nowhere to be found in the cosmos, so too for Nicholas [of Cusa], the question of non-bodily matter does not arise. In Leibniz's variety of pananimism, as well, there is no *hyle* that is not a *soma*, no matter that is not the organic body of some monad" (p. 49).

7 Remember that at any one time a monad is "pregnant" with all of its *future* states, so it was the states of the constituent monads of the "struck" ball that caused it to move when it did, not the impact of the striking ball.

8 Sensory presentations such as those of odours or tastes are in a way, "incomprehensible" and "we are persuaded, by a kind of faith which we owe to the evidence of the senses, that these perceptible qualities are founded upon the nature of things and that they are not illusions" (Th: 97).

9 Earlier, Leibniz had described each substance as "like a whole world, and like a mirror of God, or indeed of the whole universe, which each one expresses in its own fashion—rather as the same town is differently represented according to the different situations of the person who looks at it" (M: §9; see also M: §57, and Th: §147).

10 For an extended account of this topic, see especially Harries (2001).

11 Hence Leibniz takes over Anselm's early "ontological" proof of God—the idea that God's existence can be deduced from the very concept "God". Since the concept of God implies the perfection of God, and since an existing thing is more perfect than a merely imagined one, God *must* exist. Kant was to undermine this proof in the *Critique of Pure Reason*.

12 Quoted in Adams (1994: 194–95).

13 On the metaphysical bases of Leibniz's politico-moral thought see especially Riley (1996). During the civil war in England, a similar ameliorist and irenic attitude was clear among the Cambridge Platonists.

14 The controversial claim that Hobbes was a theological voluntarist has recently been argued, in Martinich (1992).

15 Against traditional readings, Darwall (1995: 110–11) identifies the Cambridge Platonists as instigating within the British moral tradition an approach to ethics based on the notion of the self-determining subject, based on the primacy of practical rather than theoretical reasoning—thus advancing "versions of a thesis we are much more familiar with in Kant: that moral obligation is self-imposed in the practical reasoning of a self-determining agent".

16 It is a common perception that Hobbes' naturalism undermines the intended *normative* role ascribed to the will as basis of obligation. "Hobbes never succeeded in distinguishing will from appetite, except insofar as will is the last appetite, though a last appetite is still an appetite. As a result, even though he urges in *Leviathan* that wills 'make the essence of all covenants,' that political legitimacy is derived from voluntary acts of consent, he was never able to show how an obligation can be derived from an appetite" (Riley 1982: 58). See also Schneewind (1998: 91).

17 While it is clear that the *plant* or *animal* soul cannot exist outside its embodiment in the plant or animal, in relation to the rational soul, Aristotle distinguishes intellect (*Nous*) from soul (*psyche*), making the former immortal and separable, and the latter mortal and inseparable (Meta: bk 12, ch. 7, 1072b27). The inseparability of the soul proved difficult for later Christian thinkers who wanted to integrate Aristotelian philosophy with Christian belief.

18 This, for Brandom, is the basis of the difference between the metaphysics of the idealists—from Leibniz through Kant, to the post-Kantians—and the empiricists. Berkeley, it will be recalled from chapter 1, having taken empiricism to the extreme, is a poor model on which to understand the philosophy of the Continental idealists. Brandom elaborates this reading of Leibniz in *Tales of the Mighty Dead* (2002: ch. 5).

19 This is at the core of a famous dispute between Leibniz and the Newtonian natural philosophy as represented by Samuel Clarke (see L-C).

20 See, for example, Sklar (1981).

21 Cf. Price (1996).

22 Augustine had specifically argued against equating God's creation of the world with the idea of atemporal emanation. The world *had* an actual beginning: we must literally believe the holy scriptures, where it is written that "In the beginning God created the heavens and the earth", although Augustine has God's *willing* as occurring in imparticible time (CG: bk 11, ch. 4). Moreover, Augustine even dates this event to less that 6,000 years before his writing (ibid.: bk 12, ch. 11). The idea of atemporal emanation had become subject to the accusation of heresy from the early fourteenth century.

23 Kristeller (2001) and Popkin (1992) have drawn attention to the *Neoplatonic* features of Spinoza's thought.

24 Consistent with this, he rejected the associated idea that the world was created *ex nihilo*. On the interaction of theological and scientific ideas in the seventeenth century, see in particular Funkenstein (1986: chs 2 and 3).

25 Hence Leibniz seemed to downplay his famous visit to Spinoza at the Hague in 1676.

26 And this implies, of course, that they could not *interact*, as interaction demands that the agents are also *acted on*.

27 Once more, the idea that "mystical" states in which the self was experienced as merging with "the godhead" were properly reached by *rational* forms of thought was to be found among early Dominican thinkers such as Meister Eckhart.

28 In general, Baruzi (1907) explores Leibniz's lifelong interest in the organisation of religious life in such a way that it gave embodiment to the harmony of monads as conceived metaphysically.

Chapter 3: Kant's development from *physical* to *moral* monadologist

1 It should be remembered, however, that neither in Newton's thinking did objects *act on* each other, not even "at a distance". *All* action, in Newton's account, came from God, his omnipresence in the universe allowing him to act directly at every point in it. All bodies were the passive recipients of God's action.

2 While Kant used the designation "physical monadology" in a paper of 1756 (TP: 1.473–87), I will use this broadly to refer to the general nature of Kant's pre-critical writings up to the mid-1760s. Cf. Michael Friedman's description of Kant's early philosophy as a "Newtonian version of the monadology" (Friedman 1992: 6). Like Leibniz, Kant in his pre-critical work conceived of the law-like behaviour of things in the world as revealed by modern physics as somehow resulting from divine legislation. But Newton *too* thought of the laws of physics as decreed by God, and so *this* aspect of Kant's view was neutral between Leibniz and Newton.

3 In the General Scholium, written for the second (1713) edition of *The Mathematical Principles of Natural Philosophy*, book 3, Newton writes that God's "duration reaches from eternity to eternity; his presence from infinity to infinity ... He is not eternity and infinity, but eternal and infinite; he is not duration or space, but he endures and is present. He endures forever and is everywhere present; and by existing always and everywhere, he constitutes duration and space" (MPNP: vol. 2, 43).

4 A force of repulsion was needed in addition to Newton's gravitational force of attraction, thought Kant, to explain why all the physical monads in the universe did not collapse into a single body under the influence of attraction.

5 This is argued in Friedman (1992: 8–9) in opposition to Vuillemin (1955), who treats Kant's early account of space as more fully Leibnizian.

6 See, for example, Leibniz's Third Letter to Clarke (L-C: paras 5 and 6, pp. 14–15).
7 Leibniz thus employs something like the principle of verificationism in this argument. See, for example, Hale (1988: 96).
8 Or, we might say today, between "levo" and "dextro" forms of molecules with their differing chemical properties.
9 Kant's "two-world" locution and his stress on the need to keep *conceptual knowledge* free from the distorting influences of the senses have strong *Platonic* resonances that were to be important in the subsequent development of idealism after Kant.
10 On Rousseau's Platonism, see, for example, Williams (D. Williams 2005, 2007) and Cooper (2002).
11 Quoted in Shell (1996: 81).
12 See also the *Critique of Practical Reason* (CPrR: 5.117).
13 Before the advent of twentieth-century analytic philosophy, influenced by the logical innovations of Frege, traditional logicians kept "sortal" predicates naming kinds distinct from attributive predicates.
14 One advantage of this term-based logic is that the kind term provides a way of restricting the range of possible attributive predicates to a thing. Thus it might be said that chairs are the kinds of thing that typically have legs. In contrast, "this number has a broken leg" has no meaning, because numbers are not the kinds of things that have (or even lack) legs.
15 As Kant was to put it later, Leibniz had *intellectualised* appearances, while Locke had *sensualised* concepts (CPuR A271/B327).
16 Gardner (1999: 22, 30–33) points out this ambiguity of Kant's use of "metaphysics" and draws from it a distinction between "analytic" and "idealist" ways of interpreting the first Critique with similarities to the distinction between what I call "weak" and "strong" TI.
17 Lest it be thought that "what exists anyway" must exhaust the role of what a science *could* be about, the exemplary notion of a "right" might be invoked. One might thus argue that while there is a fact of the matter as to whether I have, say, the exclusive right to drive *this* car (the one that I *own*), the existence of such rights is itself dependent upon the historically contingent fact that in our society we acknowledge rights of, say, private property. To put it another way, the *fact* that this car is mine is to be thought of as an "institutional fact" rather than a "brute fact".
18 See, for example, Michael Beaney's excellent account of the history of the notion of analysis (Beaney 2007).
19 Kant should *not* be taken as saying that we cannot know anything outside our individual minds, and that we can only know our own subjective ideas or representations. He was no sceptic about the "outside world", although he is often taken to have been such a sceptic. That we have sensations testifies to our interacting with substances outside ourselves. However, we cannot on the basis of these interactions assume that things are *as they appear* to us, and that they "really" have the properties that they seem to have. Those properties, spatio-temporal properties in particular, actually reflect the way that we represent to ourselves those things with which we interact. In *that sense*, space and time are "in us", and not in the "things themselves".

Chapter 4: Kant and the "Copernican" conception of transcendental philosophy

1 Thus Kant asserts in the first edition Fourth Paralogism that "the transcendental idealist is an empirical realist, and grants to matter, as appearance, a reality which need not be inferred, but is immediately perceived" (CPuR: A371).

2 In contrast, transcendental *realism*, Kant says, "finds itself required to give way to empirical idealism" (CPuR: A371), "*empirical* idealism" being yet another name for Berkeley's immaterialist doctrine.

3 Here, we might understand what it is to be an *idealist* about form by appealing to a contrasting *realist* account of form. For example, it could be said that the appeal in Armstrong (1997) to the reality of propositionally structured "states of affairs" constitutes an explicitly realist theory of logical form.

4 This is explored in the Transcendental Aesthetic.

5 Again it must be stressed that the concepts in question are ones that can be known of objects independently of experience.

6 In fact, this seems very much like an "infinitised" version of Aristotle's "enclosing-boundary" approach to space or place.

7 Kant implies that the notion of "cause" is equally entailed in a simple perceptual judgment, such as "this tomato is red". The idea is that to say something is of a particular colour is to attribute to it some property causally responsible for one's experiencing it in the way one does when deeming it to *be* that colour.

8 A generally Kantian reading of Wittgenstein's *Tractatus Logico-Philosophicus* was put forward by Stenius (1960), but for an account of the parallel more like the one suggested here see Burri (2004). Later in the twentieth century, a conception along these lines was developed in Sellars (1997) and referred to as the "space of reasons".

9 Kant has conveniently elided the verb referring to the relation between concepts and functions, but as should be clear from the following paragraph, "rests on" is inappropriate.

10 A spatiotemporal analogue might be that to judge an object at location l_1 at time t_1 is to exclude the possibility of its being at a different location l_2 at t_1 but not t_2.

11 In a similar spirit Lloyd Gerson has described the idea that the universe has a systematic unity as "Platonism's most profound legacy from the Pre-Socratic philosophers" (Gerson 2005: 260). It is because the world is a unity that "a systematic understanding of it is possible", one that is resolutely "top–down" in its explanatory structure. Gerson, however, does not distinguish between a "henology" and an "ontology". Recently, the idea of a Neoplatonic "henological" alternative to a traditionally "ontologically" conceived metaphysics has been developed in the context of medieval theology, in Narbonne (2001).

12 In his *Commentary on Plato's Parmenides*, Proclus criticises Plato for regarding being as "superior" to non-being. But to consider something as "being" is to consider it as the subject of assertion, and one should not regard "the One" in this way, as it is "above form, and it is not suitable to apply to it any of those attributes which are proper to secondary things, nor to transfer to it attributes proper to us" (CPP: 426). Considering "the One" as nonbeing thus exempts it from this mistake. This argument, based on the nature of negation, was to be highly relevant for Hegel.

13 Likewise, the knowing soul is not located in time: "In my opinion the soul is far higher than the heavens since in its highest and purest part it has nothing whatsoever to do with time" (SW: 137).

14 The passage continues, "*Where in* the world is a metaphysical subject to be noted? You say that this case is altogether like that of the eye and the field of sight. But you do *not* really see the eye. And from nothing *in the field of sight* can it be concluded that it is seen from an eye" (ibid.: §5.633).

15 From this proposition, "the sole text of rational psychology", is derived in the first instance the essential attributes of the thinking thing. It is a substance, it is simple, it is unified, and it stands in possible relation to objects in space.

16 Or alternatively, the "aporiae" from which Aristotle thought all metaphysical thought commenced.

17 For Leibniz, it is the fact that the actual world is only one of a plurality of logically *possible* ones that motivates his claim that it must have been *chosen* by an intelligence (Th: 127–28).

18 "Now no one can think a negation determinately without grounding it on the opposed affirmation. The person blind from birth cannot form the least representation of darkness, because he has no representation of light; the savage has no acquaintance with poverty, because he has none with prosperity. ... All concepts of negations are thus derivative, and the realities contain the data, the material, so to speak, or the transcendental content, for the possibility and the thoroughgoing determination of all things" (CPuR: A575/B603).

19 The actual list of categories (other than substance) that Aristotle gives is as follows: quantity (four foot, five foot); quality (white, grammatical); relation (double, half, larger); where (in the Lyceum, in the market place); when (yesterday, last year); being in a position (is lying, is sitting); having (has shoes on, has armour on); doing (is cutting, is burning); and being affected (being cut, being burned) (Cats: ch. 4, 1b25–2a4).

20 In this sense, Aristotle is closer to a modern *realist* about logical form, such as in Armstrong (1997).

21 "In this Preface I propose the transformation in our way of thinking presented in criticism merely as a hypothesis, analogous to that other hypothesis, only in order to draw our notice to the first attempts at such a transformation, which are always hypothetical, even though in the treatise itself it will be proved not hypothetically but rather apodictically from the constitution of our representations of space and time and from the elementary concepts of the understanding" (CPuR: Bxxii, note).

22 This thesis was put forward by Cassirer (1963), who stressed the role of the fifteenth-century German Neoplatonist Cardinal Nicholas of Cusa, whose theologically derived ideas on a homogeneous law-governed cosmos seemed to anticipate Copernicus and Galileo. The importance of Cusa has been emphasised more recently in Blumenberg (1983) and Harries (2001).

23 This form of explanation is in Leibniz, who effectively describes the hypothetico-deductive method (NE: 450). The appeal to such forms of explanation in the German tradition can be traced back to the Renaissance natural philosopher Jacobo Zabarella's interpretations of Aristotelian logic. For a fuller discussion of these issues see Redding (2007: ch. 4).

24 In the first edition of the *Critique of Pure Reason*, Kant describes how all connection or unity among our cognitions requires a "unity of consciousness that precedes all data of the intuitions, and in relation to which all representation of objects is alone possible", a unity of consciousness that he there names "transcendental apperception" (CPuR: A107). The unity of this apperception, he claims, stands in relation to all concepts, in an *a priori* way, just as space and time, as unified forms of representation, stand in relation to the intuitions of sensibility (ibid.). This all suggests that what secures the unity of one's *beliefs* is that they are the beliefs of a *single* rational subject. Kant's idea is that the bundling together of *true* beliefs and the holding of them apart from others taken to be *false* just is the basic function of what we think of as "the mind".

25 See Vieillard-Baron (1979: 40–56). Cf. the claim in Beiser (2003: 65) that "Kant lies far more within the Platonic tradition ... than many scholars are willing to admit".

26 CPuR: 746n86 (editors' note). This had been pointed out in Reich (1964). It is notable that Plato's crafts-worker God of the *Timaeus* neither possesses the "ideas" in the mind, nor is an omnipotent creator—like all crafts workers, this God is limited by the given materials he has to work with. Neither is Plato's God an object of worship, but one of emulation.

27 This is argued, for example, in Burnyeat (1982).
28 Later Christian thought developed this anthropomorphising of God with the idea that the human mind is made in the *image* of the divine mind, or even that God and human nature are paradigms of each other. But of course the human mind has been imprisoned in a material world that God created *ex nihilo*.
29 Pépin (2006) contests Panofsky's claim that this is the *first* reference to a divine mind in the tradition, such references being found in the works of the Middle Platonists.
30 According to Baum (2000: 206–7), it was not until Friedrich Plessing's accounts of Plato appeared in the late 1790s that a view of Plato's ideas like that currently accepted was put forward.
31 That Kant's account of Plato closely follows the Brucker's presentation was argued in Mollowitz (1935).
32 In the discussion of Plato at the beginning of the Transcendental Dialectic (CPuR: A316/B 372), Kant defends the relevance of "ideas" for political thought against Brucker's criticism of Plato.

Chapter 5: The moral framework of metaphysics

1 Most recently, the major representative of the "two-aspects" view of Kant has been Allison (2004). See also Bird (2006).
2 This idea is captured well by Stanley Cavell: "we think skepticism must mean that we cannot know the world exists, and hence that perhaps there isn't one ... Whereas what skepticism suggests is that since we cannot know the world exists, its presentness to us cannot be a function of knowing ... this is why we take Kant to have said that there are things we cannot know; whereas what he said is that something can not be known – *and* can not coherently be doubted either, for example, that there is a world and that we are free" (Cavell 1976: 324).
3 In particular, the "Refutation of Idealism", inserted into the second edition.
4 That is, we hypothesise a way the world possibly is, and from the hypothesis deduce what would also be the case, were the hypothesis true. If what can be deduced from the hypothesis turns out to in fact be true, this is evidence that the hypothesis itself is true.
5 In our moral stance we are thus able to attain that type of aperspectival indifference to our particular insertion into the world that had been part of the goal of theoretical knowledge Platonistically conceived.
6 Thus Hume, who is often taken as representative of this tradition, writes, "It appears evident that the ultimate ends of human actions can never, in any case, be accounted for by *reason*, but recommend themselves entirely to the sentiments and affections of mankind, without any dependence on the intellectual faculties" (Enq: 293). The idea that desires are "givens" upon the basis of which reason acts instrumentally is effectively the received view within analytic philosophy, although not uncontested. See, for example, Millgram (1997) for a sustained critique.
7 Thus in the practical realm too, Kant is linked to the critique of what, in the context of theoretical reason, is referred to as the "myth of the given" in Sellars (1997).
8 Although Kant is actually making a further point with this example than the one illustrated here, it clearly presupposes the point being made here.
9 In theorem II, remark 1, Kant criticises a position in moral theory which he had, himself, earlier held—one which grounds morality in desire, but a certain "higher" type of desire. For example, some people think that morality rests on

benevolent desires—we desire that people as a whole, and not simply ourselves, are happy. Thus the Scottish philosopher Francis Hutcheson thought we had a "moral sense"—a bit like our aesthetic sense, such that we feel a certain sort of pleasure in the perception of good actions. In a moral sense, we would have thus a basis for non-egoistic benevolent action. Similarly, Jean-Jacques Rousseau thought that moral behaviour is based on natural reactions, such as the tendency to feel pity in the face of another's suffering.

10 Defenders of Kant commonly point out that we should not think of the categorical imperative—especially not as expressed in *this* way, which is only one of the forms that Kant gives to it—as providing a simple test or "decision procedure" which can automatically be applied to maxims to give a definite answer. See, for example, Wood (2005: 130–43). This controversial issue of the *applicability* of the moral law will be taken up in the next chapter.

11 "A kingdom of ends is thus possible only by analogy with a kingdom of nature; the former, however, is possible only through maxims, that is, rules imposed upon oneself, the latter only through laws of externally necessitated efficient causes" (GMM: 4.438).

12 This is the approach, for example, of Korsgaard (1996).

13 And this, in turn, is reflected in the categorical imperative as expressed in the so-called "formula of humanity": "So act that you use humanity, whether in your own person or in the person of any other, always at the same time as an end, never merely as a means" (GMM: 4.429).

14 In the terms of the approach to the analysis of "speech acts" initiated in the last century by the philosopher J. L. Austin, to take a promise or undertaking *as a* type of description is to conflate the stances to another that Kant is trying to distinguish in his account of morality.

15 Defenders of Kant often lament that critics, assuming that Kant's *whole* moral philosophy is contained in the *Groundwork* and the *Critique of Practical Reason*, then find Kant's moral philosophy wanting.

16 Quoted in Adams (1994: 195).

17 Moreover, Kant was to then explain the concept of God in light of the *prior* concept of morality, rather than deriving the normativity of the moral law from the existence of God.

18 "Ethics Does Not Give Laws for Actions (*Ius* Does That), but Only for *Maxims of Actions*" (MM: 6.388).

19 "That lawgiving which makes an action a duty and also makes this duty the incentive is *ethical*. But that lawgiving which does not include the incentive of duty in the law and so admits an incentive other than the idea of duty itself is *juridical*. It is clear that in the latter case this incentive which is something other than the idea of duty must be drawn from *pathological* determining grounds of choice, inclinations, and aversions, and among these, from aversions; for it is a lawgiving, which constrains, not an allurement, which invites" (MM: 6.219).

20 On Kant's implicit egoistic account of motivation see, for example, Edwards (2000a).

21 For Kant, while moral action is the ultimate purpose behind entering into the social contract, he clearly recognises that one cannot legislate for morality.

22 In Kantian terms, Rousseau's general will/will of all distinction amounts to that between a "collective" and a "distributive" unity of wills. What unites Rousseau and Kant here is their shared Platonistic focus on unity.

23 There Kant famously claims to understand Plato better than he understood himself. Plato understood his "ideas" as objects of theoretical reason, Kant

understands them as objects of practical reason. With this, Kant has an alternative to dismissing the Platonic republic as "a dream of perfection that can have its place only in the idle thinker's brain". Anticipating the language of the categorical imperative, Kant suggests that we see Plato's ideal republic as expressing a "constitution providing for the *greatest human freedom* according to laws that permit *the freedom of each to exist together with that of others*" (CPuR: A316/B372–73). That is, it functions as a "necessary idea, which one must make the ground not merely of the primary plan of a state's constitution but of all the laws too" (ibid.).

24 Note that the *indifference* of inclination to duty does not commit Kant to a position that is often attributed to him, that acting from duty must always be an action that *opposes* that which is directed by inclination. For Kant, acting in accordance with inclination is evil when the inclination in question is consciously chosen against duty when duty would proscribe it.

25 Schiller had been educated at the famed Karlsschule military academy, in Stuttgart, and it would seem that the teaching there must have been very advanced with respect to biology. Also at Karlsschule around the same time were two students who were to later have important impacts on the emerging biological sciences, Carl Friedrich Kielmeyer and Georges Cuvier. In general, such a culture seems to have contributed to Schiller's antagonism to the implicit anthropology of Kant's transcendental idealism.

26 On the politics and culture of the "old Würrtemburg" of Hegel's youth, see in particular, Dickey (1987). On Swabian pietistic religious culture, see Stoeffler (1973) and McCardle (1986). While his early religious views had been shaped by his more orthodox Pietistic parents, as well as his local pastor, Philipp Ulrich Moser, Schiller seems to have been converted to a far more heterodox form of spirituality while a student at Karlsschule, where he was influenced by Böhmist ideas, as well as the tradition of Leibniz and Wolff, and the British Platonist "sentimentalists", Shaftesbury and Hutcheson.

27 "This tradition ... took ethical and eschatological elements from widely divergent sources in the history of Christian thought and formed from them an anthropology of fallen and restored man that allowed for – indeed, demanded – man's participation in civil life as well as in his own salvation. The thrust of the tradition was to show that through ethical activism man could transform the world in accordance with God's wishes and, by so doing, make significant 'progress' not only toward transcending his own fallen nature, but toward establishing the Kingdom of God *on earth* as well" (Dickey 1987: 12).

28 See, especially, Stoeffler (1973: 108–16).

29 Others have also detected the strong influence of the millennarian twelfth-century mystic Joachim de Fiore (Dickey 1987: 33–39) and Meister Eckhart (Crites 1998: 7). O'Regan (1994: 264) regards Joachim and Eckhart, as well as Böhme, as important influences on Hegel's heterodox form of religiosity.

30 Kant responded to Schiller's criticisms in a long footnote to *Religion within the Limits of Pure Reason Alone* (Rel: 6.23n).

31 In this and references to Schiller's *On the Aesthetic Education of Man*, the initial numeral refers to the number of the letter, the second numeral to the paragraph.

32 Kant himself had appealed to Blumenbach's concept four years earlier in *Critique of Judgment*, but had not used it in the same way. Only two years before, Kielmeyer had given his famous "Rede" of 1793, "Über die Verhältnisse der organischen Kräfte unter einander in der Reihe der verschiedenen Organisationen, die Geseze und folgen dieser Verhältnisse", in which he gave expression to his notion of the idea that organisms could be understood in terms of the "forces" determining their development. The speech was, in fact, delivered at Schiller's

old school, the *Karlsschule*. We know that Schiller at least knew of the lecture, as it is mentioned in a letter from Goethe, who had read and been influenced by it.

33 "I shall not attempt to hide from you that it is for the most part Kantian principles on which the following theses will be based" (AE: letter 1, para. 3). But later, in pointing to the tendency of a one-sided dominance of sense by reason, Schiller notes that while this way of thinking is "wholly alien to the *spirit* of the Kantian system, … it may very well be found in the *letter* of it" (ibid.: letter 13, para. 2, note 2).

34 Similar points are made in Bernstein (2001: 78) and Hare (1999).

35 It is significant that in his discussion of Schiller's objections to Kant's moral philosophy, Beiser (2005: 188–89) points to Kant's moralistic conception of the "highest good" as the real target of Schiller's dissatisfaction.

36 Schneewind (1998: 512) describes Kant's moral philosophy as combining aspects of voluntarist and anti-voluntarist traditions, equating the good with what is "willed by a will governed by the moral law", a clearly voluntarist inheritance. "In his early attempts at theodicy Kant worked with the voluntarist idea that to be good is simply to be what God wills. He gave up on the thought that God creates all possibilities; but he never abandoned the account of goodness inchoately expressed in the early fragments. In the mature theory this point emerges in Kant's identification of practical reason with a free will governed by the moral law."

37 On the central role of Augustine in the development of the notion of the will as a psychological faculty, see Dihle (1982). Menn (1998: 202–3) argues that it was the doctrine of Incarnation that required Augustine to add a will to Plotinus' God: "For the Platonists, God rules in accordance with the natures of things: everything proceeds from him in order according to the capacity of the recipient, and there is therefore no need for him to choose what he should send where. But it is not at all in accord with the nature of the recipient that Nous itself should descend into a human body: this requires a will in God, and not a will naturally directed toward what is good and appropriate for the divine nature, but a will capable of encompassing its own humiliation for the sake of the elevation of fallen human beings." On Augustine's important departures from Plotinus see Rist (1996).

38 Quoted in Coleman (2000: 321).

39 There has been a long-standing debate as to the extent to which Augustine had been an influence in Descartes' conception of the "cogito". For a strong case for the affirmative see Menn (1998). See also Taylor (1992).

Chapter 6: The later Kant as a "post-Kantian" philosopher?

1 Or more accurately, found in the section, the "Transcendental Analytic".

2 There is no easy way to characterise such a different Kant. I hesitate to use "post-critical" for the reasons given in Allison 2000: the *Critique of Judgment* is itself presented as a "critical" work, and its innovations have important continuities with those of the *Critique of Pure Reason*. I will use the paradoxical "post-Kantian Kant" to try to capture the paradox that the post-Kantians took to be internal to Kant's work, and the tensions within Kant's philosophy resulting from his attempts to solve that paradox.

3 Thus in Kuehn (2001: 131) it is noted that "The notes on moral philosophy show that Kant did indeed take the moral sense to be the basis of morality. He talked of Hutcheson and claimed that 'one should investigate the feeling of the *natural man*, and this is better than our artificial one: Rousseau has visited (*aufgesucht*) it'."

4 Thus he notes in his lectures on ethics from around this time, "The doctrine of moral feeling is more a hypothesis to explain the phenomenon of approval that we give to some kinds of actions than one which could determine maxims and first principles that hold objectively and tell us how we should approve or reject something, or act or refrain from acting" (quoted in Kuehn 2001: 201; internal quote from KGS: 19.116f.).

5 See, for example, Gill (2006: 186): "Now according to Hutcheson's view of human nature, as we've seen, every human has certain natural affections. These affections are 'rooted,' 'original,' or 'implanted' parts of our constitution. They have not been caused by anything else in the natural world. Hutcheson believed that empirical observation revealed that these natural affections are all in perfect harmony with each other—that if all of our affections were in their natural state, we'd all be benevolent and happy, in perfect accord with ourselves and with others. But how can we account for the wonderfully harmonized character of all of our implanted affections? We cannot attribute it to natural causes as our natural affections are just those that do not admit of further natural explanation. So we must attribute our natural affective harmony either to chance or to the design of a supernatural Creator."

6 Accordingly, Hutcheson was accused of voluntarism by Cudworth's defender, John Balguy, in *The Foundation of Moral Goodness* (of 1728). See Selby-Bigge (1897: vol. 2, 526–58).

7 In the *Critique of Practical Reason*, Kant points out that in contrast to the first Critique, here the "aesthetic of pure practical reason" which concerns "the relation of pure practical reason to sensibility [Sinnlichkeit] and ... its necessary influence upon sensibility to be cognized a priori, that is ... *moral feeling* [*vom moralischen Gefühle*]" must follow the "Analytic" (CPrR: 5.90).

8 Thus Munzel (1999: 126), for example, comments on the "seminal role" played by the *Critique of Judgment* "in Kant's moral thought; specifically, in relation to the task of reason becoming subjectively practical".

9 In the dialogue *Philebus*, Plato thus contrasted the pure pleasures of certain cognitive states, such as those that result from the contemplation of simple geometric designs, from the sort of false pleasures in which pleasure was somehow bound up with the contrast to its opposite, pain. The intense pleasure subsequent to the scratching of an itch, was Plato's example, but his target was the pleasure that came from the reception of dramatic art, in which pleasure seemed to be mixed up with the experience of "pains" such as pity and fear.

10 This seems deeply embedded in the Platonic notion of "harmony" or "unity in diversity", for which the opposite seems only conceivable in terms of the notion of lack—*dis*harmony, or simply "diversity" without the unity.

11 See, for example, Ferrari (1989).

12 See, for example, the survey of writings in Thiessen (2004).

13 The distinction between judgments of the agreeable and the good attests to Kant's critique of Hobbes in this regard. By treating the will naturalistically as the last appetite in a process of deliberation, Hobbes effectively reduces reflectively striven for goods to immediately "agreeable" ones.

14 The idea of judgments of beauty as bridging such a gap is explicit in Plato's account of "eros" in the *Symposium*.

15 It must be remembered that Kant believes himself to be an empirical realist—judgments of colour, for example, can "track" objective facts about colour in the *empirical* world. These judgments do not, of course, track realities in the "world in itself".

16 This process has a clear *Fichtean* ring. Positing my own interest as negated goes together with the counter-positing of some quality in the object responsible for my liking.

17 While this is the case for all judgments of taste, it is most obvious in the case of judgments of the sublime. When we contemplate the beautiful, we contemplate it as *indifferent* to our interest; in experiences of the *sublime*, however, we esteem something in *opposition* to our interests (CJ: §29, "General Comment on the Exposition of Aesthetic Reflective Judgments").

18 In his transformation of Hutcheson, Kant also changed the conception of the pleasure taken in beauty in ways that made it sit uneasily with Hutcheson's approach in that Kant opposed the pleasure taken in beauty to the *displeasure* involved in the experience of ugliness. In the Platonist picture, ugliness should be regarded as nothing more than a "privation" of beauty, but in Kant's picture it was something more. In fact Kant's attitude to ugliness reflected his earlier criticisms of Leibniz's concept of *evil*: while Leibniz had regarded evil as the privation of good, Kant had argued that evil must be regarded as a *real* presence in the world working *in opposition to* good. Leibniz's error, he claimed, was a result of conflating two different types of "negation"—"real" and "logical". Effectively this same idea would be exploited later by Hegel in his *reinterpretation* of this Platonistic approach to value.

19 In the Inaugural Dissertation, Kant had used the term *Typus* to designate a form of analogical representation—specifically the representation of periods or limits of *time* by the use of spatial lines and points (TP: 2.405). This same idea of spatial representation of temporal determinations is described in the *Critique of Pure Reason* (CPuR: B154) as "external figurative representation" (*äusserlich figürliche Vorstellung*).

20 Recently the theme of the origin, nature and significance of this "gap" in Kant's theoretical philosophy, and the extent to which it took Kant in the 1790s in the direction of post-Kantian idealists, has become a focus of the renewed debate over the significance of Kant's *Opus Postumum*. See, for example, Beiser (2002: pt 1, ch. 10), Förster (2000) and Edwards (2000c). The most extreme reading of the degree to which Kant's continuing efforts to answer this problem caused him to adopt an essentially Hegelian position is advocated in Tuschling (1971).

21 Some of these related attempts include, in the second Critique, the proposals of the "typus" of the moral law (CPrR: 5.69); the conception of the "kingdom of God" as a realm in which "nature and morals come into a harmony" (ibid.: 5.128); the "schematism of analogy" involved in the scriptural representation of Christ as described in *Religion within the Boundaries of Mere Reason* (Rel: 6.65n); the "ideals of pure reason" in the "Transcendental Dialectic" (bk 2, ch. 3) of the *Critique of Pure Reason*; and the empirical "counterpart" (*Gegenbild*) of the moral law in the "Deduction of the Principles of Pure Practical Reason" of the *Critique of Practical Reason* (CPrR: 5.42).

22 Kant had earlier discussed a similar analogy involving a state: "by analogy with the law that action and reaction are equal when bodies attract or repel one another, I can also conceive of the community between the members of a commonwealth that is governed by rules of law" (CJ: §90; see also MM: 6.232–33). Kant makes the point that despite the fact of the analogy, I "cannot transfer those specific characteristics (the material attraction or repulsion) to this [political] community, and attribute them to the citizens so that these will form a system called a state" (CJ: §90). That is, despite the analogy, "we cannot by analogy draw an *inference* from the one to the other, i.e., transfer that mark of the difference in kind between them from one to the other" (ibid.). We have seen

this at work in Kant's discussion of the ground of aesthetic judgment early in the *Critique of Judgment*. We tend to think of the ground of our favourable response to the valued object as residing *in* the object as some type of objective quality. But this is not the case; the ground of the judgment is to be located in the normative relations between the *judges*.

23 On Kant's relation to Blumenbach see Lenoir (1980, 1982).

24 On the analogy with the "intentional stance" of Dennett (1987).

25 Note that the conflation of the universal–particular distinction with the whole–part distinction here is just that of the morphologies of conceptual and intuitive species of representation.

26 "An understanding to which this distinction [between possibility and actuality] did not apply would mean: All objects cognized by me *are* (exist)" (CJ: §76). Thus for Kant, the Leibnizian idea of God's having created the best of all possible worlds could not be sustained, as the idea of alternative possibilities is no longer available.

27 As Kant argues for the concept of "noumenon" in the *Critique of Pure Reason* (CPuR: B307).

28 See especially, Tuschling (1971, 1989, 1991), Edwards (2000b, c) and Förster (2000).

29 Förster (2000) offers a helpful overview.

Chapter 7: Jena post-Kantianism: Reinhold and Fichte

1 Important among this group were Friedrich von Hardenberg, better known under his literary pseudonym "Novalis", Ludwig Tieck and Friedrich Niethammer. The relation of this group of early romantics to Fichte's idealism is complex, but in many ways they remained closer to the doctrines of Kant, rejecting Fichte's concept of the subject's "absolute self-positing". See, for example, Frank (2004).

2 In 1792 Schulze published his essay, *Aenesidemus: oder über die Fundamente der von dem Herrn Prof. Reinhold in Jena gelieferten Elementar-philosophie, nebst einer Verteidigung gegen die Anmaßungen der Vernuftkritik*. A translation of part of the essay can be found in di Giovanni and Harris (1985: 105–35).

3 In *Early Philosophical Writings* (EPW: 59–77).

4 The idea of a "category mistake" was made explicit in the mid-twentieth century by the philosopher Gilbert Ryle. It refers to a mistake involving a confusion of the *kind* of thing one is investigating. To think that ripe tomatoes are purple is to be mistaken, but to think that the number seven is purple is to be mistaken in a different way. Numbers, unlike tomatoes, are not the kind of thing that *could be* coloured.

5 We might clarify Fichte's point here by thinking of the second "inference" of which Schulze was critical, as like that made by Berkeley when he inferred the existence of a *divine* mind, rather than an external object, from the fact of the resistance of the contents of his *own* mind to his will. But Fichte alludes to the fact that for Kantian self-consciousness, it is a question not of one mind inferring to some *other* mind, but of a single mind's awareness of *itself* as somehow actively engaged in producing its own representations.

6 Cf. the following: "All the claims of Aenesidemus against this procedure are based merely on the fact that he wants the absolute existence [Existenz] or autonomy of the *ego* to be valid *in itself* (just how and for whom we do not know), whereas it should only hold *for the ego itself*. It is *for the ego* that the *ego* is *what* it is, and is *why* it is. Our knowledge cannot advance beyond this proposition" (RA: 147).

194

7 Zöller (1998: 60) neatly captures Fichte's complexly dual conception of "I-ness" as "the act-character or agility (*Agilität*) of the I, according to which the latter is not a thinglike being with a predetermined essence but a doing that first brings about what it is; and its character as intelligence or of being-for-itself, according to which nothing can have being with respect to the I that is not *for* the I".

8 Fichte apparently coined this term on the analogy with the usual term for "fact"—*Tatsache*. A *Handlung* is an "act", so the term *Tathandlung* is sometimes rendered "fact–act".

9 We might think of this as a *Platonic* ("henological") rather than *Aristotelian* ("ontological") dimension of Fichte's thought, to the extent that the focus is on the *unity* of the self rather than the self as a substance. The criticism of the idea that the mind is a type of immaterial *thing* is found in forms of Christian mysticism influenced by late antique Neoplatonist thought. Again, from this perspective, the idea that the mind is a kind of immaterial entity could be described as a category mistake. The mind is neither a material nor immaterial thing.

10 While "−A = −A" is just an instance of the principle "A = A", this has a different logical structure to the principle in question, "−A is not equal to A". This second principle is effectively a *denial* that A = −A. Thus, for example, denying that all Greeks are philosophers is not the same as asserting that all Greeks are *non*-philosophers.

11 Kant had been attacked as inconsistent on just this point. If "cause" is meant to be a concept that only applies *within* experience, how could it be invoked to explain the content *of* experience, as when Kant seems to imply that the unknowable "thing in itself" is the cause of the "matter" of our intuitions?

12 This idea that the *limits* of positing activity are reached in such "original qualities" is clearly reflected by Schelling in the context of his philosophy of nature. "*Quality* is originally absolutely *inconstructible*, and it must be, because it is the limit of all construction by virtue of which every construction is a determinable one" (FOS: 22n).

13 Actually, the idea of two opposed cognitive "drives" had been used by Reinhold in the late 1780s in his attempt to provide Kant's philosophy with a foundation in the notion of representation. See Henrich (2003: 143–46).

14 This idea of Fichte's was to have repercussions on many at Jena in that decade, especially Friedrich Schlegel and others among the "early romantics". See below, Chapter 8.

15 Fichte had in "Fundamental Principles" used the notion of *streben*, or striving, in an allusion to Spinoza (Fnds: 101; Heath and Lachs here translate *streben* as "endeavour"). It would seem, then, that it contains elements of Spinoza's *conatus*.

16 In a popular lecture from this period, Fichte talks of a "drive toward truth" (EPW: 210).

17 This idea of thought's movement beyond limits somehow self-imposed would become a central feature of Hegel's conception of the dialectical movement of thought.

18 On Fichte's primordially *striving* subject, see Zöller (1998) and N. Martin (1996: ch. 6).

19 Thus the I's basic experience presupposes a type of inarticulate desiring or "longing [Sehnen]", an "original, wholly independent manifestation of the striving that lies in the self" (Fnds: 267). It is only on the basis of this longing that the self is "driven *out of itself*; only thereby is an *external world* revealed *within* it" (ibid.: 266). Desire or longing is not an optional *addition* to consciousness. "Anyone who wants to be released from desire", as he puts it later in his 1796–99 lectures, "wants to be released from consciousness" (FNM: 295).

20 Indeed, Fichte's apparent absorption of theoretical into practical reason here might be seen as a consequence of the initial rejection of the "thing-in-itself"

doctrine. Without any independent source of an external given that in Kant's account restricted the theoretical use of reason to a "regulative" *rather than* "constitutive" role, there was now nothing to limit "pure" reason to practical use.

21 La Vopa (2001: 270–97) gives a good account of the antagonism between Fichte and Schiller.

22 There is a difference here in as much as the self-ascribed "free efficacy" is not that of moral freedom but that of the more limited rational pursuit of self-ascribed goals. Fichte was to grapple with the conditions of moral freedom in the *System der Sittenlehre* of 1798, but although there may be some suggestion there of the role of recognition, it is not as explicit as in the *Rechtslehre*.

23 "But if there is such a summons, then the rational being must necessarily posit a rational being outside itself as the cause of the summons, and thus it must posit a rational being outside itself in general" (FNR: 37).

24 This is effectively Kant's criticism of Hobbes' naturalistic conception of the will.

25 On the events leading to Fichte's dismissal, see, for example, La Vopa (2001: chs 12 and 13).

Chapter 8: The Jena romanticism of Schlegel and Schelling

1 Crucial to this development have been, in Germany, Henrich (1991, 1995) and Manfred Frank (1997, 2004), and in France (and from a different perspective), Lacoue-Labarthe and Nancy (1988). From among anglophone philosophers, see especially Beiser (2002, 2003), Bowie (1993, 1997, 2007), and Richards (2002). See also the articles in Kompridis (2006).

2 Schlegel was claimed to have read all of Plato's dialogues in Greek in the early days of his attraction to classical culture, and was also the force behind the extensive translation of Plato into German, "encouraging" Schleiermacher to undertake this massive task. Importantly, by the 1790s, Brucker's interpretation of Plato that Kant had relied upon had come to be replaced by those of Dietrich Tiedemann and W. G. Tennemann. Tennemann, a student of Reinhold, in particular accepted a Neoplatonic view of Platonic ideas, as in a mind, and interpreted Plato as a proto-Kantian transcendental philosopher. See Vieillard-Baron (1988: 81). Novalis, in particular, had become struck by this Kantian vision of Proclus, as enthused to Schlegel, in a letter in 1798 (cited in Beierwaltes 2004: 87).

3 For a detailed account of the appeal to mythology among the romantics see Williamson (2004: ch. 1).

4 In contrast to Manfred Frank, I will be treating Schlegel as an idealist. Frank's conception (2004: 177) that "idealism holds some absolute principle, whether it be at the beginning or the end of the system, to be epistemically accessible" construes the post-Kantians as reverting to traditionally conceived metaphysics, as a reaction against Kant's transcendental scepticism. In contrast, I see them as developing Kant's strong TI at the expense of the scepticism of weak TI. In Chapter 9, I contest that even Hegel, who claimed to be an "absolute" idealist, can be understood in the way suggested by Frank's formula.

5 Schlegel published many of his witty aphorisms, often turning on paradox, in the *Athenaeum*.

6 Thus in Hegel's *Lectures on the History of Philosophy*, for example, Schlegel is treated as one of the "more important followers of Fichte" (LHP: vol. 3, 506).

7 See Hegel's discussion of Friedrich Schlegel in Aes: vol. 1, 64–68; EPR: §140, remark; and LHP: vol. 3, 506–8. Moreover, Schlegel's irony was for Hegel the manifestation of a type of nihilism that is ultimately self-undermining. The ego

can fail to find satisfaction in its own subjectivity and feel "a craving for the solid and the substantial, for specific and essential interests" (Aes: vol. 1, 66). This unsatisfied craving, according to Hegel, was expressed in Schlegel's turn to Catholicism and political conservatism.

8 Beiser (2003: 68–70) stresses the importance of Plato for Schlegel. Bubner (2003: 214–15) stresses Hegel's misunderstanding of Schlegel, as well as his blindness to the proximity of their thought. Hegel's personal dislike for Schlegel seems to have been shared by his fellow Swabian, Schiller. See Richards (2002: 49).

9 Schleiermacher's revolutionary innovations in the theory of interpretation are to be seen against the background of the development of the philological sciences in the last quarter of the eighteenth century in Germany, as well as the theory of language of J. G. Herder. On the importance for this development from around the 1770s of Philological Seminar, at University of Göttingen, directed by J. G. Heyne, see Leventhal (1994: ch. 7). Schlegel had been active within this seminar during his period at Göttingen, where he was *officially* studying law.

10 Earlier Schlegel had described modern poetry as "republican speech: a speech which is its own law and end unto itself, and in which all the parts are free citizens and have the right to vote" (CF: fragment 65).

11 For a systematic treatment of the role of the fragment in modern literature from the viewpoint of Schlegel's programme, see Strathman (2006).

12 For example, as in Rorty (1989: pt 2).

13 KA: vol. 18, 512, quoted in Frank (2004: 202).

14 KA: vol. 23, 72, quoted in Frank (2004: 204). In Schlegel's "Wechselerweis", one hears the echo of the *Wechselwirkung*, the reciprocally conditioning and conditioned relation between *entities* in Kant's third category of relation in the *Critique of Pure Reason* (A80/B106).

15 Kant himself is not so straightforward. See, for example, his discussion of truth in CPuR: A57–69/B82–84. Walker (1989) argues that Kant has an "impure coherence theory".

16 KA: vol. 12, 334, quoted in Frank (2004: 213).

17 KA: vol. 18, 36, quoted in Frank (2004: 181).

18 The document is in Hegel's handwriting. When first discovered in 1917, it was thought that Schelling was the author, but opinion is now divided, authorship being variously attributed to Hegel, Schelling or Hölderlin.

19 According to the editor, this document seems to have been written in the first half of 1794.

20 While Böhme was widely cited by the Jena Romantics, Mayer (1999) has argued that only Friedrich Schlegel and Schelling had seriously read and appropriated Böhme's writings.

21 Schelling's Kantianism here seems to follow Reinhold's attempted systematisation of Kant in terms of the theory of representation. A few years earlier a similarly Kantian interpretation of Plato had been given by W. G. Tennemann, a student of Reinhold.

22 The enthusiasm of the three seminarians for the French Revolution is well known. On the political context of Schelling's *Timaeus* commentary, see Baum (2000: 200–201).

23 See, in particular, Edwards (2000c).

24 Up to Schelling's 1800 work *System of Transcendental Idealism*, he was considering his own approach as a type of "enlargement" of Fichte's own system of transcendental idealism, such that the enlarged system contained both Fichte's narrower one and Schelling's philosophy of nature. From about this time until his

departure from Jena, however, a Spinozist "parallelism" between realist and idealist structures became the predominant organising trope. Thereafter, Schelling moved further away from his early idealist starting point, becoming increasingly critical of idealism itself.

25 Fichte's absolute subject (absolute "Ich") is, we might say, *absolutely* subject.

26 The German verb "to judge", *urteilen*, contains the morpheme *teil*, which is the root of the verb "to divide", *teilen*. Hegel particularly would use the idea of separation contained in that of judging. To judge separates the subject *doing the judging* from the object as something standing over against it. But judging also separates what is *said* of the object (in the predicate of the judgment) from the object itself (represented in subject place in the subject–predicate structure of the judgment). Hence this exploits Reinhold's analysis of representation, in which he separates the *representation* from both the subject and the object to which the representation is related *by* the subject.

27 This is the attitude found in Jacobi, who thought that reflection out of the immediacy of belief–faith in the world led to nihilism.

28 Hence we can see the link to the *theological* differences here. Newton conceived of God's relation to the world in a conventionally theist way: God existed prior to the material world and created it "ex nihilo"—out of nothing. From the Spinozist perspective, the material world, conceived as a unity, *was* divine. But Schelling wasn't a conventional Spinozist, as his idea of a type of circular movement of separation and return exploited the Neoplatonic imagery of God not being the *creator* of the world, but the world being a type of emanation of God involving the reciprocal movements of "egress" and "regress".

29 Many in fact found this exile of the mind from nature, leaving it "dead" and mindless, reflected not only in Newton's physics but also in the orthodox Christian theology that Newton also held to. While the Greeks had populated the natural world with their divinities, the Christian world was one from which the "gods had flown". Other earlier thinkers such as Rousseau had also considered the human state as one of exile from a nature which had to be in some way regained.

30 "It is not an object of understanding, since understanding remains bound to limitation; nor is it one of reason, since even in *scientific* or *systematic thinking* reason can portray or present the synthesis of the absolute with limitation only ideally (archetypally). Hence, it is the object only of fantasy, which presents this synthesis in images" (PA: §31).

Chapter 9: Hegel's idealist metaphysics of spirit

1 Similarly, he says in his lectures on aesthetics that philosophy "has no other object but God and so is essentially rational theology". Philosophy, along with art and religion, belongs to what he refers to as "Absolute Spirit", and these three realms having this same content—God—"differ only in the *forms* in which they bring home to consciousness their object, the Absolute" (Aes: vol. 1, 149).

2 Most recently, this post-Kantian "modernist" interpretation of Hegel has been put forward in Pippin (1989, 1997) and Pinkard (1994, 2000, 2002). For opposing views, see, for example, Beiser (2002) and Stern (2009).

3 There is dispute over the degree to which his early theological writings were "anti-Christian". That Hegel's early views were based in a *criticism* of Christianity that appealed to the social life of the classical polis was forcefully put forward in Lukács (1975). The anti-Christian impulse of the early writings is challenged by more recent scholarship, however, which stresses the role of Hegel's unorthodox form of "Swabian" Christian belief. See, especially, Dickey (1987).

4 It is said that reading her husband's posthumously published lectures on the philosophy of religion had caused the devout and pious widow, Marie Hegel, considerable distress. See Pinkard (2000: 577).

5 This has led some to see Aristotle as putting forward an early "functionalist" account of the mind. See, for example, Nussbaum and Putnam (1992).

6 Proclus, in contrast, held that when the soul "descends" into the realm of generation and corruption, it does so *completely*, such that there could be no separable "part of it that remains above" (ET: prop. 211), as had been held by Plotinus.

7 Hegel's conception of the Trinity is more like that of the pagan Neoplatonists than their early Christian appropriators, such as Victorinus and Augustine. For Hegel, "the Father" is simply the indeterminate universality of Plotinus' "One" which by necessity unfolds into *Nous*, which is identified with "the Son". As has been pointed out, Victorinus, in the first systematic treatment of the Trinity doctrine, "telescopes" Plotinus' first two hypostases by making "Nous" or "logos" consubstantial with "the Father". See Rist (1996: 403). Such telescoping results in the traditional picture of "God's mind" as found in Augustine. On Hegel's Neoplatonic conception of the Trinity see, for example, LPR: pt III, A ("The First Element: The Idea of God in and for Itself").

8 For an excellent account of Hegel's blend of Aristotelian and Neoplatonic conceptions of *Nous* and the Soul see Ferrarin (2001: ch. 8).

9 As we have seen, this is just how Brucker had understood the Neoplatonic philosophy.

10 Following Plato, who had famously compared the structure of the soul to that of a city in the *Republic* (473c), Plotinus had even conceived of souls as embodied in *groups* of individuals, as in a city.

11 At least this is how Hegel had seemed to regard "phenomenology" when he wrote the *Phenomenology of Spirit*. He later seemed to waver between thinking of it as an *introduction* to the system of philosophy and thinking of it as a *part* of that system.

12 This tendency is further perpetuated by translating *Wissen* as "knowledge". Unlike English, German allows one to form a noun out of the infinitive of a verb, in this case, the verb *wissen*—"to know". The meaning of the nominalised infinitive, however, is closer to an English *gerund*, in this case, the term "knowing" rather than "knowledge".

13 Frank (2004: 178–79) attributes this idea that "the concept of finitude is dialectically bound to that of infinity and cannot be isolated from it" as occurring first to Friedrich Schlegel.

14 For Fichte, any particular form of positing of an object or non-self in response to the "check" must simultaneously posit the self *as* determined by the non-self. But in self-positing the positing and posited are identical, and so *qua* absolute activity the self must surpass this finite form in which it finds itself.

15 The mind is rational because it is self-correcting. This is an idea found later in the pragmatist philosophies of C. S. Peirce and Wilfrid Sellars.

16 Consciousness had started out taking the immediate qualitatively determined "this" of Sense-certainty as the *truth* of its object and had come to learn that such immediately perceivable quality is just an aspect of the more complex object of *Perception*. In contrast to the simplicity of the "this" of Sense-certainty, the perceived object has an internal structure such that an underlying substance has changeable phenomenal properties. But in turn *Perception* learns that *its* object is in truth more complicated again, the distinction between it and the Understanding roughly enacting that between the everyday common-sensical and scientific or "nomological" views of the world. While from the point of view of

Perception we might think of the world as simply an assemblage of propertied objects, from the point of view of the Understanding, such objects will be integrated as interacting components of a single, unified, law-governed world.

17 Hegel's thought here seems to be related to Leibniz's principle of the "identity of indiscernibles". It is unclear that a word like "here" has a content if we are deprived of making any contrasts between a "here" and a "there". But one needs to be able to *discern* a difference between "here" and "there" by appeal to different things that *are* here and there.

18 This view is often thought to derive from the work of the early twentieth-century linguist, Ferdinand de Saussure, but the principle, which is extensively used by Hegel, is found also in Fichte and the early romantics, particularly Novalis. Hegel thinks it is at least implicit in Plato.

19 Of course not every term other than red excludes that colour from *being* red, as is shown with the term "scarlet" for example.

20 See, for example, Vieillard-Baron (1988: 189–210).

21 Plotinus, in imaging the "One" as a spring from which flow all the rivers of life, nevertheless notes that "we are always brought back to The One" (Enn: Ennead III, treatise 8, ch. 10).

22 Moreover, it is clear that even Hegel himself never came to a stable position concerning the role of the *Phenomenology of Spirit* within his philosophy as a whole.

23 The analogy here would be with Aristotle's conception of a philosophical inquiry into "being *qua* being", which is presupposed by inquiries into different *types* of being.

24 Horstmann's idea that, for Hegel, the doing of ontology *requires* epistemological reflection on the type of knowledge involved clearly captures the idea of a Kantian prolegomenon to metaphysics, *minus* the unwanted "transcendental scepticism" of Kant's perspective.

25 For a recent helpful account of Hegel's relation to Proclus see Beierwaltes (2004: 154–87). The logico-semantic aspects of Proclus' approach to negation have been explored in Lloyd (1990) and J. Martin (2004).

26 Spinoza starts *The Ethics* with a series of definitions, comprehending *substance* as "what is in itself and is conceived through itself, that is, that whose concept does not require the concept of another thing, from which it must be formed" (E: pt 1, def. 3).

27 "By God I understand a being absolutely infinite, that is, a substance consisting of an infinity of attributes, of which each one expresses an eternal and infinite essence" (E: pt 1, def. 6).

28 Hegel conceives of the Neoplatonists as effectively trying to reconcile Plato and Aristotle, an account in broad agreement with contemporary approaches. See, for example, Gerson (2005: 259). On Hegel's Neoplatonic reading of Aristotle's *noesis noeseos* doctrine, see Ferrarin (2001: 98–101).

29 Thus Spinoza belongs to what Lawrence Horn calls the "asymmetricalist" tradition in the treatment of the semantics of negative statements, which are seen as "less primitive, less informative, less objective, less godly, and/or less valuable than their affirmative counterparts" (Horn 2001: 3).

30 The notion derives from Proclus' treatment of negation (CPP: 424–40, 523), and the phrase "negatio negationis" is found in Christian Platonists such as Meister Eckhart. See McGinn (2005: 46–47). See also Hegel's extensive discussion of the "unity of positive and negative" in the context of his account of contradiction in the *Science of Logic* (SL: 435–38).

31 Extracts from Bruno's *De la Causa*, which reproduced key arguments of Cusa's *On Learned Ignorance* concerning the identity of the absolute maxima and minima,

were appended to Jacobi's *Über die Lehre des Spinoza*, and this seems to be the transmission route for the Cusan conception of *coincidentia oppositorum* into German idealism. See, for example, Düsing (1988: 114, 151).

32 I have charted some of this terrain in Redding (2007).

Chapter 10: Schopenhauer, Nietzsche and the ambiguous end of the idealist tradition

1 It will be remembered that Berkeley had denied that we can infer knowledge of material objects from that of their representations and then had *explained* the causation of our positing material objects—the fact that our representations are, as it were, not under our control—by appealing to their originating in the *mind of God*.

2 That is, like other post-Kantian idealists, Schopenhauer "corrects" Kant by formulating Kant's claims in terms of the "two-aspects" approach that many contemporary Kantians believed to be Kant's own view.

3 In this category Schopenhauer puts pornography, but also the depiction of food in Dutch still-life painting!

4 This trajectory had been charted by Heinrich Heine in his 1835 critique of the romantic school in Heine (1985).

5 A. W. Schlegel had regarded the *Nibelungenlied* as a type of "holy text" for the Germans, their equivalent of Homer's Odyssey. See Williamson (2004: 86). In Wagner's understanding of the Nibelungen myths, he had apparently been influenced by the theories of F. J. Mone (ibid.: 188). Mone was a follower of Friedrich Creuzer who, as we will see below, played a crucial role in Nietzsche's interpretation of the Dionysus myth.

6 See, for example, B. Magee (2001: 50–51). Wagner's theoretical writings from around this time such as "Art and Revolution" (of 1849) and "The Art-Work of the Future" (of 1850) show the heavy influence of Feuerbach. The latter is dedicated to Feuerbach and the title is taken from Feuerbach's own "The Philosophy of the Future" (AWF: 394–95).

7 Wagner started work on the *Parsifal* project in 1857, but it did not premier until 1882.

8 This is convincingly argued by N. Martin (1996: ch. 1). As Martin points out, Nietzsche is often portrayed as unilaterally antagonistic to Schiller, but while this may be true of his later work from around the time of *Thus Spoke Zarathustra*, Nietzsche's references to Schiller up until the mid-1870s had been predominantly positive.

9 Creuzer's four-volume *Symbolik und Mythologie der alten Völker, besonders der Griechen* went through multiple editions after its first appearance between 1810 and 1812. While Creuzer was influenced by the idealists, the relationship was not entirely one way. In particular, Creuzer seems to have influenced Hegel who was his philosophical colleague at Heidelberg during 1816–18 (Vieillard-Baron 1988: 211–20). Moreover, their continuing correspondence after Hegel's departure for Berlin suggests a lasting friendship.

10 He also emphasised the sexual basis of ancient Asian religions, based on the polarity of male and female.

11 In his later work Nietzsche became particularly fixated on the distinction between Dionysus and Jesus.

12 Such a view was expressed by the character Silenus, who, when asked what was the best and most desirable thing for humans answered "not to be born, not to *be*, to be *nothing*. But the second best for you is—to die soon" (BT: §3).

13 Nietzsche's early period, dominated by Wagner and Schopenhauer, is usually said to have ended around 1876. It is clear that Nietzsche was deeply disturbed by the first Bayreuth Festival, staged in that year. He had believed that *The Ring* was about the spiritual renewal of a decadent society, but it had become the triumphalist symbol of that society: in short, Wagner had "sold out". But the causes of the changes in Nietzsche's outlook are clearly complex.

14 While the child's feeling of eternity came from it having no remembered past or anticipated future, this latter feeling of eternity comes from one's radical cognitive detachment from one's present and so from a past or future.

15 The full passage taken from Nietzsche's notebooks in the 1880s runs as follows: "Against positivism which halts at phenomena—'There are only facts'—I would say, No, facts is precisely what there is not, only interpretations. We cannot establish any fact 'in itself': perhaps it is folly to want to do such a thing" (WP: §481). The Kantian nature of this claim should be apparent. Facts need logical form, but Kant is an idealist about form, so there can be no facts "in themselves".

16 Nietzsche's "middle period" is usually said to have spanned the texts *Human, All Too Human* (of 1878), "Assorted Opinions and Maxims" (of 1879), "The Wanderer and His Shadow" (1880), *Daybreak* (1881), and the first four books of *The Gay Science* (1882). On the orientation of Nietzsche's writings in this period see, especially, Abbey (2000).

17 Thus in *Daybreak*, a work dedicated to Voltaire, he appeals to a type of radicalisation of the Enlightenment criticism of religion, by historically exposing the mechanisms of its genesis: "In former times, one sought to prove that there is no God – today one indicates how the belief that there is a God could arise and how this belief acquired its weight and importance: a counter-proof that there is no God thereby becomes superfluous. ... in former times ... atheists did not know how to make a clean sweep" (D: §95).

18 In Redding (1993) I try to characterise the continuities and discontinuities between the more naturalistic approach to genealogy, that of the "English Genealogists", and Nietzsche's mature stance.

19 Evidence for and against regarding the eternal recurrence as a cosmological thesis is well treated by Alexander Nehamas (1985: ch. 5). Nehamas's own interpretation is a non-naturalistic one and closer to the "idealist" reading suggested here.

20 Pippin (1997: 333) resists this type of reading of Nietzsche in a different context, helpfully setting out *three* ways of viewing Nietzsche as related to the notion of modernity—*pre*modern or "atavistic", modern, and *post*modern. In affirming his status as a modern thinker, Pippin brings Nietzsche within the scope of Kant and post-Kantian thinkers such as Hegel. It should be noted, however, that many of the characteristics of what is intended as a postmodern philosophical position are themselves within the enlarged orbit of post-Kantian idealism as treated here. In particular, the "postmodern" Nietzsche has many of the characteristics of the "ironism" of the early Friedrich Schlegel.

21 The spirit of this "hurdy-gurdy song" might be compared to that of the account of space and time given in Sense-certainty. "The *Here pointed out*, to which I hold fast ... in fact, is *not* this Here, but a Before and Behind, an Above and Below, a Right and Left. The Above is itself similarly this manifold otherness of above, below, etc. The Here, which was supposed to have been pointed out, vanishes in other Heres, but these likewise vanish" (Phen: §108).

22 Harries (2001: 61) suggests that we see Nietzsche's eternal recurrence as an extension of Cusanus' use of the infinite sphere metaphor and its "coincidence of opposites", but without the implication of direct influence.

23 In Schopenhauer, however, it reverts to a much more *realist* metaphysical conception.

24 This was the part of the *Enneads* translated by the Schelling-inspired philologist, Friedrich Creuzer, who had done much to introduce *both* Plotinus and Dionysus into idealist and romantic thought.

25 It is significant that Plotinus actually presents his account as a form of *play*, "before entering upon our serious concern" (Enn: Ennead III, treatise 8, ch. 1).

Postscript: idealism after the end of (its) history

1 As Marx put it in 1873 in his Afterword to the second German edition of *Das Kapital* (Cptl: 29).

2 See, for example, De Caro and Macarthur (2004).

3 In Redding (2007) I have charted the emergence of an Hegelian approach within analytic philosophy with the work of Sellars, Brandom and McDowell.

4 Williams (B. Williams 1978) first introduced the idea of an "absolute conception of the world", and later developed the idea of the non-objective or irreducibly perspectival nature of moral claims (B. Williams 1985: ch. 5).

5 Our accounts of semantics (like those of ethics) must, of course, be *consistent* with physics, but "any attempt to *reduce* semantic relations to concepts of physics is doomed" (B. Williams 2000: 484).

6 On the extent of Williams's Hegelian tendencies, especially in relation to his critique of Kantian moral philosophy, see Jenkins (2006: 84–86).

7 And this benign form of teleology, I suggest, is what is to be expected from Hegel's logical considerations. "Ontologically" conceived, a teleological development could only mean something like the progressive realisation of features "implicitly" found in the earlier form. On this reading, Hegel's teleology could be seen in either of two ways, either as the development of a "divine" self-consciousness for which finite human beings provided the vehicle, or as the realisation of some "species character" implicit in human beings, but which needed the development of certain social and cultural conditions for its expression. But both of these alternatives ignore Hegel's "Proclean" refusal to consider "negation" asymmetrically, as dependent on some semantically prior non-privative term. He recognised no ultimate "thing", like Spinoza's substance, prior to the negations via which it achieves determinacy.

BIBLIOGRAPHY

Primary sources on Continental idealism

Anon

OSP "The Oldest Systematic Programme of German Idealism", in *The Early Political Writings of the German Romantics*, ed. and trans, Frederick C. Beiser, Cambridge: Cambridge University Press, 1996.

J. G. Fichte

EPW *Early Philosophical Writings*, trans. and ed. Dainiel Breazeale, Ithaca: Cornell University Press, 1988.

FISK "First Introduction to the Science of Knowledge" in *The Science of Knowledge*, ed. and trans. Peter Heath and John Lachs, Cambridge: Cambridge University Press, 1982.

Fnds *Foundations of the Entire Science of Knowledge*, in *The Science of Knowledge*, ed. and trans. Peter Heath and John Lachs, Cambridge: Cambridge University Press, 1982.

FNM *Foundations of Transcendental Philosophy* (*Wissenschaftslehre*) Nova Methodo (1796–99), trans. and ed. Dainiel Breazeale, Ithaca: Cornell University Press, 1998.

FNR *Foundations of Natural Right*, ed. Frederick Neuhouser, Cambridge: Cambridge University Press, 2000.

GA *Gesamtausgabe der Bayerischen Akademie der Wissenschaften*, ed. Reinhard Lauth and Hans Jacob, Stuttgart–Bad Cannstatt: Frommann, 1962–.

RA "Review of Aenesidemus", in George di Giovanni and H. S. Harris, *Between Kant and Hegel: Texts in the Development of Post-Kantian Idealism*, Albany: SUNY Press, 1985.

G. W. F. Hegel

Aes *Aesthetics: Lectures on Fine Art*, trans. T. M. Knox, Oxford: Clarendon Press, 1975.

EL *The Encyclopaedia Logic: Part I of the Encyclopaedia of Philosophical Sciences with the Zusätze*, trans. T. F. Geraets, W. A. Suchting and H. S. Harris, Indianapolis: Hackett, 1991.

EPR   *Elements of the Philosophy of Right*, ed. Allen W. Wood, trans. H. B. Nisbet, Cambridge: Cambridge University Press, 1991.

FK   *Faith and Knowledge*, trans. Walter Cerf and H. S. Harris, Albany: SUNY Press, 1977.

LHP   *Lectures on the History of Philosophy*, trans. E. S. Haldane, 3 vols, Lincoln: University of Nebraska Press, 1995.

LPR   *Lectures on the Philosophy of Religion: One-volume Edition—The Lectures of 1827*, ed. Peter C. Hodgson, Berkeley: University of California Press, 1988.

Phen   *Phenomenology of Spirit*, trans. A. V. Miller, Oxford: Oxford University Press, 1977.

PM   *Hegel's Philosophy of Mind: Being Part Three of the "Encyclopaedia of the Philosophical Sciences"* (1830), trans. William Wallace and A. V. Miller, Oxford: Clarendon Press, 1971.

PN   *Hegel's Philosophy of Nature*, ed. and trans. M. J. Petry, 3 vols, London: George Allen & Unwin, 1970.

SL   *Science of Logic*, trans. A. V. Miller, London: Allen & Unwin, 1969.

W   *Werke*, ed. Eva Moldenhauer and Karl Markus Michel, 20 vols, Frankfurt am Main: Suhrkamp Verlag.

Immanuel Kant

For all reference to texts of Kant except CPuR and CJ, page numbers are given to the relevant volume of KGS, for example, 5.232 is vol. 5, p. 232.

CJ   *Critique of Judgment*, trans. W. S. Pluhar, Indianapolis: Hackett, 1987.

CJFI   First introduction to the *Critique of Judgment*, in CJ, pp. 385–441.

Corr   *Correspondence*, ed. and trans. A. Zweig, Cambridge: Cambridge University Press, 1999.

CPrR   *Critique of Practical Reason*, ed. and trans. Mary Gregor, Cambridge: Cambridge University Press, 1997.

CPuR   *Critique of Pure Reason*, ed. and trans. Paul Guyer and Allen W. Wood, Cambridge: Cambridge University Press, 1998.

GMM   *Groundwork of the Metaphysics of Morals*, ed. Mary Gregor, intro. Christine M. Korsgaard, Cambridge: Cambridge University Press, 1997.

KGS   *Kants Gesammelte Schriften*, Berlin: Preußische Akademie der Wissenschaften, 1900–.

LL   *Lectures on Logic*, ed. and trans. J. Michael Young, Cambridge: Cambridge University Press, 1992.

MM   *The Metaphysics of Morals*, trans. Mary Gregor, Cambridge: Cambridge University Press, 1996.

OP   *Opus Postumum*, ed. E. Förster, trans. E. Förster and M. Rosen, Cambridge: Cambridge University Press, 1993.

Prol   *Prolegomena to Any Future Metaphysics*, in Immanuel Kant, *Philosophy of Material Nature*, trans. J. W. Ellington, Indianapolis: Hackett, 1985.

Rel   *Religion within the Boundaries of Mere Reason*, in Immanuel Kant, *Religion and Rational Theology*, ed. Allen W. Wood and George di Giovanni, Cambridge: Cambridge University Press, 1996.

TP   *Theoretical Philosophy, 1755–1770*, ed. and trans. D. Walford and R. Meerbote, Cambridge: Cambridge University Press, 1992.

G. W. Leibniz

DM   "Discourse on Metaphysics" in *Philosophical Texts*, trans. and ed. R. S. Woolhouse and Richard Francks, Oxford: Oxford University Press, 1998.

L-C   G. W. Leibniz and Samuel Clarke, *Correspondence*, ed. and intro. Roger Ariew, Indianapolis: Hackett, 2000.

M   "Monadology" in *Philosophical Texts*, trans. and ed. R. S. Woolhouse and Richard Francks, Oxford: Oxford University Press, 1998.

NE   *New Essays on Human Understanding*, trans. and ed. Peter Remnant and Jonathan Bennett, Cambridge: Cambridge University Press, 1996.

PE   *Philosophical Essays*, trans. R. Ariew and D. Garber, Indianapolis: Hackett, 1989.

PT   *Philosophical Texts*, trans. and ed. R. S. Woolhouse and Richard Francks, Oxford: Oxford University Press, 1998.

Th   *Theodicy: Essays on the Goodness of God, the Freedom of Man and the Origin of Evil*, ed. and intro. A. Farrer, trans. E. M. Huggard, Chicago: Open Court, 1985.

Friedrich Nietzsche

BT   *The Birth of Tragedy out of the Spirit of Music*, in *Basic Writings of Nietzsche*, trans. and ed. Walter Kaufmann, New York: Random House, 1968.

D   *Daybreak: Thoughts on the Prejudices of Morality*, trans. R. J. Hollingdale, intro. Michael Tanner, Cambridge: Cambridge University Press, 1982.

GS   *The Gay Science, with a Prelude in Rhymes and an Appendix of Songs*, trans. Walter Kaufmann, New York: Vintage Books, 1974.

UDH   "On the Uses and Disadvantages of History for Life", in *Untimely Meditations*, trans. and ed. R. J. Hollingdale, Cambridge: Cambridge University Press, 1983.

TI   *Twilight of the Idols*, in *The Portable Nietzsche*, trans. and ed. Walter Kaufman, New York: Viking Press, 1959.

TSZ   *Thus Spoke Zarathustra: A Book for Everyone and No One*, trans. R. J. Hollingdale, Harmondsworth: Penguin, 1961.

WP   *The Will to Power*, ed. Walter Kaufmann, trans. Walter Kaufmann and R. J. Hollingdale, New York: Random House, 1967.

Karl Leonard Reinhold

FPK   "The Foundation of Philosophical Knowledge" (partial translation of *Über das Fundament des philosophischen Wissens* [1791]), in *Between Kant and Hegel: Texts in the Development of Post-Kantian Idealism*, ed. George di Giovanni and H. S. Harris, Albany: SUNY Press, 1985, 52–106.

LKP   *Letters on the Kantian Philosophy*, ed. Karl Ameriks, trans. James Hebbeler, Cambridge: Cambridge University Press, 2005.

BIBLIOGRAPHY

F. W. J. Schelling

FOS *First Outline of a System of the Philosophy of Nature*, trans. and intro. K. R. Peterson, Albany: SUNY Press, 2004.
HMP *On the History of Modern Philosophy*, trans. and intro. Andrew Bowie, Cambridge: Cambridge University Press, 1994.
IPN *Ideas for a Philosophy of Nature*, trans. E. E. Harris and P. Heath, New York: Cambridge University Press, 1988.
PA *Philosophy of Art*, ed. and trans. Douglas W. Stott, Minneapolis: University of Minnesota Press, 1989.
STI *System of Transcendental Idealism (1800)*, trans. Peter Heath, intro. Michael Vater, Charlottesville: University Press of Virginia, 1978.
T *Timaeus* (1794), ed. Hartmut Buchner, Stuttgart: Frommann-Holzboog, 1994.

See also *Schriften*, ed. Manfred Frank, Frankfurt am Main: Suhrkamp, 1985.

Friedrich Schiller

AE *On the Aesthetic Education of Man: In a Series of Letters*, ed. and trans. Elizabeth M. Wilkinson and L. A. Willoughby, Oxford: Clarendon Press, 1967.
NSP *Naïve and Sentimental Poetry and On the Sublime*, trans. and intro. Julius A. Elias, New York: Frederick Ungar.

Friedrich Schlegel

AF "Atheneum Fragments" in *Philosophical Fragments*, trans. Peter Firchow, Minneapolis: University of Minnesota Press, 1991.
CF "Critical Fragments" in *Philosophical Fragments*, trans. Peter Firchow, Minneapolis: University of Minnesota Press, 1991.
DP "Dialogue on Poetry", in *Dialogue on Poetry and Literary Aphorisms*, trans. E. Behler and R. Struc, University Park: Pennsylvania State University Press, 1968.
KA *Kritische Friedrich-Schlegel-Ausgabe*, ed. E. Behler, J. J. Anstett and H. Eichner, 35 vols, Munich: F. Schöningh, 1958–2002.

Friedrich Schopenhauer

WWR *The World as Will and Representation*, trans E. G. F. Payne, Dover, New York, 1969.

Other primary sources

Aristotle

Cats *Categories*, in *The Categories, On Interpretation, and Prior Analytics*, ed. and trans. H. P. Cooke, Loeb Classical Library, Cambridge, Mass.: Harvard University Press, 1960.

DA *De anima*, ed., with intro. and commentary, David Ross, Oxford: Clarendon Press, 1961.
Meta *Metaphysics*, trans. Hugh Tredennick, Loeb Classical Library, Aristotle XVII–XVIII, Cambridge, Mass.: Harvard University Press, 1960.
OH *On the Heavens*, trans. W. R. C. Guthrie, Loeb Classical Library, Cambridge, Mass.: Harvard University Press, 1960.
Phys *Physics*, trans. P. H. Wicksteed and F. M. Cornford, Loeb Classical Library, Cambridge, Mass.: Harvard University Press, 1960.

Augustine

CG *The City of God against the Pagans*, ed. and trans. R. W. Dyson, Cambridge: Cambridge University Press, 1998.

George Berkeley

WGB *The Works of George Berkeley, Bishop of Cloyne*, ed. A. A. Luce and T. E. Jessop, London: Thomas Nelson & Sons, 1948–57.
PHK *A Treatise Concerning the Principles of Human Knowledge*, ed. Jonathan Dancy, Oxford: Oxford University Press, 1998.
TD *Three Dialogues between Hylas and Philonous*, Amherst: Prometheus Books, 1988.

Ralph Cudworth

TISU *The True Intellectual System of the Universe*, with new intro. G. A. J. Rogers, Bristol: Thoemmes Press, 1995.

Meister Eckhart

ES *The Essential Sermons, Commentaries, Treatises, and Defense*, trans. and intro. Edmund Colledge and Bernard McGinn, New York: Paulist Press, 1981.
SW *Selected Writings*, trans. Oliver Davies, London: Penguin, 1995.

Ludwig Feuerbach

EC *The Essence of Christianity*, trans. George Eliot, New York: Harper, 1957.
PPF *Principles of the Philosophy of the Future*, trans. M. H. Vogel, intro. T. H. Wartenberg, Indianapolis: Hackett, 1986.

Hugo Grotius

CLPB *Commentary on the Law of Prize and Booty*, trans. G. L. Williams and W. H. Zeydel, Oxford: Oxford University Press, 1950.

Thomas Hobbes

HEW   *Hobbes' English Works*, ed. W. Molesworth, London, 1841.
L   *Leviathan, with Selected Variants from the Latin Edition of 1668*, ed. Edwin Curley, Indianapolis: Hackett, 1994.

David Hume

Enq   *Enquiries Concerning Human Understanding and Concerning the Principles of Morals*, ed. L. A. Selby-Bigge and P. H. Nidditch, Oxford: Clarendon Press, 1975.
THN   *A Treatise on Human Nature*, ed. L. A. Selby-Bigge and P. H. Nidditch, Oxford: Clarendon Press, 1978.

John Locke

EHU   *An Essay Concerning Human Understanding*, Oxford: Clarendon Press, 1975.

Karl Marx

Cptl   *Capital: A Critique of Political Economy*, vol. 1, trans. Samuel Moore and Edward Aveling, ed. Frederick Engels, Moscow: Progress Publishers, 1996.

Henry More

AAA   *An Antidote against Atheism, or, An Appeal to the Naturall Faculties of the Minde of Man, Whether There Be Not a God*, London: J. Flesher, 1665.

Isaac Newton

MPNP   *Mathematical Principles of Natural Philosophy, and His System of the World*, trans. Andrew Motte in 1729, trans. rev. Florian Cajori, 2 vols, Berkeley: University of California Press, 1962.
NPN   *Newton's Philosophy of Nature: Selections from His Writings*, ed. H. S. Thayer, intro. J. H. Randall Jr, Mineola, N.Y.: Dover, 2005.

Nicholas of Cusa

OLI   *On Learned Ignorance*, in *Selected Spiritual Writings*, trans. and intro. H. Lawrence Bond, New York: Paulist Press, 1997.

Plato

CW   *Complete Works*, ed. J. M. Cooper, Indianapolis: Hackett, 1997.

Plotinus

Enn   *The Enneads*, trans. Stephen Mackenna, intro. and notes John Dillon, London: Penguin, 1991.

Porphyry

Int   *Introduction*, trans., with commentary, Jonathan Barnes, Oxford: Oxford University Press, 2003.

Proclus

ET   *The Elements of Theology* trans. and commentary, E. R. Dodds, Oxford: Clarendon Press, 1933.
CPP   *A Commentary on Plato's Parmenides*, trans. John M. Dillon and Glenn R. Morrow, Princeton, N.J.: Princeton University Press, 1987.

Jean-Jacques Rousseau

SC   *The Social Contract*, in *The Social Contract and Discourses*, trans. G. D. H. Cole, London: Dent, 1973.

Spinoza

E   *The Ethics*, in *A Spinoza Reader*, ed. and trans. Edwin Curley, Princeton, N.J.: Princeton University Press, 1994.

Richard Wagner

AWF   *The Art Work of the Future and Other Works*, trans. W. A. Ellis, Lincoln: University of Nebraska Press, 1993.

Secondary and other works

Abbey, Ruth (2000) *Nietzsche's Middle Period*, Oxford: Oxford University Press.
Adams, Robert Merrihew (1994) *Leibniz: Determinist, Theist, Idealist*, Oxford: Oxford University Press.
Allison, Henry E. (1990) *Kant's Theory of Freedom*, Cambridge: Cambridge University Press.
Allison, Henry E. (2000) "Is the *Critique of Judgment* 'Post-Critical'?" in Sedgwick (2000).
Allison, Henry E. (2004) *Kant's Transcendental Idealism: An Interpretation and Defense*, rev., enlarged edn, New Haven, Conn.: Yale University Press.
Antognazza, Maria Rosa (1999) "*Immeatio* and *Emperichoresis*: The Theological Roots of Harmony in Bisterfeld and Leibniz", in *The Young Leibniz and His Philosophy* (1646–76), ed. Stuart Brown, Dordrecht and London: Kluwer Academic.

Antognazza, Maria Rosa (2007) *Leibniz on the Trinity and the Incarnation: Reason and Revelation in the Seventeenth Century*, trans. Gerald Parks, New Haven, Conn.: Yale University Press.

Armstrong, David M. (1997) *A World of States of Affairs*, Cambridge: Cambridge University Press.

Ayers, Michael M. (2005) "Was Berkeley an Empiricist or a Rationalist?" in *The Cambridge Companion to Berkeley*, ed. Kenneth P. Winkler, Cambridge: Cambridge University Press.

Baruzi, Jean (1907) *Leibniz et l'organisation religieuse de la terre*, Paris: Félix Alcan.

Baum, Manfred (2000) "The Beginnings of Schelling's Philosophy of Nature", in Sedgwick (2000).

Beaney, Michael (2007) "Analysis", *The Stanford Encyclopedia of Philosophy* (Fall 2007 edn), ed. Edward N. Zalta, < http://plato.stanford.edu/archives/fall2007/entries/analysis/ > .

Beck, Lewis White (1960) *A Commentary on Kant's "Critique of Practical Reason"*, Chicago: University of Chicago Press.

Beierwaltes, Werner (2004) *Platonismus und Idealismus*, Frankfurt am Main: Vittorio Klostermann.

Beiser, Frederick C. (1987) *The Fate of Reason: German Philosophy from Kant to Fichte*, Cambridge, Mass.: Harvard University Press.

Beiser, Frederick C. (1996) *The Sovereignty of Reason: The Defense of Rationality in the Early English Enlightenment*, Princeton, N.J.: Princeton University Press.

Beiser, Frederick C. (2002) *German Idealism: The Struggle against Subjectivism*, 1781–1801, Cambridge, Mass.: Harvard University Press.

Beiser, Frederick C. (2003) *The Romantic Imperative: The Concept of Early German Romanticism*, Cambridge, Mass.: Harvard University Press.

Beiser, Frederick C. (2005) *Schiller as Philosopher: A Re-Examination*, Oxford: Oxford University Press.

Beiser, Frederick C. (2006) "Moral Faith and the Highest Good", in *The Cambridge Companion to Kant and Modern Philosophy*, ed. Paul Guyer, Cambridge: Cambridge University Press.

Bernstein, Richard J. (2001) "Radical Evil: Kant at War With Himself", in *Rethinking Evil: Contemporary Perspectives*, ed. Maria Pia Lara, Berkeley: University of California Press.

Bird, Graham (2006) *The Revolutionary Kant: A Commentary on the "Critique of Pure Reason"*, Peru, Ill.: Open Court.

Blumenbach, Johann Friedrich (1781) *Über den Bildungstrieb und das Zeugungsgeschäft*, Göttingen: J. C. Dieterich.

Blumenberg, Hans (1983) *The Legitimacy of the Modern Age*, trans. Robert M. Wallace, Cambridge, Mass.: MIT Press.

Bowie, Andrew (1993) *Aesthetics and Subjectivity: From Kant to Nietzsche*, Manchester: Manchester University Press.

Bowie, Andrew (1997) *From Romanticism to Critical Theory: The Philosophy of German Literary Theory*, London: Routledge & Kegan Paul.

Bowie, Andrew (2007) *Music, Philosophy and Modernity*, Cambridge: Cambridge University Press.

Brandom, Robert B. (2000) *Articulating Reasons*, Cambridge, Mass.: Harvard University Press.

Brandom, Robert B. (2002) *Tales of the Mighty Dead: Historical Essays in the Metaphysics of Intentionality*, Cambridge, Mass.: Harvard University Press.

Brient, Elizabeth (2002) *The Immanence of the Infinite: Hans Blumenberg and the Threshold to Modernity*, Washington, D.C.: Catholic University Press of America.

Brown, Stuart (1995) "The Seventeenth-Century Intellectual Background", in *The Cambridge Companion to Leibniz*, ed. Nicholas Jolley, Cambridge: Cambridge University Press.

Brown, Stuart (1998) "Some Occult Influences in Leibniz's Monadology", in Coudert *et al.* (1998).

Brucker, Johann Jakob (2001) *The History of Philosophy from the Earliest Periods: Drawn up from Brucker's Historia Critica Philosophiæ*, ed. W. Enfield, Bristol: Thoemmes Press.

Bruno, Giordano (1995) *The Ash Wednesday Supper*, ed. and trans. Edward A. Gosselin and Lawrence S. Lerner, Toronto: University of Toronto Press.

Bubner, Rüdiger (2003) *The Innovations of Idealism*, trans. Nicholas Walker, Cambridge: Cambridge University Press.

Burnyeat, Myles (1982) "Idealism and Greek Philosophy: What Descartes Saw and Berkeley Missed", *Philosophical Review* 91: 3–40.

Burri, Alex (2004) "Facts and Fictions", in *The Literary Wittgenstein*, ed. John Gibson and Wolfgang Huemer, London: Routledge.

Cassirer, Ernst (1963) *The Individual and the Cosmos in Renaissance Philosophy*, trans. M. Domandi, Oxford: Blackwell.

Cavell, Stanley (1976) "The Avoidance of Love", in *Must We Mean What We Say? A Book of Essays*, Cambridge: Cambridge University Press.

Christianson, Gale E. (1984) *In the Presence of the Creator: Isaac Newton and His Times*, New York: Free Press.

Clarke, Edwin and L. S. Jacyna (1987) *Nineteenth-Century Origins of Neuroscientific Concepts*, Berkeley: University of California Press.

Cohen, Norman (1970) *The Pursuit of the Millennium: Revolutionary Millenarians and Mystical Anarchists of the Middle Ages*, rev. edn, London: Paladin.

Coleman, Janet (2000) *A History of Political Thought: From Ancient Greece to Early Christianity*, Oxford: Blackwell.

Cooper, Laurence D. (2002) "Human Nature and the Love of Wisdom: Rousseau's Hidden (and Modified) Platonism", *Journal of Politics* 64: 108–25.

Coudert, Allison P., Richard H. Popkin and Gordon M. Weiner (eds) (1998) *Leibniz, Mysticism, and Religion*, Dordrecht: Kluwer Academic.

Crites, Stephen (1998) *Dialectic and Gospel in the Development of Hegel's Thinking*, University Park: Pennsylvania State University Press.

Darwall, Stephen (1995) *The British Moralists and the Internal "Ought": 1640–1740*, Cambridge: Cambridge University Press.

Darwall, Stephen (2006) *The Second-Person Standpoint: Morality, Respect and Account-ability*, Cambridge, Mass.: Harvard University Press.

De Caro, Mario, and David Macarthur (2004) *Naturalism in Question*, Cambridge, Mass.: Harvard University Press.

Dennett, Daniel C. (1987) *The Intentional Stance*, Cambridge, Mass.: MIT Press.

Dickey, Lawrence (1987) *Hegel: Religion, Economics, and the Politics of Spirit, 1770–1807*, Cambridge: Cambridge University Press.

di Giovanni, George, and H. S. Harris (1985) *Between Kant and Hegel*, Albany: SUNY Press.

Dihle, Albrecht (1982) *The Theory of Will in Classical Antiquity*, Berkeley: University of California Press.

Duhem, Pierre (1985) *Medieval Cosmology: Theories of Infinity, Place, Time, Void, and the Plurality of Worlds*, ed. and trans. Roger Ariew, Chicago: University of Chicago Press.

Düsing, Klaus (1988) "Absolute Identität und Formen der Endlichkeit: Interpretationen zu Schellings und Hegels erster absoluter Metaphysik", in *Schellings und Hegels erste absolute Metaphysik (1801–2)*, ed. K. Düsing, Cologne: Jürgen Dinter.

Edwards, Jeffrey (2000a) "Self-Love, Anthropology, and Universal Benevolence in Kant's Metaphysics of Morals", *Review of Metaphysics* 53: 887–914.

Edwards, Jeffrey (2000b) "Spinozism, Freedom, and Transcendental Dynamics in Kant's Final System of Transcendental Idealism", in Sedgwick (2000).

Edwards, Jeffrey (2000c) *Substance, Force, and the Possibility of Knowledge: On Kant's Philosophy of Material Nature*, Berkeley: University of California Press.

Ferrari, Giovanni (1989) "Plato on Poetry", in *The Cambridge History of Literary Criticism*, ed. George A. Kennedy, Cambridge: Cambridge University Press.

Ferrarin, Alfredo (2001) *Hegel and Aristotle*, Cambridge: Cambridge University Press.

Flathman, Richard E. (1992) *Willful Liberalism: Voluntarism and Individuality in Political Theory and Practice*, Ithaca: Cornell University Press.

Force, James E. (1990) "Newton's God of Dominion: The Unity of Newton's Theological, Scientific and Political Thought", in *Essays on the Context, Nature, and Influence of Isaac Newton's Theology*, ed. James E. Force and Richard H. Popkin, Dordrecht: Kluwer.

Förster, Eckhart (2000) *Kant's Final Synthesis*, Cambridge, Mass.: Harvard University Press.

Frank, Manfred (1997) *Unendliche Annäherung: Die Anfänge der Philosophischen Frühromantik*, Frankfurt am Main: Suhrkamp.

Frank, Manfred (2004) *The Philosophical Foundations of Early German Romanticism*, trans. Elizabeth Millán-Zaibert, Albany: SUNY Press.

Franks, Paul W. (2005) *All or Nothing: Systematicity, Transcendental Arguments, and Skepticism in German Idealism*, Cambridge, Mass.: Harvard University Press.

Franz, Michael (2003) "Der Neuplatonismus in den philosophiehistorische Arbeiten der zweiten Hälfte des 18. Jahrhunderts", in *Platonismus im Idealismus: Die platonische Tradition in der klassischen deutschen Philosophie*, ed. Burkhard Mojsisch and Orrin F. Summerell, Munich: K. G. Saur.

Frazer, Alexander Campbell (1908) *Berkeley and Spiritual Realism*, London: Constable.

Friedman, Michael (1992) *Kant and the Exact Sciences*, Cambridge: Cambridge University Press.

Funkenstein, Amos (1986) *Theology and the Scientific Imagination from the Middle Ages to the Seventeenth Century*, Princeton, N.J.: Princeton University Press.

Gadamer, Hans-Georg (1992) *Truth and Method*, 2nd, rev. edn and trans., ed. and trans. Joel Weinsheimer and Donald G. Marshall, New York: Crossroads.

Garber, Daniel (1985) "Leibniz and the Foundations of Physics: the Middle Years", in *The Natural Philosophy of Leibniz*, ed. K. Okruhlik and J. R. Brown, Dordrecht: Reidel.

Garber, Daniel (2005) "Leibniz and Idealism", in *Leibniz: Nature and Freedom*, ed. D. Rutherford and J. A. Cover, Oxford: Oxford University Press.

Gardner, Sebastian (1999) *Kant and the "Critique of Pure Reason"*, London: Routledge.

Gersh, Stephen, and Dermot Moran (2006) *Eriugena, Berkeley, and the Idealist Tradition*, Notre Dame: University of Notre Dame.

Gerson, Lloyd P. (2005) "What Is Platonism?" *Journal of the History of Philosophy* 43: 253–76.

Gibbons, B. J. (1996) *Gender in Mystical and Occult Thought: Behmenism and Its Development in England*, New York: Cambridge University Press.

Gill, Michael B. (2006) *The British Moralists on Human Nature and the Birth of Secular Ethics*, Cambridge: Cambridge University Press.

Gillespie, Michael Allen (1995) *Nihilism before Nietzsche*, Chicago: University of Chicago Press.

Grant, Edward (1981) *Much Ado about Nothing: Theories of Space and Vacuum from the Middle Ages to the Scientific Revolution*, Cambridge: Cambridge University Press.

Hale, Susan C. (1988) "Spacetime and the Abstract/Concrete Distinction", *Philosophical Studies* 53: 85–102.

Hall, A. Rupert (1990) *Henry More—Magic, Religion, and Experiment*, Oxford: Blackwell.

Hammer, Espen (2007) *German Idealism: Contemporary Perspectives*, New York: Routledge.

Hare, John E. (1999) "Augustine, Kant, and the Moral Gap", in *The Augustinian Tradition*, ed. Gareth M. Mathews, Berkeley: University of California Press.

Harries, Karsten (1975) "The Infinite Sphere: Comments on the History of a Metaphor", *Journal of the History of Philosophy* 13: 5–15.

Harries, Karsten (2001) *Infinity and Perspective*, Cambridge, Mass.: MIT Press.

Haym, Rudolf (1870) *Die romantische Schule: ein Beitrag zur Geschichte des deutschen Geistes*, Berlin: Gaertner.

Heine, Heinrich (1985) *The Romantic School and Other Essays*, ed. Jost Hermand and Robert C. Holub, New York: Continuum.

Henrich, Dieter (1991) *Konstellationen: Probleme und Debatten am Ursprung der idealistischen Philosophie (1789–1795)*, Stuttgart: Klett-Cotta.

Henrich, Dieter (1995) *Der Grund im Bewusstsein: Hölderlins Denken in Jena 1794–95*, Stuttgart: Klett-Cotta.

Henrich, Dieter (2003) *Between Kant and Hegel: Lectures on German Idealism*, ed. David S. Pacini, Cambridge, Mass.: Harvard University Press.

Hill, R. Kevin (2003) *Nietzsche's Critiques: The Kantian Foundations of His Thought*, Oxford: Oxford University Press.

Horn, Laurence (2001) *A Natural History of Negation*, Stanford, Calif.: CSLI Publications.

Horstmann, Rolf-Peter (2006) "Hegel's Phenomenology of Spirit as an Argument for a Monistic Ontology", *Inquiry* 49: 103–18.

Hotson, H. (1994) "Alsted and Leibniz: A Preliminary Survey of a Neglected Relationship", *VI Internationale Leibniz Kongress: Leibniz und Europa*, vol. 1, Hanover: G. W. Leibniz Gesellschaft.

Hutin, Serge (1960) *Les disciples anglais de Jacob Boehme aux xvii et xviiie siècles*, Paris: Editions Denoël.

Jacob, Margaret C. (2006) *The Radical Enlightenment: Pantheists, Freemasons and Republicans*, 2nd rev. edn, Lafayette, La.: Cornerstone Books.

Jammer, Max (1954) *Concepts of Space: The History of Theories of Space in Physics*, Cambridge, Mass.: Harvard University Press.

Jenkins, Mark P. (2006) *Bernard Williams*, Chesham, UK: Acumen.

Jolley, Nicholas, (1986) "Leibniz and Phenomenalism", *Studia Leibnitiana* 18: 39–51.

Kelly, George Armstrong (1969) *Idealism, Politics and History: Sources of Hegelian Thought*, Cambridge: Cambridge University Press.

Kessler, Eckhard (1990) "The Transformation of Aristotelianism during the Renaissance", in *New Perspectives on Renaissance Thought: Essays in the History of Science, Education and Philosophy in Memory of Charles B. Schmitt*, ed. J. Henry and S. Hutton, London: Duckworth.

Knuuttila, Simo (2001) "Time and Creation in Augustine", in *The Cambridge Companion to Augustine*, ed. Eleonore Stump and Norman Kretzmann, Cambridge: Cambridge University Press.

Kompridis, Nikolas (ed.) (2006) *Philosophical Romanticism*, London: Routledge.

Korsgaard, Christine (1996) *Creating the Kingdom of Ends*, Cambridge: Cambridge University Press.

Koyré, Alexandre (1957) *From the Closed World to the Infinite Universe*, Baltimore, Md.: Johns Hopkins Press.

Kristeller, Paul Otto (2001) "Stoic and Neoplatonic Sources of Spinoza's *Ethics*", in *Spinoza: Critical Assessments*, ed. Genevieve Lloyd, London: Routledge, vol. 1: 111–25.

Kuehn, Manfred (2001) *Kant: A Biography*, Cambridge: Cambridge University Press.

Kuhn, Thomas S. (1957) *The Copernican Revolution: Planetary Astronomy in the Development of Western Thought*, Cambridge, Mass.: Harvard University Press.

Kuhn, Thomas S. (1962) *The Structure of Scientific Revolutions*, Chicago: University of Chicago Press.

Lacoue-Labarthe, Philippe, and Jean-Luc Nancy (1988) *The Literary Absolute: The Theory of Literature in German Romanticism*, trans. Philip Barnard and Cheryl Lester, Albany: SUNY Press.

La Vopa, Anthony J. (2001) *Fichte: The Self and the Calling of Philosophy, 1762–1799*, Cambridge: Cambridge University Press.

Laywine, Alison (1993) *Kant's Early Metaphysics and the Origins of the Critical Philosophy*, Atascadero, Calif.: Ridgeview.

Lenoir, Timothy (1980) "Kant, Blumenbach, and Vital Materialism in German Biology", *Isis* 71: 77–108.

Lenoir, Timothy (1982) *The Strategy of Life: Teleology and Mechanics in Nineteenth Century German Biology*, Dordrecht: Reidel.

Leventhal, Robert S. (1994) *The Disciplines of Interpretation: Lessing, Herder, Schlegel and Hermeneutics in Germany, 1750–1800*, Berlin: W. de Gruyter.

Lloyd, A. C. (1990) *The Anatomy of Neoplatonism*, Oxford: Clarendon Press.

Loemker, Leroy E. (1961) "Leibniz and the Herborn Encyclopedists", *Journal of the History of Ideas* 22: 323–38.

Loemker, Leroy E. (1972) *Struggle for Synthesis: The Seventeenth Century Background of Leibniz's Synthesis of Order and Freedom*, Cambridge, Mass.: Harvard University Press.

Longuenesse, Béatrice (2007) "Point of View of Man or Knowledge of God: Kant and Hegel on Concept, Judgment, and Reason", in *Hegel's Critique of Metaphysics*, trans. Nicole J. Simek, Cambridge: Cambridge University Press.

Louden, Robert B. (2000) *Kant's Impure Ethics*, Oxford: Oxford University Press.

Luce, A. A. (1945) *Berkeley's Immaterialism: A Commentary on His "A Treatise Concerning the Principles of Human Knowledge"*, London: T. Nelson & Sons.

Lukács, Georg (1975) *The Young Hegel: Studies in the Relation between Dialectics and Economics*, trans. R. Livingstone, Cambridge, Mass.: MIT Press.

Magee, Bryan (2001) *Wagner and Philosophy*, London: Penguin.

Magee, Glenn Alexander (2001) *Hegel and the Hermetic Tradition*, Ithaca: Cornell University Press.

Magnus, Bernd (1978) *Nietzsche's Existential Imperative*, Bloomington: Indiana University Press.

Mahnke, Dietrich (1937) *Unendliche Sphäre und Allmittelpunkt: Beiträge zur Genealogie der Mathematischen Mystik*, Halle: Max Niemeyer.

Martin, John N. (2004) *Themes in Neoplatonic and Aristotelian Logic: Order, Negation and Abstraction*, Aldershot, UK: Ashgate.

Martin, Nicholas (1996) *Nietzsche and Schiller: Untimely Aesthetics*, Oxford: Clarendon Press.

Martin, Wayne M. (1997) *Idealism and Objectivity: Understanding Fichte's Jena Project*, Stanford, Calif.: Stanford University Press.

Martinich, A. P (1992) *The Two Gods of "Leviathan": Thomas Hobbes on Religion and Politics*, Cambridge: Cambridge University Press.

Mayer, Paola (1999) *Jena Romanticism and Its Appropriation of Jakob Böhme: Theosophy, Hagiography, Literature*, Montreal: McGill-Queen's University Press.

McCardle, Arthur W. (1986) *Friedrich Schiller and Swabian Pietism*, New York: Peter Lang.

McGinn, Bernard (2005) *The Harvest of Mysticism in Medieval Germany*, New York: Herder & Herder.

McGuire, J. E. (1995) "Force, Active Principles, and Newton's Invisible Realm", in *Tradition and Innovation: Newton's Metaphysics of Nature*, Dordrecht: Kluwer.

Meerbote, Ralf (1990) "Kant's Functionalism", in *Historical Foundations of Cognitive Science*, ed. J.-C. Smith, Dordrecht: Kluwer.

Menn, Stephen (1998) *Descartes and Augustine*, Cambridge: Cambridge University Press.

Mercer, Christia (2002) "The Aristotelianism at the Core of Leibniz's Philosophy", in *The Dynamics of Aristotelian Natural Philosophy from Antiquity to the Seventeenth Century*, ed. C. Leijenhorst, C. Lüthy and J. M. M. H. Thijssen, Leiden: Brill.

Mercer, Christia (2004) "Leibniz, Aristotle, and Ethical Knowledge", in *The Impact of Aristotelianism on Modern Philosophy*, ed. Riccardo Pozzo, Washington, D.C.: Catholic University of America Press.

Merchant, Carolyn (1979) "The Vitalism of Anne Conway: Its Impact on Leibniz's Concept of the Monad", *Journal of the History of Philosophy* 17: 255–69.

Millgram, Eliah (1997) *Practical Induction*, Cambridge, Mass.: Harvard University Press.

Mojsisch, Burkhard, and Orrin F. Summerell (eds) (2003) *Platonismus im Idealismus: die platonische Tradition in der klassischen deutschen Philosophie*, Munich and Leipzig: K. G. Saur.

Mollowitz, Gerhard (1935) "Kants Platoauffassung", *Kant-Studien* 40: 13–67.

Moran, Dermot (2006) "*Spiritualis Incrassatio*: Eriugena's Intellectualist Immaterialism: Is It an Idealism?" in *Eriugena, Berkeley, and the Idealist Tradition*, ed. Stephen Gersh and Dermot Moran, Notre Dame: University of Notre Dame.

Morison, Benjamin (2002) *On Location: Aristotle's Concept of Place*, Oxford: Oxford University Press.

Müller-Sievers, Hulmut (1997) *Self-Generation: Biology, Philosophy, and Literature around 1800*, Stanford, Calif.: Stanford University Press.

Munzel, G. Felicitas (1999) *Kant's Conception of Moral Character: The "Critical" Link of Morality, Anthropology, and Reflective Judgment*, Chicago: Chicago University Press.

Nagel, Thomas (1986) *The View From Nowhere*, Oxford: Oxford University Press.

Narbonne, Jean-Marc (2001) *Hénologie, ontologie et Ereignis (Plotin-Proclus-Heidegger)*, Paris: Belles Lettres.

Nehamas, Alexander (1985) *Nietzsche: Life as Literature*, Cambridge, Mass.: Harvard University Press.

Nussbaum, Martha C., and Hilary Putnam (1992) "Changing Aristotle's Mind", in *Essays on Aristotle's "De Anima"*, ed. Martha C. Nussbaum and Amélie Oksenberg Rorty, Oxford: Oxford University Press.

O'Regan, Cyril (1994) *The Heterodox Hegel*, Albany: SUNY Press.

Ospovat, Dov (1981) *The Development of Darwin's Theory: Natural History, Natural Theology, and Natural Selection, 1838–1859*, Cambridge: Cambridge University Press.

Panofsky, Erwin (1968) *Idea: A Concept in Art Theory*, trans. Joseph J. S. Peake, New York: Harper & Row.

Peirce, C. S. (1992) "Frazer's *The Works of George Berkeley*" in *The Essential Peirce: Selected Philosophical Writings*, vol. 1 (1867–1893), ed. N. Houser and C. Kloesel, Bloomington and Indianapolis: Indiana University Press.

Pépin, Jean (2006) "Saint Augustine and the Indwelling of the Ideas of God", in *Eriugena, Berkeley, and the Idealist Tradition*, ed. Stephen Gersh and Dermot Moran, Notre Dame: University of Notre Dame.

Pinkard, Terry (1994) *Hegel's Phenomenology: The Sociality of Reason*, Cambridge: Cambridge University Press.

Pinkard, Terry (2000) *Hegel: A Biography*, Cambridge: Cambridge University Press.

Pinkard, Terry (2002) *German Philosophy 1760–1860: The Legacy of Idealism*, Cambridge: Cambridge University Press.

Pippin, Robert B. (1989) *Hegel's Idealism: The Satisfactions of Self-Consciousness*, Cambridge: Cambridge University Press.

Pippin, Robert B. (1997) *Idealism as Modernism: Hegelian Variations*, Cambridge: Cambridge University Press.

Popkin, Richard (1992) "Spinoza, Neoplatonic Kabbalist?" in *Neoplatonism and Jewish Thought*, ed. Lenn. E. Goodman, Albany: SUNY Press.

Pozzo, Riccardo (2004) "Kant on the Five Intellectual Virtues", in *The Impact of Aristotelianism on Modern Philosophy*, ed. Riccardo Pozzo, Washington, D.C.: Catholic University of America Press.

Price, Huw (1996) *Time's Arrow and Archimedes' Point: New Directions for the Physics of Time*, New York: Oxford University Press.

Putnam, Hilary (1992) *Renewing Philosophy*, Cambridge, Mass.: Harvard University Press.

Rawls, John (2000) *Lectures on the History of Moral Philosophy*, Cambridge, Mass.: Harvard University Press.

Reath, Andrews (1989) "Kant's Theory of Moral Sensibility: Respect for the Moral Law and the Influence of Inclination", *Kant-Studien* 80: 284–302.

Redding, Paul (1993) "Nietzsche and the English Genealogists", in *Nietzsche, Feminism and Political Theory*, ed. P. Patton, London: Routledge.

Redding, Paul (1996) *Hegel's Hermeneutics*, Ithaca, N.Y.: Cornell University Press.

Redding, Paul (2007) *Analytic Philosophy and the Return of Hegelian Thought*, Cambridge: Cambridge University Press.

Reich, Klaus (1964) "Die Tugend in der Idee", in *Argumentationen: Festschrift für Josef König*, ed. Harald Delius and Günther Patzig, Göttingen: Vandenhoeck & Ruprecht.

Richards, Robert J. (1992) *The Meaning of Evolution: The Morphological Construction and Ideological Reconstruction of Darwin's Theory*, Chicago: University of Chicago Press.

Richards, Robert J. (2002) *The Romantic Conception of Life: Science and Philosophy in the Age of Goethe*, Chicago: University of Chicago Press.

Richie, A. D. (1967) *George Berkeley, A Reappraisal*, ed., with preface G. E. Davie, Manchester: Manchester University Press.

Riley, Patrick (1982) *Will and Political Legitimacy: A Critical Exposition of Social Contract Theory in Hobbes, Locke, Rousseau, Kant, and Hegel*, Cambridge, Mass.: Harvard University Press.

Riley, Patrick (1996) *Leibniz' Universal Jurisprudence: Justice as the Charity of the Wise*, Cambridge, Mass.: Harvard University Press.

Rist, John (1996) "Plotinus and Christian Philosophy", in *The Cambridge Companion to Plotinus*, ed. Lloyd P. Gerson, Cambridge: Cambridge University Press.

Roberts, John Russell (2007) *A Metaphysics for the Mob: The Philosophy of George Berkeley*, New York: Oxford University Press.

Rorty, Richard (1989) *Contingency, Irony and Solidarity*, Cambridge: Cambridge University Press.

Rudy, Gordon (2002) *Mystical Language of Sensation in the Later Middle Ages*, New York: Routledge.

Rutherford, Donald (1995) *Leibniz and the Rational Order of Nature*, Cambridge: Cambridge University Press.

Rutherford, Donald (1998) "Leibniz and Mysticism" in Coudert *et al.* (1998).

Schneewind, J. B. (1996) "Voluntarism and the Foundations of Ethics", *Proceedings and Addresses of the American Philosophical Association*, 70: 25–41.

Schneewind, J. B. (1998) *The Invention of Autonomy: A History of Modern Moral Philosophy*, Cambridge: Cambridge University Press.

Schönfeld, Martin (2000) *The Philosophy of the Young Kant: The Precritical Project*, Oxford: Oxford University Press.

Scuchard, Marcia Keith (1998) "Leibniz, Benzelius and Swedenborg", in Coudert *et al.* (1998).

Sedgwick, Sally (ed.) (2000) *The Reception of Kant's Critical Philosophy: Fichte, Schelling, and Hegel*, Cambridge: Cambridge University Press.

Selby-Bigge, L. A. (1897) *British Moralists, Being Selections from Writers Principally of the Eighteenth Century, in two volumes*, Oxford: Clarendon Press.

Sellars, Wilfrid (1997) *Empiricism and the Philosophy of Mind*, intro. Richard Rorty and Study Guide Robert Brandom, Cambridge, Mass.: Harvard University Press.

Shell, Susan Meld (1996) *The Embodiment of Reason: Kant on Spirit, Generation, and Community*, Chicago: University of Chicago Press.

Shim, Michael K. (2005) "What Kind of Idealist Was Leibniz?" *British Journal for the History of Philosophy* 13: 91–110.

Siorvanes, Lucas (1996) *Proclus: Neo-Platonic Philosophy and Science*, New Haven, Conn.: Yale University Press.

Sklar, Lawrence (1981) "Up and Down, Left and Right, Past and Future", Noûs 15: 111–29.

Sloan, Phillip R. (ed.) (1992) Richard Owen: The Hunterian Lectures in Comparative Anatomy May–June, 1937, intro. and commentary Phillip R. Sloan, Chicago: University of Chicago Press.

Smith, Justin Erik Halldór (2004) "Christian Platonism and the Metaphysics of Body in Leibniz", British Journal for the History of Philosophy 12: 43–59.

Stenius, Erik (1960) Wittgenstein's Tractatus: A Critical Exposition of Its Main Lines of Thought, Oxford: Blackwell.

Stern, Robert (2002) Hegel and the "Phenomenology of Spirit", London: Routledge.

Stern, Robert (2009) "Hegel's Idealism" in The Cambridge Companion to Hegel and Nineteenth Century Philosophy, ed. Frederick C. Beiser, Cambridge: Cambridge University Press.

Stoeffler, F. Ernest (1973) German Pietism during the Eighteenth Century, Leiden: Brill.

Stoneham, Tom (2002) Berkeley's World: An Examination of the Three Dialogues, Oxford: Oxford University Press.

Strathman, Christopher A. (2006) Romantic Poetry and the Fragmentary Imperative: Schlegel, Byron, Joyce, Blanchot, Albany, N.Y.: SUNY Press.

Taylor, Charles (1992) Sources of the Self: The Making of the Modern Identity, Cambridge, Mass.: Harvard University Press.

Thiessen, Gesa Elsbeth (ed.) (2004) Theological Aesthetics: A Reader, Grand Rapids, Mich.: William B. Eerdmans.

Thompson, Manley (1983) "Philosophical Approaches to Categories", Monist 66: 336–52.

Tonelli, Giorgio (1975) "Conditions in Königsberg and the Making of Kant's Philosophy", in bewusst sein: Gerhard Funke zu eigen, ed. Alexius J. Bucher, Hermann Drüe and Thomas M. Seebohm, Bonn: Bouvier.

Tuschling, Burkhard (1971) Metaphysische und transzendentale Dynamik in Kants "Opus Postumum", Berlin: Walter de Gruyter.

Tuschling, Burkhard (1989) "Apperception and Ether: On the Idea of a Transcendental Deduction of Matter in Kant's Opus Postumum", in Kant's Transcendental Deductions: The Three "Critiques" and the "Opus Postumum", ed. Eckart Förster, Stanford, Calif.: Stanford University Press.

Tuschling, Burkhard (1991) "The System of Transcendental Idealism: Questions Raised and Left Open in the Kritik der Urteilskraft", in System and Teleology in Kant's "Critique of Judgment", ed. Hoke Robinson, Southern Journal of Philosophy, 30 (supp.): 109–27.

Van Cleve, James (1999) Problems from Kant, New York: Oxford University Press.

Vieillard-Baron, Jean-Louis (1979) Platon et l'idéalisme allemand (1770–1830), Paris: Beauchesne.

Vieillard-Baron, Jean-Louis (1988) Platonisme et interprétation de Platon à l'époque modern, Paris: Vrin.

Vohler, Martin (2002) "Christian Gottlob Heyne und das Studium des Altertums in Deutschland", in Disciplining Classics – Altertumswissenschaft als Beruf, ed. Glenn W. Most, Göttingen: Vandenhoeck & Ruprecht.

Vuillemin, Jules (1955) Physique et métaphysique kantiennes, Paris: Presses Universitaires de France.

Walker, Ralph C. S. (1989) The Coherence Theory of Truth: Realism, Anti-Realism, Idealism, London: Routledge.

Westfall, Richard S. (1980) *Never at Rest: A Biography of Isaac Newton*, Cambridge: Cambridge University Press.

Williams, Bernard (1978) *Descartes: The Project of Pure Enquiry*, Harmondsworth: Penguin.

Williams, Bernard (1985) *Ethics and the Limits of Philosophy*, Cambridge, Mass.: Harvard University Press.

Williams, Bernard (2000) "Philosophy as a Humanistic Discipline", *Philosophy* 75: pp. 477–96.

Williams, David Lay (2005) "Justice and the General Will: Affirming Rousseau's Ancient Orientation", *Journal of the History of Ideas* 66: 383–411.

Williams, David Lay (2007) *Rousseau's Platonic Enlightenment*, University Park: Pennsylvania State University Press.

Williams, Robert R. (1997) *Hegel's Ethics of Recognition*, Berkeley: University of California Press.

Williamson, George S. (2004) *The Longing for Myth in Germany: Religion and Aesthetic Culture from Romanticism to Nietzsche*, Chicago: University of Chicago Press.

Wilson, Catherine (1989) *Leibniz's Metaphysics: A Comparative and Historical Study*, Princeton, N.J.: Princeton University Press.

Winkler, Kenneth P. (ed.) (2005) *The Cambridge Companion to Berkeley*, Cambridge: Cambridge University Press.

Wittgenstein, Ludwig (1922) *Tractatus Logico-Philosophicus*, trans. C. K. Ogden, London: Routledge & Kegan Paul.

Wood, Allen W. (2005), *Kant*, Oxford: Blackwell.

Zarka, Charles (1996) "First philosophy and the Foundation of Knowledge", in *The Cambridge Companion to Hobbes*, ed. Tom Sorell, Cambridge: Cambridge University Press.

Zöller, Günter (1998) *Fichte's Transcendental Philosophy: The Original Duplicity of Intelligence and Will*, Cambridge: Cambridge University Press.

INDEX

Adams, R. M. 182, 183, 189
aesthetic judgment:
  disinterestedness of, 92, 93;
  logic of in Kant, 92;
  recognitive underpinning of in Kant, 93;
  subjective universality of in Kant, 94
aesthetic socratism, Nietzsche's critique of, 166
aether, Kant's notion of, 127
Albert the Great, 137
Allison, H. 74, 188, 191
Alsted, J. H. 182
analytic philosophy, critique of British idealism of, 175
Antognazza, M. R. 25, 182
Aristotle, 30, 81, 200;
  account of the soul of, 28, 29, 138, 148, 183, 199;
  approach to physics of, 22;
  categories of, 63;
  concept of divine pleasure in, 91;
  conception of God in, 152–53;
  conception of space, 6–7, 9, 10, 31, 63, 186;
  conception of substance, 21, 22, 62, 63, 64, 152;
  cosmology of, 22;
  notion of "inference to the reason" in, 47
Armstrong, D. M. 186, 187
Athenaeum, 116
Augustine, St. 11, 69, 100, 199;
  account of creation in, 33, 184;

conception of the will in, 87,191;
  influence on Descartes of, 191;
  relation to Neoplatonism of, 87;
  voluntarism of, 67
Austin, J. L. 189

Balguy, J. 192
Baruzi, J. 34, 184
Baum, M. 188, 197
Beaney, M. 185
beauty, symbolic dimension of in Kant, 95
Beierwaltes, W. 126, 196, 200
Beiser, F. C. 2, 18, 68, 86, 123, 187, 191, 193, 196, 197, 198
Berkeley, G. 105, 182, 183, 186, 201;
  erroneous attribution of idealism to, 1–2, 5, 12, 17, 19, 175;
  nominalism of, 17–19, 181;
  objections to Newton's view of space of, 13, 16 181;
  spiritual realism of, 5, 17, 19, 107, 154;
  voluntarism of, 19
Bernstein, R. 191
Bird, G. 188
Bisterfeld, J. H. 171, 182
Blumenbach, J. F. 85, 129, 190, 194;
  Kant's relation to, 99;
  notion of formative force in, 98
Blumenberg, H. 15, 183, 187
Böhme, J. 34, 84, 126, 180, 190, 197
Böhmer, Caroline, 116
Bowie, A. 196
Brandom, R. B. 30, 183, 203

Hegel

Frederick Beiser

Hegel (1770-1831) is one of the major philosophers of the nineteenth century. Many of the major philosophical movements of the twentieth century - from existentialism to analytic philosophy - grew out of reactions against Hegel. He is also one of the hardest philosophers to understand and his complex ideas, though rewarding, are often misunderstood.

In this magisterial and lucid introduction, Frederick Beiser covers every major aspect of Hegel's thought. He places Hegel in the historical context of nineteenth-century Germany whilst clarifying the deep insights and originality of Hegel's philosophy.

A masterpiece of clarity and scholarship, *Hegel* is both the ideal starting point for those coming to Hegel for the first time and essential reading for any student or scholar of nineteenth century philosophy.

ISBN 10: 0-415-31207-8 (hbk)
ISBN 10: 0-415-31208-6 (pbk)

ISBN 13: 978-0-415-31207-3 (hbk)
ISBN 13: 978-0-415-31208-0 (pbk)